Shariati on *Shariati* and the Muslim Woman

Who was Ali Shariati?

for *Muslim Women:*

•**Woman in the Heart of Muhammad**(ﷺ)•
•**The Islamic Modest Dress**•
•**Expectations From the Muslim Woman**•
•**Fatima is Fatima**•

and

•**Guide to Shariati's Collected Works**•

LALEH BAKHTIAR

ABC INTERNATIONAL GROUP, INC.

Library of Congress Cataloging-in-Publication Data
Laleh Bakhtiar
      Shariati on Shariati and the Muslim Woman:
      Who was Ali Shariati? for Muslim Women: The Islamic
      Modest Dress, Expectations From the Muslim Woman,
      Fatima is Fatima and Guide to Shariati's Collected Works
         p. cm.
         1. Islam—20th century—Addresses, essays,
         lectures. 2. History (Islamic Revolution)—
         Addresses, essays, lectures. I. Bakhtiar, Laleh
         II. Title
      BP163.55164   1996   297'.09'04   86-82499
      Bibliographical References   Index

ISBN: 1-871031-50-8

Published by

ABC Group International, Inc. (USA)

Distributed by
KAZI Publications, Inc.
3023 W. Belmont Avenue
Chicago IL 60618
Tel: 312 (773)-267-7001; FAX: 312 (773)-267-7002

To Ali With Love

CONTENTS

PREFACE

Ali Shariati (1933-1977), a contemporary Muslim social activist, devoted his life to paving the way for the return to what he and those who followed him believed to be a non-distorted Islam. In Part One, "Who was Ali Shariati?," his life is seen through his own journals and letters as well as through the words of his first teacher, his father, Muhammad Taqi Shariati. Asterisks indicate words defined in the glossary.

Part Two consists of four lectures/essays of Shariati's view of the Muslim woman. Three, "Woman in the Heart of Muhammad (ﷺ)" (Vol. 30 *CW* pp. 511-547), "The Islamic Modest Dress," and "Expectations From the Muslim Woman," are translated and published for the first time here. The third is Shariati's "Fatima is Fatima," long out of print. (The last three are in Vol. 21, *CW*).

Ali Shariati left over 15,000 pages of lectures, letters, books and journals which were gathered together, divided into subjects and published from 1976-1986 in Persian in 35 volumes called *The Collected Works*. As no more than 500 pages of his works have been translated into English, the appendices address the need for a "Guide to Shariati's Collected Works" in order to give those interested in Shariati's ideas and his place in history an understanding of the extent and breadth of his work as well as an insight into his creative abilities which were so strong that the titles themselves call out to be heard.

The "Guide" gives all information heretofore available on each of the titles including date, place where the lecture was given, and the surrounding circumstances where known. Page numbers are given showing where a lecture can be found in the Persian *Collected Works* and indication of English translation where relevant.

There are five additional indices given in the appendices in order to facilitate access to (A) the translated titles and (B) transliterated titles of the 35 volumes. In the third and fourth indices, every title that appears within the Collected Works

(*CW*) is listed (C) alphabetically in translation and (D) transliteration followed by the number assigned to the work in the "Guide to Shariati's Collected Works." The fifth (E) is a list of the Dated Works According to Dates produced during his most prolific period of 1968-1972. Through this one can follow, day by day, the blossoming of the creative energies of this son of Islam and Iran, a man about whom Jean Paul Sartre said, "I have no religion, but if I were to choose one, it would be that of Shariati's."

It is hoped that this work will be viewed as an attempt to give wider scope to Shariati's ideas and that interested readers will contact the publisher with any information or criticism that they may have. This then can be passed on to other readers. *Inshallah.*

Laleh Bakhtiar
Chicago, 1996

PART ONE
WHO WAS ALI SHARIATI?

I.
FINAL MIGRATION

On the dawn of Ali Shariati's last day in Iran, May 16, 1977, just before his final migration to Europe, he wrote to his beloved father Muhammad Taqi Shariati[1] saying:

"Presently I am preparing for a journey.... I will be gone for one or two months to study and seek treatment. With the Will of God, I shall return. The reason why I did not say good-bye to you was because I knew how you were feeling and how you would worry. Now in these last few minutes in my home and in my country, I kiss your hand. I will await you....

"....Now that it is near dawn on Monday, after the morning prayer and two or three hours before we leave (turning to the Holy Quran) I asked for guidance from Him in regard to this journey.[2] The top of the page said 'bad'. Shaken, I read the verse and cried in happiness. I will record it from a few verses before:

"Those who believed in God and have migrated and striven with their wealth and their lives in God's Way are of much greater worth in God's sight. These are they who are the achievers (of salvation) [9:20].

And then the verses that first appeared: *"O believers, what is amiss with you that when it is said to you, 'Go forth in the way of God,' you sink down heavily to the ground? Are you so content with this present life, rather than the world to come? Yet the enjoyment of this present life, compared with the world to come, is a little thing. If you go not forth, He will chastise you with a painful chastisement, and instead of you He will substitute another people; and you will not hurt Him anything, for God is powerful over everything.*

"....Then God sent down on him His Tranquility and confirmed him with legions you did not see; and He made the word of the unbelievers the lowest; and God's Word is the uppermost; God is All-mighty, All-wise. Go forth, light and heavy! Struggle

*in God's way with your possessions and your selves; that is bet-
ter for you, did you know"* [9:38-41].[3]

A little over a month later, on June 19, 1977, Ali Shariati
died. According to popular belief, his death was directly and/or
indirectly connected to SAVAK*.

Mourning ceremonies were held for him throughout the
world as his body was flown to Damascus to be buried beside his
beloved Zaynab,* whose role he described as 'greater than martyrdom' for it was she who carried the message of Imam Husayn
(爐)* to the world and without her, Karbala* would have been
an event lost in history. To many, he played the same role in contemporary history. His message—greater than martyrdom—
was to command good and prevent evil, the very cause for which
Imam Husayn (爐) set out from Makkah and the beloved
Zaynab, from Karbala. So he lived his life in the cause of Imam
Husayn (爐), dying, many believe, a martyr on the 3rd of
Shaban, the anniversary of the birth of Imam Husayn (爐), having delivered his message as had the beloved Zaynab, beside
whom he is buried.

Many years later, after the victory of the Revolution, his
father, Muhammad Taqi Shariati was interviewed[4] and asked
to describe his son who was born in the environs of Mazinan, a
village in north east Iran on November 23, 1933.

II
FROM MAZINAN TO FRANCE

His father describes his son saying, "A quality that he had from early childhood was his love for learning and studying. Even in the fifth and sixth grades of primary school, he would stay up late into the night reading. When one of his eyes developed a spot on it, I became very worried. I did not want him to study so much at such an early age. At night, around midnight, I would go to his room and turn off his light. He would dutifully pretend to go to bed, and I would leave his room. Many times when I would go to check again, I would see his light was on until 2:00 am and he was still reading.

"As a child, he had no desire for any of the games children play or toys children play with. He was not even interested in sports. He loved reading and learning. Among the gifts which God the Most High blessed him with were this desire for learning, the strength of his power of deduction and the wealth of his literary talents."[1]

Ali, recalling his relationship with his father, wrote: "My father fashioned the first dimension of my spirit. It was he who first taught me the art of being human. As soon as my mother weaned me, he gave me a taste for freedom, nobility, purity, steadfastness, faith, chastity of soul and independence of heart. It was he who introduced me to his friends—his books. They were my constant and familiar companions from the earliest years of my schooling. I grew up and matured in his library which was, for him, the whole of his life and his family. Many things that otherwise I would have had to learn much later, in adult life, in the course of long experience and at the cost of long-lasting effort and struggle, he gave to me as a gift in my childhood and early youth, simply and spontaneously. My father's library is now a world full of precious memories for me.

I can remember each of his books, even their bindings. I love greatly that good, sacred room which is, for me, the summation of my sweet good, but distant, past."2

His father continued, "All of our family for generations had been ulama.* My grandfather was one of the outstanding pupils of Haj Mulla Sabzevari, known as the Seal of Philosophers. Thus, I was, myself, born into such a family of scholars and ulama, and I followed their way. I established the Center for the Propagation of Islamic Truth in the early 1940s in Mashhad when there was a brief spell of freedom after Reza Khan resigned from the monarchy.

"I had two purposes in mind. One was to activate the people in an organization similar to one established in Tabriz. I began by teaching classes and then we bought a center where we were actively involved in confronting Marxism and communism.

"The other work that we did, which was more difficult, was to confront the traditionalists whose faith and belief had become inundated with superstitions and distortions to the point that the real Islam had become transfigured and metamorphosized. It had been changed from a dynamic, moving, active religion of *jihad** into a religion of indifference in the face of what destiny supposedly had in store. The human being was at the mercy of forces around him.

"One of the events in history which can best awaken the people to *jihad* (activity and struggle) is the story of Karbala and the rising of Imam Husayn (صلى). You will notice to what extent the message of Imam Husayn (صلى) has been distorted. The goal of his supporters has simply become crying once a year. The people have been told for centuries: Imam Husayn (صلى) arose to die so we would cry for him and go to heaven!' Do you see to what extent the truth has been metamorphosized?

"The first Muharram after I had opened the center, I began by stressing this point: I do not oppose tears and the expression of emotions, as you will see. When I narrate the story, I cry more than anyone else. What I object to is making crying and tears the goal for a great movement like that of Imam Husayn (صلى).

"Then I would begin to narrate from the time Imam Husayn (صلى) left Madinah and went to Makkah, left Makkah and went to lraq, to Karbala, and the time spent in Karbala. I spoke of his sermons, his letters, the conversations he had with various people. I pointed out that in none of those did he indicate we should cry. In his last will and testament written in the first hours there and given to his brother Muhammad Hanifi, in order to prevent the spread of rumors begun by the Umayyids,* he said: 'I did not arise for mutiny or revolt. I arose to command to good and prevent evil,'* and not a commanding to good or preventing of evil by going down a street and calling out to an oppressor, 'Do not oppress' or sitting upon the *minbar** and saying, 'Do not oppress' or 'Do not drink wine.' No. Rather he meant to prevent the evil from which Islamic states are suffering, from the rule of Yazids.*

"Imam Husayn (☞) arose to prevent an evil. He arose because the rule was not an Islamic rule. Neither was the rule of Yazid an Islamic rule, nor was that of his father, Muawiyah.* They had metamorphosized Islam. They were not Islamic rulers and had not understood Islam in the least bit.

"Therefore, this great arising, which can revive an entire nation, and enliven a whole nation by calling it to movement and *jihad,* has been so distorted that it has become exclusively a means to cry. How far this is from fairness. How unfair it is!

"My son, Ali, was born into a home in which he heard stories like this from the beginning. He heard all aspects of lslam discussed. He would come to the center and attend the classes I gave and naturally was very effected. I was sure from the beginning that Ali would choose to study lslam, to come to know Islam and to help others understand Islam because of his special talents.

"He was seven when he first went to primary school (Ibn Yamin) and from there to secondary school," (Ferdowsi High School) "in 1948. It was when he was in high school that he became actively involved in the new Islamic movement through the Center for the Propagation of lslamic Truth. Through his activities, he became familiar with young people and university students. He began writing articles. He also became familiar with the works of the Socialist Movement of Believers-in-God towards which he became most supportative."3

The Socialist Movement of Believers-in-God was a group founded as an underground movement in Tehran in 1944-45. This movement was founded by young devoted Muslims. While stressing their belief in the One God and accepting the world view of monotheism, they believed that from the economic point of view, the Islamic economic system was, in truth, a kind of socialism and that a revolutionary movement was required in which all of the stagnant values of society would be destroyed and a new society formed based upon monotheistic values. Their method was an underground one. The first phase was one of ideological struggle and training people.

Later a difference of opinion arose between the members as to whether or not the work should continue underground or openly in support of the movement to nationalize the oil industry led by the Prime Minister, Dr. Mohammad Mosaddeq. The group which believed in open activities under those conditions separated from this movement. It was this group which was later to form the People's Party of Iran. The other faction of the Socialist Movement of Believers-in-God continued its organizational work and by establishing some open and semi-open groups, it was able to print magazines like *Mahd-i-ilm* (Cradle of Knowledge) and *Danesh-juyan wa danesh-amuzan-i-fars* (University and High School Students of Fars Province) without mentioning the association behind them.

The interview with Muhammad Taqi Shariati continued, "After the first cycle of high school, he had been accepted at a male Teachers Training College (1950). The condition was that a student who graduated would have to work for five years as a teacher in the provincial areas. When he finished the course work, he taught in Ahmadabad which was then outside the city limits of Mashhad.

"During the time he was teaching, the College of Arts and Sciences was formed at Mashhad University. He applied for his M.A. and was accepted."

In pursuance of the ideas that Ali Shariati had developed on the social views of Islam, he published one of his first articles in June/July, 1955 entitled "The Median School of Islam—the History of the Evolution of Philosophy."[4]

He wrote, "The movements of Muslim nations seeking independence will only attain victory when they follow clear intellectual principles and when they understand the *maktab* (school of thought and action of Islam) as a school of thought in which philosophical, economic, ethical, rational, social, political, etc. issues are clearly expressed. The important point to note is that the structure of this school is built with material provided to us by Islam. Inspiration for its reconstruction must come directly from the salvation-bringing, sacred teachings of the Quran and the *Sunnah* of the Prophet (ﷺ).

"If one day the Muslim nations, that is, those very men and women who are now struggling for the great reconstruction of Islam, gather around the axis of one thought and have clear and determined social goals, there is no doubt they will easily remove the obstinate and merciless rivals from their lands and

guarantee their movement against decline forever, attain outstanding progress and reconstruct their civilization with its
past greatness.

"The bases of this movement have been placed on the shoulders of each and every individual among the Muslim peoples. It
is these very simple people who must regain the lost suprema-
cy of Muslims because it was these very people who strengthened the Islamic movement in the world with their self-sacrifices.

"Fourteen hundred years ago a few slaves, date sellers,
camel herders and wage earners followed the religion of
Muhammad (ﷺ) and brought about the world movement of
Islam. Today it is the workers, farmers, merchants, office
employees, university and high school students who must
revive it. Yea! Movements always arise from among the people
because it is the aristocratic and ruling class who most often
refuse to limit conservatism in order to preserve their own position. Their efforts are inevitably directed towards preventing
any social change for change could endanger their interests. If
there are a few people from this class who have believed in the
movement of the deprived and strugglers upon the way, they
are very exceptional. Many scholars and ulama also take on the
color of the aristocrats either because of the fame and success
they thereby attain or because the aristocrats hire them to preserve their interests.

"Thus, there is no choice but that we ourselves must get to
work. We must seek our inspiration from God alone. We must
endeavor to revive the salvation-giving religion of Islam and
the flourishing civilization that we lost by bringing about a
change which will transform the total present lslamic society.
Then we will have once again found the way of truth and the
right way to guarantee our well-being in both this life and in
the life that is awaiting us. In order to do this, we must first
arm ourselves with education and knowledge and put forth the
progressive school of thought and action of Islam.

"The school of Islam is a median school which humanity has
once put into practice and from which outstanding results were
attained. This is not a method that we have initiated. Rather, it
is a way which, with the blossoming of Islam, carried the caravan of civilization during the golden centuries on its way to
well-being and progress. The program of the 'middle-way' or
median school of Islam can be summarized in the following
three points:

"First, as opposed to the schools of materialism and idealism, Islam has a method particular unto itself and this method can be called 'realism'.

"Second, the social and economic system of Islam is a practical socio-economic system based upon a belief in God and located in the middle between the two corrupt systems of capitalism and communism.

"Third, the political method of Islam (from the international point of view) is between the two blocs of the East and the West. The base of Islam is a median bloc which cannot be affiliated to either of the other two. It is a natural tree which is neither of the East nor the West but rather, a third between the two contradictory poles. This bloc is composed of all Islamic countries."[5]

Then in September/October, 1957, he and his father, among others at the Center for the Propagation of Islamic Truth were arrested in Mashhad and flown by military plane to Tehran. When his father was asked about this arrest, he said, "Ali was active in the National Front which had been begun by Mosaddeq. Later when the religious faction of the National Front separated and Mehdi Bazargan formed the National Resistance Movement, Ali joined them. He liked Mehdi Bazargan very much. He went to the meetings of the movement in Mashhad. They did some things, but it was mostly just keeping busy.

"In 1957, there were sixteen of us in the center who were accused of participating in the publication of a booklet disclosing the oil situation and, because of this, they tried to tie us into the movement. It was basically because of their dislike of the work of the center because of its connection with the National Front. Ali was always involved in political activities, whether they be in the National Front, the National Resistance Movement or whatever."[6]

As Shariati was the youngest among those arrested, only 23 at the time, he received the brunt of the torture. They shaved his head and beat him severely. During the eight months imprisonment, Ali became familiar with the torture of the regime. From his small, dark cell, he opened a window onto the world and onto history. He sensed the oppression and tyranny of the criminals and oppressors of history. A deep union was formed between him and all of the prisoners and oppressed of history as a result of his anguish and torture.

Ali Shariati bore all the blows of prison and all his bitter experiences with the power of his faith, with patience and trust in God. He left prison with a spirit full of hope and an iron will to continue his struggle against oppression, *kufr** and ignorance. He returned to Mashhad* to continue his education where he received his M.A. from the College of Arts and Sciences in 1958, finishing first in his class. The legal commitment of the university was to send the one who graduated first in his class to Europe to continue his studies. His political record, however, was a barrier to the rule automatically being carried out. He taught in the Mashhad area, married Pouran Shariat-Razavi and was finally given permission to leave and to study in France. He was then allowed to take advantage of the scholarship he had won.[7]

III.
To France and Back

Ali's father described Ali's departure in 1959 from Iran and his chosen field of study. "As he was leaving for France for graduate studies, his mother and I accompanied him to Tehran. When we were saying good-bye at the airport, I said to him, 'Ali, when you had asked me what I thought you should study abroad, I realized that I was not experienced enough to suggest a field to you. I told you to wait until we got to Tehran to ask our friends. We discussed it with Mehdi Bazargan and others. They said you showed a lot of promise in the area of sociology, and since there was no professor trained in this at Tehran University, you should study that which you liked best.'

"I then recited the prayer for a safe journey in his ear and said, 'I have a favor to ask of you. Please do not bring us a gift of anti-religion from Europe. Do not lose your faith. You will be in touch with great professors who believe in religion. You can bring us the gift of new issues and approaches in regard to lslam." Then (in order to show that he had accepted what I had said) he sent us the translation of Alexis Carrel's* work called *Prayer* after just a few months while his mother and I were still in Tehran.

"After seven or eight months abroad, he wrote me saying, 'Father, we thought once I came to Europe to study, I would be free to study what I wanted, but the dry rules and regulations of our country dictate certain things so that we are not free even here. It has become clear that I must choose a field of study for my Ph.D. which follows the field I studied for my M.A.—otherwise I cannot be hired as a professor at a university and my credentials will not be accepted. I will take the exams for Persian literature so that there will be no problem in my getting hired in Iran, but l will not put aside the study of sociology which I have begun and which I am very strongly inclined towards. That is, I will also study sociology.' He did this. He also studied Islamic history and Persian literature, which he had to study, and the sociology of religion, which he loved."[1]

It is the general opinion among his friends that Shariati had not gone to Europe to get a degree so much as to become familiar at close hand with the way of thinking in the contemporary Western world. Full of ideas on Islam, having studied and applied them to his life from an early age, his familiarity with other ideas was not obtained in the corners of quiet libraries or in such and such academies of study. Rather, it was in the social arena itself that he learned of the prevalent ideas among Westerners, just as he had learned about Islam.

During the first few years Shariati was in France, new resistance activities began in Iran and abroad by communists and nationalists. In Iran, it was the continuation of the efforts of the National Resistance Movement which grew into the Second National Front and then became the Freedom Movement of Iran. In response to this movement, patriotic young Muslim students abroad became active.

Shariati joined this group as soon as he arrived in France. The National Front and Freedom Movement had still not been fully formed in Iran when he formed a group of Muslims called the Young National Movement of Iran in Europe. They began to work actively once the National Resistance Movement in Iran was fully organized. On February 25, 1962 the National Movement of Iranians in America was formed. He played a leading role in the movement abroad. The first Congress was held in Weisbaden, West Germany in August, 1962. A newspaper was published of which Shariati agreed to act as editor. The first issue of the monthly *"Iran-i-Azad"* ("Free Iran") appeared on November 15, 1962. Before Shariati resigned as editor, it was among the best and richest political papers. It was the only publication which reflected the struggle of the Iranian people in the best way in all dimensions. His analyses, which he sometimes signed with the name Sham (candle), were among the best.

His migration to Europe also coincided with the peak of the Algerian Liberation Movement. He was hopeful that this movement would help in freeing Iran from monarchial rule. Instead of just sitting and writing in support of the Algerian Muslims, he joined the Movement for the Liberation of Algeria and was actively involved. He was put in prison in Paris for six months in 1961 and, in prison, got to know others who shared his opposition to colonialism and imperialism, among whom was Franz Fanon,* a man who sought out struggles of liberation but who knew little about Islam. Shariati told him about Islam.

During the last days of his life, Fanon wrote Shariati saying, "Islam struggled against the West and colonialism sooner than Asia and Africa....these two ancient enemies of theirs. Even though I may not share your feelings in regard to lslam, I stress what you have said perhaps recognizing its importance more than you do, concerning the fact that in the Third World, Islam has a greater anti-colonial capacity than all other powers, social possibilities and ideologies and that Islam is anti-Western by nature.

"I hold the hope that this spirit of Islam will again find life within the dying Muslim form through your genuine intellectuals. I hope that they will succeed in giving consciousness to their people and mobilizing them in the defensive battle against the assault of thoughts, occupations and poisoned and questionable European solutions, that they will be able to exploit the great and powerful spiritual, cultural and social resources hidden in the depths of their spirit; and that they will help Muslim societies to save humanity and lay the foundation for another kind of human being and civilization. This is a mission which to the same extent that I am unable to play a role in it, I believe that you and those who think like you are appointed to. Of course, I know that your efforts upon this way—as opposed to what they may first seem to be—will not contradict my dreams for the formation of a united people with common interests in the countries of the Third World. That which unites you and I now makes me believe that this is a great and wise step in growing closer to this dream of mine.

"At the same time, however, I believe the revival of the religious spirit will make the realization of this dream more difficult for the nation which is in a state of 'becoming' (i.e. the Third World)....but the particular view that you have of the revival of the religious spirit and your endeavors to give movement to this great power....in order to bring great salvation to the human being of today who has fallen into the stagnation of abasement, has been metamorphosized and drawn into imitation and personality cults will mean the return to Islam is a return to 'selfhood' as you view it.... Even though my way differs from yours and perhaps is even opposite yours, yet I know that we will meet at the end, at the stage where human beings live well...."[2] Ali, in truth, had found a brother in Franz Fanon. Later, giving a lecture called "Knocking on the Door of Truth,"[3] he was to describe Fanon's death and burial.

Ali also became familiar with Marxism and socialism. While he developed a deep knowledge of both, he always remained a Muslim. He learned Western philosophy and sociology. He also got to know men like Louis Massignon,* Schwartz, Jean Paul Sartre* and Gurvitch.* He helped some of his professors in their research projects. He became familiar with Gurvitch's complicated thought. They called him a 'Gurvitchite' as he was considered to be one of his followers. Students would come to him to have the lessons of Gurvitch explained to them.

Later, in his classes on Islamology in Mashhad, he spoke about the role of the prophets, as compared with social thinkers and philosophers like Jean Paul Sartre and the success of the former and lack of success of the latter. "What did the prophets do and of what did their victory consist? We know that the most successful reformers of society have been the prophets. There is no doubt about it whether one approve of prophethood or not. Socrates was one of the greatest geniuses of humanity, but if you compare his success with that of Jesus or our own Prophet...., you see they are incomparable. The prophets guided a society, a culture and a history, whereas Socrates just gave beautiful lectures but did not develop a society.

"The art of the prophets and other reformers of humanity, which brought them success, was their discovery of social laws. They understood their society very well. Their mission was coordinated with existing social traditions and history. They succeeded whereas idealists and utopians from Plato to Thomas More and many of the contemporary reformers like August Comte,* Saint-Simon,* Proudhon,* Russell* and Sartre failed. Various other contemporary philosophical, social, political and economic schools have developed philosophies, but have not understood social laws. They have sat in their homes and written about utopias and sacred cities. They have conceived of the best of societies in books alone, in their minds. They have conceived of things that are incapable of realization. Plato said, 'Now that my utopia cannot be developed upon the earth, it will be implemented in heaven.' The prophets did not create laws in the structuring of society. They discovered laws of society and, based upon that, their mission of training and discipline was implemented and realized....[4]

In a footnote he recalled an experience to explain the lack of success of men like Jean Paul Sartre. "Jean Paul Sartre was sitting in a cafe on St. Germain des Pres in Paris several years ago expressing disgust at the way people had come to understand his school of existentialism and, in particular, the ugly and degenerated reaction which his school created in young people. This shows how social thinkers and philosophers such as himself produce a concept to guide people before they even recognize people and their times. As he himself admitted, these ideas not only met with defeat but gave negative results as well. His school of guidance resulted in error and loss."[5]

Shariati spent the little money that he received while in Paris on the needs of the movement and in purchasing books. He lived on the verge of poverty in one room with his wife and two small children.

After completing his graduate studies in 1964 when he was 31 years old, he returned to Iran. He was arrested at the border between Turkey and Iran because of his activities abroad against the regime. He was imprisoned. After six months, during which time he was not able to contact or see his family or his father, he was freed because of objections his professors in France made against his imprisonment and because of the efforts of friends in international organizations.

IV.
FROM THE CITY OF MARTYRDOM TO THE HUSAYNIYAH

After releasing him from prison, the Shah's regime, in spite of his higher degrees, sent Shariati to teach at a high school in a small town outside of Mashhad, a job he held before going to Europe. After a time he was also allowed to teach at the Agricultural College in Mashhad. Due to objections raised on his behalf, the authorities had to finally give him a position teaching history at Ferdowsi University in Mashhad in 1966. He taught there until 1972 when he was 39.

The university was completely transformed and his classes became high points for all students. They came from other colleges to hear his lectures. A class of 50 students suddenly had 300, 400 and 500 students until the university announced that no student from any other college could attend classes at the College of Arts and Sciences although students from the College of Arts and Sciences could still attend classes at, for instance, the Physician's College.

They suggested he do research instead: "Do research and collect your pay every month." They offered him a higher salary for this work. He was offered high positions by the ministers and by lawyers who sat on the train with him between Mashhad and Tehran. Some even offered him their positions, but he did not accept any offers they made. He joined no party or group. He stood alone.

During the six years at Mashhad University, in spite of the barriers placed before him, he began his constructive efforts to create and develop his thoughts on the school and foundations of Islam. The young generation of Iran received him with great enthusiasm as their thirst for an undistorted Islam had been aroused. University students from all over Iran invited him to lecture at their respective universities. He accepted these invitations in spite of all the difficulties he faced.

In Mashhad he taught Islamology, including lectures on: "Of What Use the Study of Islam?" (30.1); "Who is Muhammad (☙)?" (30.2); "Knowing Muhammad (☙)" (30.3); and the "Visage of Muhammad (☙)" (30.4). His course on the History of Civilization included: "Description of History" (11.4); "Schools of History and Methods of Research" (11.5); "Impressive Events in History" (12.1); "Characteristics of the Recent Centuries" (12.2); "Characteristics of Today's Civilization" (12.7); "A General Discussion on Civilization and Culture" (12.3); "Political Tendencies in the Contemporary World" (12.5); "The Problem of Finding Self" (12.6); "What does 'civilization' mean?" (11.2); "General Discussion on World View and Culture" (11.3); "Why is mythology the spirit of all civilizations?" (11.6); "History of the Chinese Civilization" (11.7); and "World View and Environment" (12.4).

A center had been formed in 1967 in Tehran called the Husayniyah* Irshad by a group of ulama and other Muslim thinkers. They invited Shariati, among others, to participate in programming the works of the organization. He accepted their invitation and began a series of lectures under the title of History of Religions and Islamology. Unprecedented numbers of students participated in his classes. In addition to his regular classes, he gave lectures upon special occasions of the Islamic calendar as well as in response to unfolding political events.

Beginning in the fall of 1968, at the same time that he had been teaching at Mashhad University (four years before his expulsion), he commuted to Tehran giving lectures at the Husayniyah Irshad. His first dated lecture was "Approach to the Understanding of Islam" (28.2), October 25, 26, 1968. In December he gave lectures on "A Complete Human Being" (25.6) and "The Human Being and History" (24.5).

In the spring of 1969 he gave ten days of lectures: "Ali (☙): A Myth-like Reality" (26.6); "Appointment with Abraham" (consisting of four lectures which form the second volume of the *hajj*) (29.1); "Civilization and Modernism" (31.9); and his famous "*Ummah* (Community) and *Imamate* (Leadership)" (26.10).

He wrote "Totemism" (13.4) during this time as well as "The Fall" (13.1) and "The Human Being in Islam" (24.1). He gave a lecture on "Existentialism" (24.6) at Melli University.

In the fall of 1969 he gave the lectures, "A Glance at

Tomorrow's History" (31.6); "History of Islamic Iran" (27.1); "Art Fleeing from What Exists" (32.2); "Ali (ﷺ) is Alone" (24.6); "Ali:(ﷺ): His Life after Death" (26.9); "The Scientific Method" (31.2); "About the Book" (25.9); and "Migration and Civilization" (23.11).

At the beginning of 1970, he lectured on "Advice and a Story" (32.8); "Prayer" (8.1); and "The School of Imam Sajjad" (8.2); and then in the spring he wrote, "Iqbal: The 20th Century Reformer" (5.2); its Preface and "The Philosophy of History in the View of Islam" (19.8). In the summer, he lectured on "History and its Value in Islam" (29.20); "Religion vs. Religion" (22.1); and "The Intellectual and His Responsibility to Society" (20.2). In the fall, he continued his History of Civilization courses and spoke on "The Economic Roots of the Renaissance" (31.3).

In the winter of 1970-71, he went on the *hajj* and lectured in Madinah, Arafah, Mina, Makkah and Mt. Hira where he spoke on "Madinah: The City of Migration" (29.2); "Civilization: The Logical Outcome of Migration" (29.3); "Study of Types of Migration" (29.4); "The Salvation of the Young Generation" (29.5); "Migration, *Ummah* (Community) and *Imamate* (Leadership)" (29.6); "Reflections on the *hajj* Rituals" (29.7); "Sacrifice Your Ishmael" (29.9); "Selection and/or Election" (29.10); "What must be done?" (29.11); "A Glance at the Life of Muhammad (ﷺ)" (29.12); and "Monotheism and Multitheism" (23.2).

He returned and spoke on "An Insight into Shi'ite History" (19.6) and "Husayn: Adam's Heir" (19.7). He continued his lectures in the History and Knowledge of Religions and History of Civilization Courses. He spoke on "Permanent Standards of Education" (29.23) and published his translation of the reply of Kashif al-Ghita (31.18). He lectured on "Fatima is Fatima," (21.1); "Death: A Message for Life" (29.26); "The Machine at the Service of Machinism" (31.8); and wrote volume one of *Hajj: Reflections on its Rituals*. (6).

In the fall of 1971, continuing his course on History and Knowledge of Religions, he lectured on "Mothers! Fathers! We are to blame!" (22.2); "Awaiting the Religion of Protest" (19.7); "Alid Shi'ism/Safavid Shi'ism" (9.2); "The Responsibility of Being a Shi'ite" (7.3); "Ali (ﷺ): Founder of Unity" (26.6); "Yea Brother! That's the way it was!" (22.3); "World View" (23.1); "Ideology I" (23.3); and "From where should we begin?" (20.6).

In January of 1972, he again went on the *hajj* and spoke in

Madinah, Makkah, Arafah and Mina on "Twenty-three Years in Twenty-three Days" (29.13); "The Importance of Migration in Islam" (29.14); "A Sketch of the Prophet's Mosque" (29.15); "Monotheism: The Infrastructure of Our Actions" (29.10); "Now that you have reached the Ka'bah, do not remain there" (29.17); and "Promise for the Future" (29.19).

He then began his famous Islamology courses at Husayniyah Irshad in Tehran in February of 1972. On the 9th of Muharram (February 24, 1972) he gave his lecture on "Martyrdom" (19.3). In the spring of 1972, he was expelled from Ferdowsi University in Mashhad. He wrote, "Good-bye City of Martyrdom" (22.5).

V.
FROM THE HUSAYNIYAH
TO THE ZAYNABIYAH

He moved to Tehran and continued his lectures on Islamology. Just seven months later the Husayniyah was closed until after the Islamic Revolution in 1979 which he did not live to see.

Because of these circumstances, his lectures on Islamology in Tehran were limited to twenty-seven lectures including topics such as: "School of Thought and Action" (16.1); "School of Thought and Action of Islam" (16.2); "Monotheism: A Philosophy of History" (16.7); "The Philosophy of Ethics" (16.8); "History in the View of the Quran and Schools of Thought" (17.1); "Toynbee's Thesis" (17.2); "Marxism in the Three Cycles of His Life" (17.3); "The Relationship Between Thought and Action" (17.5); "Marxism in the 19th Century" (17.3); "Capitalism and Surplus Value" (18.1); "Historic Determinism" (18.4); "Commentary on *Surah Anbiya*" (18.8); and "The School of Existentialism" (18.9).

He spoke on "Expectations From the Muslim Woman" (21.2); and gave seminars. He spoke on "And Once Again Abu Dharr" (3.2); "Our Century in Search of Ali (ﷺ)" (26.3); "Revolutionary Role of the Reminders and Reminding" (7.2); "The Most Beautiful Worshiped Spirit" (8.4); "The Third Way" (20.4); and "Consciousness and Deception" (20.5).

He was succeeding beyond anyone's imagination in drawing the young people to Islam. As he grew stronger, the opposition increased. He had to face the Shah's entire regime and the Shah's security forces, as well as groups as diverse as leftist intellectuals and those clothed in very religious conservative garb. They stopped at nothing. Accusations of mistakes and errors by the regime's agents disguised as both religious men and leftist intellectuals only served to increase the interest among the young people in Shariati.

His father was asked about this: "Do you recall any mistakes in Dr. Shariati's works and if so, do you feel they are so extensive that they have mislead our young people?"[1]

His father replied, "God forbid. The greatest service that Ali did was that he made the religion of Islam relevant to the class of the enlightened and educated. If it had not been for him, perhaps these young people who today practice lslam would have deviated from Islam and would not be the strong followers of Ayatullah Khomeini that they are today because they would not have been familiar with the school of thought and action of Islam. His greatest service to our society and the greatest obligation our society has to him is because he expressed religious truths among these people and groups.

"One of our friends has said, 'Before Ali began preaching Islam, university professors would profess to be great intellectuals by degrading Islam, but today these very professors know that his success among young people was due to his belief in Islam. The difference between these two is the service of what Ali did. He made religion relevant in the university among young enlightened and educated people. Before him, religion was not a relevant and pertinent issue in these institutions.'

"When I was in jail, a communist came up to me and said, 'You have a son who is greater than a whole society.' I asked, 'How can you say that when you have taken a way which is separate from our way?' He said, 'While I have been in prison, I have read several of his lectures and writings like "From Migration to Death," "The Visage of Muhammad (ﷺ)" and two or three other lectures but the title, cover and author of these were changed so the guards would not know whose book we were reading. These were sent to us as was the lecture he gave at the Petroleum College. I was able to read several and I swear by God that if we had had a teacher and preacher like Shariati, our fate would have been much different than just receiving the religion that our parents had inherited and passed to us or going to hear irrelevant sermons. None of that was acceptable to our type. If we had had a teacher like him, our destiny would have been very different.'

"This, then, was his greatest service. Now in regard to mistakes or errors, who is there who has not made mistakes in speeches, lectures or in his writings? Ali made no terrible mistakes or errors which would harm public thought or belief.

Some things are a question of taste. For instance, in regard to the books of such and such an ulama or scholar copied centuries ago, in some cases, there are errors. He said this should be pointed out so that people not think that they must accept everything that has been copied down. Now perhaps there is a person who objects to this kind of criticism. This is a question of taste. It cannot be called a mistake. He and I also had differences of opinion. I would say that he should not criticize these people because society respects them. He would say the reason why he criticized was because the preachers memorized whatever the gentleman in question wrote and repeated it word for word to the people. He believed that criticism must be made so that people allow for the possibility that such a book may have errors in it.

"One cannot say that Ali Shariati's work has errors because the things are so minor. They are nothing for which he should be criticized—especially in comparison to the work that he did for society, for Islam. His errors were minimal. There was nothing said or written that would harm a person's beliefs or the religion of Islam."

Sometimes 6000 students would participate in Shariati's lectures. More than 40,000 people saw the play on Abu Dharr Ghifari in September/October, 1972 before the regime applied pressure to close it.

It was Aban (October-November) 1972. In addition to the last three lectures on Islamology, he spoke on "Shi'ism: A Complete Political Party" (7.1); "Followers of Ali (ﷺ)" (26.8); "Message of Hope to Responsible Intellectuals" (20.1); and "*Qasitin* (those who deviate), *Mariqin* (those who miss the truth of religion), *Nakithin* (those who break their allegiance)" (26.7). Then on Friday, November 12 of that same year, following the second part of "Shi'ism: A Complete Political Party" (7.1), after a congregational ritual prayer, when all other conspiracies failed to stop the movement, the Shah's forces closed the Husayniyah Irshad.

THE HUSAYANIYAH

Writing to his friends at the Husayniyah two weeks after it was closed, Shariati summarized what he felt his work at the Husayniyah had been and began planning for the work to be done once it was reopened, something he would not live to see.[2]

"...The Husayniyah has ended its second season...it is closed until the opening of its third—which will most certainly be more glorious. This is a crucial time, full of tests and difficulties for us...

"...And on these nights and days when I have had the opportunity to pray to God and consider my efforts and endeavors, think about them, and evaluate whatever it was I accomplished, study my weak and strong points, without wanting to exaggerate the results of our work and fall into the difficulty of 'pride' and without covering over the errors and mistakes, I think that, in truth, much has been accomplished and that which has been accomplished is beyond any merit we may have had.

"Today—tonight—as I am sitting here alone, in hiding, expecting at any moment for something to happen, it is 5:05 am, the 26th of November and just like every other weak person who at the time of trouble thinks about God, and, being all alone, realizes to a greater degree that the only One we can have is God. I sense the presence of God with the clarity and directness of the morning dawn rising before my eyes of anticipation. I sense Him. I see Him. I touch His subtle and supportative Hand upon my shoulders. I am drowned in wonder and shame at all the kindness and affection which He gave to this, His humble and worthless servant.

"In truth, how great is God's kindness and understanding. After all, who were we to stand before and confront all of the power of those who deviate (*qasitin*), the crimes of treason of those who break their allegiance (*nakithin*) and the frightening prejudice of those who miss the truth of religion (*mariqin*)? The power of the Pharaoh, the gold of Korah and the edicts of Balaam all joined together.... In this aloneness and this anxious and shaky 'place of retreat' where each moment a doubt arises, more than ever before and more than on those glorious nights packed with people at the Husayniyah, I am certain about the successes of the Husayniyah and its future. It is the same certainty that I have in regard to the rising of the sun on this very morning at 6:00 am.

"THIS WAS NOT A DREAM..."

"This was not a dream....it would be most unfair to think that He would leave us half-way there. Does He not know that just because of Him and with the hope of His support and guidance, we took steps upon His Way? Does He not know that upon the Way we have taken towards Him, we put everything else aside? We wanted to gain absolutely nothing for ourselves. He knows that the Way was more narrow than a strand of hair, sharper than a sword and that it passed through hell. Yet throughout all of this, we had our hand in His alone.

"Perhaps we have erred upon this Way, but we have committed no crime, no treason. Perhaps we moved forward too slowly, but we never hesitated for a moment. We never stepped off His path. Does He not know that from the beginning we solely devoted our lives to Him, we never allowed even sleep or food or visiting friends or life or wife or children to interfere. From the time we pledged our pen to Him, we have written no article for our profession, not even a letter throughout all of these months to my wife...

AND THAT OF THE UNKNOWN HEROES...

"And that young unknown youth who lived in a hole and (in order to meet the costs of riding the bus to the Husayniyah and buying pamphlets) would not eat on Fridays or what of the university students— boys and girls—who reciting their communal ritual prayer beside the mosque, were beaten. In return for the curses and slander made against them, they cried out, 'Allah *akbar*'—all of them. And what of that girl who, after the ritual prayer, the beatings and arrests saw that everything had ended and saw the only home she had in the world in which she had faith, was closed. She did not go elsewhere. She returned to her family in the middle of the night only after she had circumambulated the Husayniyah. Silent, and in anguish, she cried alone.

DOES GOD NOT KNOW?

"Does God not know all of these things? Does He not see? He would never turn away from a zealous man who with total sincerity and certainty called the people to His Way, and the people came. It is true that whenever a journey reaches steep slopes, the climb becomes more difficult. He tests those who are upon this Way. If they are unable to continue, unable to move forward, He holds them back and seeks out more rugged people to continue up the dangerous slopes. If He finds them patient, people who reflect no weariness, people who are overflowing with faith, certainty and trust, they will begin the move....

"We are presently undergoing such a test. Once we who have God as our Employer are certain that this is His Way, that we have thought with consciousness and acted with the purest of intentions, I do not believe that we need to prove anything to ourselves because we are aware that that which can never be doubted in regard to the work of the Husayniyah was the piety (*taqwa*) behind every act. What sign could be clearer than the fact that the Husayniyah played no political games of 'opportunism' or 'advisability'. We consciously sensed the effects of a deep and penetrating transformation of society as a result of our work which changed the orientation and direction of a generation in a relatively short period of time.

"This proves that we correctly determined our duty and accurately carried it out. It is clear that we understood the expedient nature of the time and necessities of the place....This all shows that it was in line with God's Will. God had Willed that His religion be saved from the hands of those who used it to set up shop or who sold it for a price and in so doing reflected the level of their awareness and extent of their honor. It had been His Will that Islam be removed from the monopoly of an eroded generation and given, instead, to the time, to consciences that are alive and awake and to aware scholars of this generation. Faith was removed from the stagnant mire of deteriorated thoughts, books and frameworks. It was allowed to flow and fill the fertile lands of tomorrow thus making possible the growth of verdant fields of thought and emotion.

"The tomorrow of the thought, literature and attitudes of our intellectuals will not be weary and wary of religion. We took the Quran from the cemetery back to the city, from the environs of perfumed shrines to the very fabric of life, from the end of the bazaar to the heart of the university, from poetry and poets, from prayers and eulogy, from tears and crying, from machine-like repetitions, from being an unclear, unfunctional thing to being a movement of a conscious, constructive faith which gives power, motion and consciousness, created values and built a new generation, a new age.

TOMORROW'S SOCIAL MOVEMENT

"There is no doubt about the fact that our social movement of tomorrow will be neither a movement based on materialism nor on nationalism. It will be a movement based on Islam—a conscious, progressive Islam whose political party will be formed from the ideology of Islam.

"These are the principle lines of the clear and determined design which the Husayniyah drew. The generation who will complete it are those who showed their faith, consciousness and power of decision-making in an exemplary manner on that

Friday afternoon (when the Husayniyah was closed by the security forces).

"That which you laid the foundation for was the construction of a building. Today it has become a faith. Every brick that you placed one upon another has today become a heart, a heart which is illuminated by the sacred ray of God's Light, which has been lit by the flame of the light of Islam.

"The flames of this fire have arisen to the farthermost distances of the world and leaped out from the depths of souls. When I hear it said, 'They have closed the Husayniyah!' I begin to laugh. They have mistaken a place for a school of thought and action. They do not know that 'closing the Husayniyah' will only fan the flames! A university student said, 'At the Literacy Corps Base during free time, a group gathered in a corner and were playing cards. The rest? They were reading the books printed at the Husayniyah and in the evening when news came that they had closed the Husayniyah, only two people were left playing cards!'

"I who have always confessed to my inabilities, who have always seen myself drowned in God's Grace, never sensed with such completeness as I do today that we did this work. Never before today have I sensed with such certainty that the decisive and extensive success of the Husayniyah over time and the conquest of the body of thoughts of our society has been guaranteed by God's Will.

"Who has ever had the success of planting stucco and earth and growing love and thought? The events which took place at the Husayniyah broke through the election at Thaqifah* and the act of the Khawarij.* Criteria were buried. Barriers eliminated....and then my vows to give my nights and days to the Husayniyah. Every moment. No home. No family. All given to the Husayniyah. The result—the opportunity to speak, to write, to gather together all those potentials, all that love and devotion....

"These were all preparation for the groundwork of a concept which had been created by the Unseen without any of us being aware of it, predicting it, or affecting it. He implemented it. He drove everyone to where He wanted them to go. He made friend and foe, alike, His agent to implement His design. Whoever learns what the Husayniyah was will either not believe it or will be obliged to admit to its miraculous-like work.

"This is what should assure us that the director, designer and responsible authority of the legal Husayniyah institute is Him, and that He has a plan for the future which He will undoubtedly not leave undone. We should know that no edict, ruling, command or sign will have any effect when confronted by His Will. There is no doubt that the movement of time and the cycle of thought in our age are real Signs and Divine Traditions, in truth, and that the victories and ideals of the Husayniyah are but assignments from Him.

THE ISLAM OF TOMORROW

"The Islam of tomorrow will not be the Islam of the pseudo-religious scholars. The Islam of Qum and Mashhad will also change. The young theological students have shown that they will no longer accept things which are dictated to them without first questioning them. The defeat of this group (of pseudo-religious scholars) confirms the fact that (in spite of the weapons at their disposal and the strong support they received behind the front lines in their war on the unarmed) the Husayniyah will stand. From this point onwards, the power of religion will never again be given into the hands of official custodians who are satisfied with simply inheriting it.

"The new educated class has also shown that in spite of all of the efforts over the past fifty years to turn them from religion and to cause disgust in them in regard to Islam, they answer in a positive way to the call of Muhammadic Islam. In much the same way, responsible, conscious, determined preachers have joined our ranks.

"Tomorrow's Islam will not be the Islam of the book of prayers. It will be the Islam of the Quran. Tomorrow's Shi'ism will not be the Shi'ism of the Safavid Shah Sultan Husayn. It will be the Shi'ism of Husayn (ﷺ). Tomorrow's religion will no longer be the religion of ignorance, tyranny, prejudice, ancient superstitions, habit, repetition, tears, weakness and abasement, for it has become the religion of consciousness, justice, awareness, liberation, revolutionary movement, knowledge, civilization, art, literature, social, responsibility, progress, new ways of thinking, looking to the future and domination over time and over historic destiny.

"These are the realities which tell us that the Husayniyah chose the right path. It carried out its duty correctly. Its watchwords were expressed at the right time and in the right place.

THE HUSAYNIYAH IS A MOVEMENT

"The Husayniyah is not a place. It is not an accident, a gathering or a meeting. It is an event, a phenomenon which came into being in response to the necessities and needs of the time. The Divine Law created and ruled over its time and its society so that it was able to carry out its dangerous assignment to reject a trinity in Islam,[3] to negate a deviated Shi'ism, to design monotheistic Islam and to prove the existence of red Shi'ism.[4] Rest assured that never will ignorance or deviation effect an assignment which God has given and historic determinism accompanied.

"The edicts of Kab al-Ahbars,* the hoarded gold of Abd al-Rahmans* and the exiles by the Uthmans* are nothing more than a few useless stones thrown in a stream to momentarily block its flow before it reaches the sea. The Husayniyah is like a spark which falls on dry wood. It will, at any moment inflame a thought even if the body be cold....

"Part of the agenda is that every penny spent here has become a word. Each brick has become a thought, and the building has become a school of thought and action. Even if they destroy the building, its flattened earth will remain as its address directing history to the evolution of thought, the Islamic movement and the consciousness of the people. The people will occupy it whenever they want, no matter who tries to stop them for it belongs to them.

"The concept of 'what must be done?'[5] will be implemented. That is why from the beginning you were the founders of a building and, now you are the heirs of a movement, a current movement which daily grows in power and in extent.

"What about me? As a teacher, speaker or writer at the Husayniyah, I sense that God put forth the work of the Husayniyah as a most difficult responsibility. It is as if His Words can be heard: The third season of the Husayniyah is about to begin. Do not lose hope. Do not become indifferent. Do not return to normal life. Do not take another way. Do not turn to your homes. Leave aside your professions. Sacrifice your wife and children. Forget your 'self'. During whatever remains of your life, wherever you are in the world, under whatever conditions you live and in whatever work you do, direct others to it.

"To me the Husayniyah was not just a place to go to speak or to teach. The Husayniyah has been kneaded with my blood, thought, personality and faith. The Husayniyah Irshad is the base of a political party, a party which chose Islam as its ideology. Its intellectual school of thought and action and world view is Islamology. I designed the basis of it in lectures like "Shi'ism:

A Complete Political Party," "Monotheism," "The Philosophy of History," "Husayn (﷽): Heir of Adam," "*Ummah* (Community) and *Imamate* (Leadership)," "Red Shi'ism," "Ali (﷽): School of Thought and Action, Unity, Justice," "The School of Thought and Action of Imam Sajjad (﷽): Consciousness, Love, Need and Jihad," "Prayer," "Awaiting the Religion of Protest," (that is, whenever you arise, the Mahdi* will come; he is awaiting us!), "The Story of Adam," (the philosophy of the nature of the human being), "The Islam of the *Imamate* (Leadership) and Justice," "Alid Shi'ism/Safavid Shi'ism," "Islam as Ideology in the Triangle of Gnosis, Marxism and Existentialism," and "The Revolutionary Role of the Reminders and Reminding in History."

Then he began defining certain key terms in terms of the Quran and the *Sunnah*: "Family and kinship are not to be considered as a third principle alongside the Quran and the *Sunnah* but rather as an objective embodiment of these two sources and the entrance into these two bases.

"Selection: of a revolutionary regime more committed than a democracy and opposed to beliefs that are simply inherited rather than chosen; implementing the 'greater occultation'*; a time of responsibility for all people and an age of committed democratic rule; guidance of a progressive and intellectual philosophy of historic determinism.

"Monotheism: a philosophical world view, a unified philosophy of history, an anti-class social infrastructure and an equality among people—that is, world, social and human unity embodied in a complete, progressive, intellectual and social party meeting such needs and insights of this era as the strategies and tactics of struggle, the method of social work, the study of goals and even revolutionary programs in a social environment....

"*Jihad*.

"*Ijtihad*. The various methods used by the Imams in the realization of a unified mission...

"Such an Islam chosen not only as a heart-felt religious faith or as a particular religious sect but also as the perfect, progressive and powerful ideology of a political party, a divine-like party of the masses. Once so equipped, such an Islam will make itself known in the contradictions of the social arena, for intellectual conflicts and in powerful ideological wars of the world.

"Armed decisively (unlike traditional religions which flee from conflict out of fear and weakness) and with the assurance of intellectually armed *mujahid*,* Islam is on the alert and ready to challenge eastern and western intellectual fronts.

"Islam must stake out an intellectual claim by relying upon its ideological bases and its own cultural sources. It must do so with honor, consciousness and power. At the same time, in the name of progressive intellectuals, it must awaken the people, give movement to society, provide intellectual leadership appropriate to this time and salvation to its people in the best form possible.

"Know that you stand in the front ranks of the intellectuals of your time and that you have two added values that other committed but anti-religious intellectuals lack.

"First, with the ideological infrastructure of monotheism and resurrection, you offer meaning to life and existence. Second, by having a faith and a religious culture, you develop a relationship of understanding and spiritual kinship with your people—while other intellectuals become estranged from them. This is why Muslims in their present degenerated form have fallen behind and are weaker than the progressive anti-religious intellectual. Yet armed with the above ideology and faith, you can take on the form of progressive, aware, powerful human beings—something which anti-religious intellectuals are deprived of by their materialism.

"These are issues which the Husayniyah Irshad addressed. These issues form a school of thought and action and movement which the Husayniyah has conceptualized at this time in the conscience and ideas of this generation. As both friends and enemies are astonished to realize, never before have the people of one particular time or the conscience of a generation so quickly and deeply accepted the call of an intellectual base, found faith and sincerity in it and, above all else, sensed a commitment.

"These are the Articles of Association of the Husayniyah recorded in the events of our time, recorded upon the hearts of an aware generation who seek truth and recorded upon the will of educated, enlightened, anguished and responsible believers who have decided to reclaim their faith from the deviation into which it has been made to fall....

"The Husayniyah Irshad which you built several years ago has been smelted down with the use of a powerful divine elixir and has been transformed. It has become a movement, an intellectual current. It has become faith, love, belief, idea, responsibility, way, goal, and ideology. It has become a political party....The message cannot be deterred by any conspiracy, deceit or force whatsoever.

"A man must live and enjoy material benefits, have work which occupies him, see to his wife and children, enjoy life, rest and relax and, in his free time, he must serve society or his faith. Yea. But sometimes it happens that the heavy weight of responsibility (the responsibility for a thought, the responsibility for the destiny of a nation, a faith, a time) is placed upon the shoulders of one or of several people. Here the 'musts' change. When cholera strikes a city or when a faith is being quickly destroyed by conscious enemies assisted by unconscious or criminal friends or when the salvation of a people, a generation, is dependent upon the cry and self-sacrifices of one or several people, such people must give their lives for all the years they are alive. The issue of living is no longer relevant. Whatever has been approved, recommended or, even obligatory, becomes forbidden.

"Our time, our young generation, our faith, our Quran, our Prophet and...our beloved culture; and our tomorrows all in anticipation of those who discern the dangers, the conspiracies, and the disgraceful destiny of tomorrow, who know the message in a prophetic-like way and who continue to announce the *jihad*....Muslim intellectuals (who are very few in number) are messenger-like persons, messengers whose Gabriel is Muhammad (ﷺ) and that's all!...

"The Husayniyah Irshad began this invitation. It awoke our times. It created a great wave. The salvation of our people, the salvation of our faith is in the group who know 'what must be done?'"

THE FINAL JOURNEY

Nine months later, on September 12, 1973, the Shah's authorities issued a warrant for Shariati's arrest. He was then imprisoned without trial, tortured and placed in solitary confinement for 550 days until March 20, 1975. They tortured his friends and followers in his presence trying to make him support their regime, but none of this had any effect upon him.

After the closing of the Husayniyah and the imprisonment of Shariati, his books were banned. Anyone possessing one was arrested and the book was confiscated. As policies of suppression increased, the resistance of the people increased. His books were distributed both in Iran and outside of Iran. They were found in India, Pakistan, Afghanistan, the countries in the Persian Gulf, Europe and America.

He was finally released from prison because of the activities of two fronts. First, the tactics of his friends and students through international organizations, disclosures about the regime's activities and political pressure on Iran. Second, the pressure applied by friends and allies of the Liberation Movement in Algeria (who by then held responsible positions in the government) when the Shah went to Algeria. Algeria at that time was acting as the mediator between Iran and Iraq in the signing of the Algeries Accord.[6]

After his release in the spring of 1975, SAVAK's (the Shah's secret police) tactics changed and through various agents they tried to have Shariati agree to a debate in exchange for permission to leave Iran. He refused. They then issued orders to eliminate him. They printed some of his works without his permission. They spread rumors that Shariati had done this himself trying to show that he cooperated with the regime. The leftist communists fanned the flames of this rumor. Shariati quickly denied this in circulars published in the winter and spring of 1976.

He was under surveillance after his release from prison. The Shah's regime did not allow him to continue his work. It so restricted his activities that he decided to migrate from Iran with the help of his friends. He published his will and testament. He wrote the last letter he would ever write to his father, whom he loved a great deal. He said good-bye to his wife and children and on May 16, 1977, began a new migration from Iran.

But he did not live beyond Sunday, June 2, 1977, dying in London under mysterious circumstances. His body was taken by friends to Damascus on June 17, 1977 to be laid beside the grave of the beloved Zaynab.

VI.
EPILOGUE

His father was asked to what he felt Ali owed his success. He said: "His success was both outward and inner. Outwardly it was his powerful pen and literary ability. In many cases his pen turned to magic. He had a most alluring way of presenting his ideas....This in addition to the substance of his work, the study he had done, and the powerful quality of his pen and speech. All of these were outward causes for his success.

"The inner cause was that whatever Ali said, he was himself committed to and believed in. He would never express anything—no matter how attractive—that he did not himself believe in. Whatever he said, he believed. And because what he said came from the heart, it entered the heart of those who heard it or read it.

"This method was, at that time, very dangerous. The regime was extremely sensitive in regard to him. They would continuously and repeatedly send people who would warn him and threaten him. 'Don't say this.' 'Do that.' This is why they expelled him from Mashhad University.... He paid no attention to danger when it came to what he believed. It was such that he felt each speech that he gave would be his last. In this way he rejected all dangers at the cost of his very life. He expressed his beliefs to the people as much as possible in the time available to him.

"Take the book on Abu Dharr.* The head of the Farhang Library brought it to me in 1950 to translate into Persian. I translated the introduction but because of the extent of my work over a period of many years and as I could not sleep more than three or four hours at night, my nervous system was affected. The doctors forbade my working. I suggested Ali trans-

late the book because he had a good literary style. He was in the
11th grade.

"He translated it. I helped him when I could. That is, he
would translate several pages and then read them to me. If
there was a word or phrase that was not correct, I would tell
him. He would then return to his room and continue translating.

"The amazing thing about it was that this book and the
introduction he wrote fit exactly into the style of writing of his
later works. That is, the style he used when in the 11th grade
was very similar to his style of writing after earning his graduate degrees. A person who studies literary styles would know
immediately that his works are written by the same person.

"It was Shaykh Ali Agha Tehrani, a great and respected
scholar, who first noted this. He compared Ali's first work, the
Introduction to and translation of Abu Dharr and the last thing
he wrote, the story of Hurr,* and found remarkable similarity of
style. In order to show the belief and line of thought of Shariati,
he compared these two."[1]

Shaykh Ali Agha Tehrani wrote, "The spiritual and human
qualities of this scholar and great *mujahid*, Ali Shariati, amaze
the mind. Genius, faith, sincerity, consciousness, perseverance,
the amount of work he accomplished, his anguished soul—and
the certainty of belief in the way he had taken—all overwhelm
anyone who knew him or studies his work. From his very first
work until his last, all had a unified goal and direction. For
example, one of his books is called "Two Martyrs." The first,
about Abu Dharr, is a product of his high school years and the
second, about Hurr, is one of the last things that he wrote.

"They are both oriented towards the same way: struggle
against corruption, aggression, satanic desires and finally, gaining victory over all corruption and attaining one's Absolute
Beloved. The themes are similar in each: the struggle of truth
over falsehood, of intellect over whims, and ideas and thoughts
of God over the advice and desires of the ego. Both concern the
victory of truth over selfish interests."[2]

Shaykh Ali Agha Tehrani goes on, "In my mind, his perseverance upon the Straight Path is the best reason for the right-
ness of his way and his lacking any kind of selfish inclinations
and goal other than divinely inspired ones. If this were not so,
he would have become like others who have taken advantage of
golden material opportunities that came their way.

"One of the reasons the Quran gives for proof that it was

revealed by God and not a product of man's imagination is its very uniformity. *'Will they not ponder on the Quran? If it had been from other than God, they would have found in it much incongruity.'* (4:82) With this inspiration, the genius of Shariati took flight beyond the horizons of time and place."[3]

Shariati's father then continues the story of how Ali came to write and speak about Hurr as one of his last works, "When Ali came to Mashhad before leaving for the last time for Europe, he went to the home of his eldest sister. He could never remain unoccupied for a moment. Even when he went to call on people, he spent his time reading or writing. He would never sit at a social gathering and waste two or three hours just making conversation.

"This was also true the last time that he went to his eldest sister's house. He looked through her books and took one which just happened to be *Muntahiil-amal*. He opened the book. It fell open at the report of Imam Jafar Sadiq (ﷺ) concerning Hurr. He paid no heed to the late Shaykh Qummi's Persian translation of the report. Instead, he paced the floor, translating the report of Imam Jafar (ﷺ) about Hurr from Arabic to Persian himself saying, 'Hurr (meaning inwardly liberated), in every state is still Hurr. Let the hammer of the times beat down upon him. The anvil teaches him patience. Let every blow bring an onslaught of torments. Never does he break, neither when lashed down and bound in misery nor when comfort flees from him and the very world is his scourge.'

"Then Ali sat down and began to speak. His niece, who was familiar with his habits, unbeknownst to him, placed a tape recorder in the room. He spoke out loud for well over an hour. Later the tape was transcribed. I do not know if Ali then checked the text and changed it or if it was the exact words recorded in that room.

"All I know is that later when he returned to Tehran, he called upon Mr. Humayun, may God rest his soul in peace, the man who had funded the establishment of the Husayniyah Irshad. There were a group of scholars there, as well, who asked him to read them the story of Hurr which he did and which was recorded.

" Several well known scholars later came to see me in Mashhad—Dr. Mufattah, Dr. Bahonar, etc. I said to them, 'You are well informed about books and literature.' Then I asked, 'From the day of Ashura when Hurr was martyred until today, when we sit here together, has any scholar, any historian, any thinker had such a beautiful realization about Hurr. Has any-one taken this small event in all of history and spoken about it for over an hour without one single extra word appearing and with all of the material being used?'

"This is something which only my son Ali did. There is not one scholar, writer, thinker or great ulama throughout history, any gathering in which the name of Hurr is mentioned or in all the histories where his name is mentioned who had this beau-tiful realization about him and could so explain his life from the sociological point of view or express the purification of the soul, self-sacrifice, etc. as Ali did in the story of Hurr.

"I asked them if they knew of any other who had realized this aspect of Hurr's life, and they all agreed that it was a real-ization exclusive to Ali.

"Thus, he had these talents and abilities and realizations. The ability to think in this way was exclusive to him among his contemporaries or even among society as a whole. His words bear witness to the quality of his intuitions and the quality of his deductions."[4]

Ali wrote about Hurr, "On the morning of Ashura he was an officer in the army of Yazid and after a few hours, he was among the victims in the ranks of Imam Husayn and one of his dear-est helpers.

"How could just one or two hours be sufficient for all of this? Did he change his mind as a result of studying? Did his view of faith and belief change? Did his principles of jurisprudence change?

"Never. The only change that took place between the Hurr of Ta'sua and the Hurr of Ashura was the change in his choice of leadership. In this great transformation it is only his choice of leader that changes. It is this change which transforms an individual criminal into the highest station one can attain in life. The change in choice of leadership developed him from one who should have suffered the eternal fires of hell into an inspir-ing person who is full of nobility and self-sacrifice. The story of Hurr retells this reality: how the change in leadership and the knowledge of a rightful leader can effect a human being" (*CW*, vol. 2, pp. 215).

PART TWO
FOR MUSLIM WOMEN

WOMAN IN THE HEART
OF MUHAMMAD (ﷺ)

INTRODUCTION

There has been a great deal said about this subject while, at the same time, much has been left unsaid. What has been said has been either the words of an enemy whose remarks a combination of lies, slanders and distortions of historical reality, or has been the words of a friend who has attempted, frequently unsuccessfully, to overstate, paraphrase and justify the view of the Muslim woman in order to suit the mores of the people of his time. Neither of these two views is that of a researcher, a person free from prejudice, who investigates only in search of truth.

The question of woman, whether from the emotional or social point of view, continues to be relevant. Whether we wish it or not, the issue has remained in the realm of opinion. Of necessity, therefore, schools of thought, religion, preference, or need interpret and explain it. In this way, in every school, age and society different conclusions are obtained. It is natural that writers who have studied this subject as related to the life of the Prophet have been unable to free themselves from the snare of pre-judgment resulting from these five factors: school of thought, religion, custom, preference [i.e. social zeal and emotional inclination] and need [individual or social].

It is in this context that the interpretation by men of women in society is colored to a great extent by time and environment. Obviously, a scientist who does research on such a topic, which in every age and society takes on a particular form, is faced with a difficult task. If he does not free himself from the opinions, customs and prejudices of his own society as well as rid himself of the blight of pre-judgment and, in the words of Professor Jacques Berk, "...view and weigh a subject which is of a different time and surroundings with the eyes of his own age and surroundings....," he will remain unable to perceive historical reality as it was. In this case, all that he says will be futile. In fact, the question of woman in all of its many aspects is so dependent on the conditions prevailing in a particular age that what may be the most humane principles and customs can, when viewed from a different era and surroundings, appear to be crimes against humanity.

Polygamy is one example. Without doubt, the conscience of our time is wounded by such an ugly affront to women However, this principle protected many bereaved women in the past who lacked a guardian. In many cases it is clear that it also protected their orphaned children who otherwise would be permanently deprived of a man and a secure and healthy family. Such people were, therefore, threatened with poverty, distress and corruption. They were entrusted into the care of a man with polygamy. He provided what was, in those days, the only shelter for women and children. He provided a new home to a family disintegrated by the loss of its head, frequently as a result of a violent death.

A second example is modest dress. Today it is considered to be a shackle restricting women. It is viewed within the spirit of this century as ugly and contemptible. However, in the past it was construed as the sign of distinction of a certain group, as a special social prestige, as the sanctuary of honor and respect for women. It continues to be so construed today in rural areas and by distinguished urban families who have remained faithful to religious practice.

In recent years researchers have studied the subject of the rights of women in Islam. I shall not reiterate their statements here. What is certain is that of all the great reformers and thinkers of history [most of whom viewed women with contempt], Prophet Muhammad (ﷺ) is the only one who took the fate of woman seriously and returned human respect and social rights to her. Islam bestows the right of and economic independence on woman. At the same time it obliges the male to provide for her to whatever extent she may demand even to the point of compensating her for nursing her own infant. She is entitled to a gift from her bridegroom, and although today this right is usually relinquished, in the past it represented the independent character of the woman and provided economic security against inauspicious future circumstances. She is also granted civil and religious equality with men, factors which make women powerful within society and independent of men who have always desired dictatorial domination over them.

What can I say concerning the touchy and complicated subject of women in society from the point of view of Islam. My conclusion reached, after exact and complete study of the social, moral and human rights of women within Islam, is that, while struggling vehemently against the existing discrimination between men and women, Islam does not support the equality of the two. To phrase it differently, it believes neither in discrimination nor in equality. **Rather, it emphasizes equity by assigning to both their natural places within society**. It knows discrimination to be a crime and equality to be wrong. The intention of the heart is against the former and nature against the latter.

Nature knows woman to be neither inferior to man nor the same as him. Nature has molded the two to be complements of one another in life and society. It is for this reason that Islam, in contrast to Western civilization, favors that both be granted their natural rights which are equal and identical. This point is the most important one to be made on the subject. The depth and value of this view is not unknown to those aware readers who have the courage to think, without first seeking the permission of Europe, and who see with their own eyes.

Prophet Muhammad (ﷺ) in practice attempted to give woman the rights which Islam maintains to be hers. He took allegiance (a political and social guarantee and contract according to Islam) from women as well as men. He included women as well as men within the ranks of his followers. He placed his daughter Fatima on his knees in public. While speaking, he stroked and caressed her in a loving and endearing manner. In showing some special attention to her, it seems he intended to show the Arabs that a girl is not shameful but, just as a boy, is a dear offspring.

Previous to this time, it was the Arabs, who according to the Koran, would turn black upon hearing that their newborn was a girl and would try to hide their indignation. Sometimes they would not hide it, but would bury her alive under the earth.

When Ali (ﷺ) asked the Prophet's permission to marry Fatima (ﷺ), Prophet Muhammad (ﷺ) sought her consent and did so with courtesy and with frankness mixed with shyness and modesty. He stood outside the door of her room and said, "Fatima, Ali ibn Abu Talib mentions your name." He remained silent in anticipation of her reply. If Fatima had meant to give a negative response, she would have slowly closed the door. However, she did nothing. Thus to answer in the positive was to give no answer—to remain silent.

When Fatima (ﷺ) went to live in her husband's house, Prophet Muhammad (ﷺ) visited her daily. He stood outside her door and asked her permission to enter and anticipated her in offering greetings.

Prophet Muhammad (ﷺ)'s behavior with his wives is of the same caliber—a mixture of courtesy, softness and affection which appeared surprising in the harsh society of that day. This man, who outside his home was the manifestation of power and firmness, within his home behaved so gently, simply and affectionately with his wives that they dared to speak out fearlessly and openly disputed with him even to the point of tormenting him. At one point they so plagued him that, in contrast to the usual custom of throwing the wife out of the house (a practice frequently followed by today's believers), the Prophet himself left his home and went to reside in a site on one side of which grain had been strewn. This silo was situated on a small hill. The Prophet would place the trunk of a tree against it, climb the tree trunk and, upon reaching the top, remove the trunk so that no one could disturb him. On this occasion he quarreled with his wives for one month and was so tormented that he even stopped going to the mosque. The people became very anxious and distressed. They sent Umar (ﺮ) as their representative. He went to see the Prophet and asked permission to speak with him. His request was refused; whereupon Umar sent the Prophet the message, "I don't want to talk to you about my daughter because I am disgusted with her. If you give me permission, I will cut off her head."

The Prophet gave Umar permission to enter. Umar said, "When I entered I saw that he had rolled out a straw mat in a corner of the area. When he rose, the imprint of the straw mat showed on his side. I began weeping profusely." Seeing Umar's sorrow, the Prophet talked to him about the pleasure of abstinence. He calmed Umar.

The behavior of his wives was one of the greatest problems

of the Prophet's life, which is natural, as his thought was greatly distant from theirs. Moreover, women of that day were considered to be inferior, humble slaves. They were thought to be
unworthy of the freedom and respect which they felt only in the
home of the Prophet. Today, we more than ever before, are
familiar with this truth. For one who has had no such experience, changing one's personality in the beginning may involve
unhealthy and sometimes even dangerous reactions.

The words of Umar reveal clearly a deep-rooted revolution
in the social rights of women and, especially, in the relationship
between man and woman during the time of the Prophet. He
said, "I swear to God that in our ignorance we did not take
women into consideration in any affair until God sent down
verses and established a portion for them. As I was asking
advice on a certain matter, my wife told me to do this and that.
I said, "What business is it of yours to meddle in my affairs?"

"She said, 'How is it that while you don't want anyone to
meddle in your affairs, your daughter disputes with the Prophet
of God and carries on to such a point that she spends the whole
day sulking and in anger?'"

Umar said, "I took my cloak and left my house. I went to
Hafsa and said, 'My little girl, do you quarrel with the Prophet
of God to the point that you spend the whole day sulking?' Hafsa
said, Yes, I quarrel with him.' I said to her, 'My daughter,
beware of the punishment of God and the anger of the
Prophet.'"

One day Umar and Abu Bakr (؇) saw the Prophet sitting sur-
rounded by his wives who, with much yelling and commotion in
harsh, impudent tones, complained of their hard lives and
demanded allowances from him while he sat quietly and sadly
with a bitter smile on his lips. When his eyes fell upon Abu Bakr
and Umar, he complained, "They ask of me something which I
do not have."

Umar and Abu Bakr arose and began to chastise their
daughters who, being more familiar with such language, quiet-
ed down and promised not to demand something of the Prophet
which he did not have. Their behavior was unbearable even for
their fathers (let alone the Muslims who suffered seeing the
pain the Prophet suffered) but the Prophet bore it all in order
to teach a new lesson to the harsh and uncivilized men of his

society and to give a new sense of individuality to the helpless
and deprived women.

Another reason for the perennial dissatisfaction of the
Prophet's wives was that to a certain extent they had heard how
the wives of the kings of Iran, the ceasars of Rome, and even the
sultans and rulers of Yemen and Egypt lived in magnificent
courts and were immersed in gaming, dancing, wine, and mirth,
while they, the wives of the King of the Arabs, saw months go
by without any smoke arising from the roofs of their kitchens.
They cooked gruel from unshelled barley bran and ate it. This
was their warm food, but usually their tables held water and
dates and nothing else!

This conflict between the Prophet and his wives grew until
a revelation intervened and suggested: Whoever of you with
desire for this world should take your complete dowry and continue your life freely as you desire and whoever of you with
desire for God and the Hereafter should accustom yourself to
Muhammad and the hard life and destitute house of
Muhammad. The wives choose poverty and the Prophet. Only
one among them choose this world, but the world was unfaith-
ful to her and her fate, inauspicious.

The Prophet would say, "I love three things in this world:
perfume, women and the brightening of my eyes during prescribed prayer." After the migration when he had more than one
wife, he behaved equitably towards them spending a night with
each of them, but his heart overflowed with love for Ayisha (R).
She was the only virgin he married. All of his other wives were
widows whom he had married on the basis of political or moral
advisability.

Ayisha, besides being beautiful and young, was a very intelligent, well-mannered, well-spoken and knowledgeable woman
who truly loved the Prophet. She was very jealous of his other
wives. By talking with her, the Prophet soothed the hardships
and great weariness of his political life. Whenever the pressure
of deep contemplation and reflection disquieted him, whenever
he could no longer bear the pressure of his many thoughts, he
called Ayisha and said, "Speak with me, my rose!"

Christian missionaries and biased or unknowledgeable
writers who have been influenced by their religious and political propaganda have attempted to find a weak point in the
strong soul of the Prophet. Since Christians view the beauty of

women as a deception of the devil, any attraction to it is thought immoral and degenerate (even to the extent that abstinence from marriage is believed to be pleasing to God and a preservation of piety), and since the conscience of Europe considers polygamy to be ugly and repellent, westerners attempt to make an eastern Don Juan of the Prophet, a man infatuated with women who, like the sultans of the East, formed harems.

These people create a great uproar over two issues: first, the Prophet's many marriages and second, the story of Zaynab bint Jahsh. Since the noise of this uproar has even reached Muslim countries and has preoccupied many of our own intellectuals [i.e. certificate holders], I shall reveal the truth as I have understood it.

I believe that the question of women in the life and feelings of the Prophet is not only not a point of weakness in his character but is, in truth, one of the bright and beautiful aspects of this great soul. As Abbas Mahmood Aghad, an Egyptian, states, "Christian missionaries and colonial writers wanted in this way to strike Islam a death blow, while in reality, they are greatly astray on this for to a Muslim who is familiar with his religion and the life story of his Prophet, the truth is clearly manifest. Contrary to being a point of weakness, this very point to a Muslim is sufficient proof in itself of the greatness of the Prophet and the exoneration of his religion, despite the various slander spread against it. For a Muslim, for the verity of the prophethood of Muhammad, there is no more truthful argument than his behavior with his wives and his manner of choosing them..." Here let us first study the story of Zaynab and then that of his many wives, Thus we may know what this love really was and see how what is called passion and having a 'harem' was really love for his community. We will see that this situation serves as a model for future generations.

ZAYNAB BINT JAHSH

Zaynab was the daughter of Jahsh and the sister of Abd Allah, an important Emigrant who ended his glorious life in martyrdom. The Jahsh family was of the celebrated nobility of the Quraysh. Zaynab, the beautiful daughter of Jahsh, was related to the family of Abd al-Muttalib through his daughter. She was the result of the union of two parents of noble birth and therefore, the cousin of the Prophet.

Zayd ibn Harith was a slave captured in Damascus whom fate had brought to the home of Khadija (﷽). Khadija gave him to Muhammad (ﷺ) when she and Muhammad (ﷺ) were married. Harith, Zayd's father, who was from among the nobility of Damascus, went to Makkah in search of his son. Upon finding him, he offered to buy him back from his master. The Prophet accepted, but Zayd did not, preferring bondage and exile in the house of Muhammad and Khadija to freedom in his own country at the side of his father and mother. Without hesitation Zayd told his father who, having suffered greatly in his search for his captured son, had now become impatient in his desire to take him, "I see in the face of Muhammad a purity from which I cannot tear my heart..."

The Prophet recognized his great loyalty and now saw himself as dearer in Zayd's eyes than was Harith. He immediately freed him and claimed him as his son, asking everyone henceforth not to call him Zayd ibn Harith Abd al-Muhammad (Zayd ibn Harith the slave of Muhammad), but rather to call him Zayd ibn Muhammad ibn Abd Allah (Zayd the son of Muhammad, the son of Abd Allah). In this way Zayd regained the father and country which he had lost and, the Prophet filled the empty place left by his two recently deceased offspring, Ghassem and Abd Allah [Tayib and Tahir].

The strong wonderful friendship between these two souls is one of the most beautiful events of the Prophet's life. Zayd grew up in the house of the Prophet! And this intelligent young Damascene who had inherited ability from his rich society and outstanding family background became the fifth member of this family whose sixth was God. How blessed Zayd was because he recognized the good fortune which had come his way and opened the door towards it. How well he chose his wonderful fate.

The adoption of children into families was a common practice among Arabs. Slaves sometimes became very dear in the eyes of their masters. They were freed and elevated from slave to offspring. However, at the same time, the memory of having been a slave remained alive in the social environment of the master. While his change of status provided the freed slave with new social rights, his social prestige remained blemished. A **freed** person was never viewed as a **free** person. A step-child did not take the place of a child. He or she was still regarded as psychologically and spiritually inferior and was, thus, deprived of many social rights and discriminated against. One such discrimination involved the community's public outrage and shame over a man marrying a woman who had previously been the wife of his freed slave. The outrage was so great that they prohibited such marriages and threatened public shunning if they were to occur.

The Prophet, trying to end all discrimination which separated the freed from the free to insure the absolute equality of the two—wanted to remove the stigma of having been a former slave, from the memory of the people. He also wanted to rid the former slaves of their feelings of social inferiority and, thereby, grant them social distinction as well as freedom so that he would be considered in his own estimation as well as in society's as a free, not freed, person.

It was with this intention that the Prophet entrusted Zayd with important and sensitive missions which would introduce him as an honorable and clear Emigrant and Companion. He made him his successor at Madinah and made him the commander of the largest army against Byzantium in which important figures such as Jafar ibn Abu Talib, Abd Allah ibn Ruwaha and Khalid ibn Walid were common soldiers. He consulted with him on the most sensitive matters and made him supervisor of many important affairs. He even consulted with Zayd's young son, Usama, in the company of such men as Ali ibn Abu Talib, on a crucial and serious subject of jurisprudence, involving a family matter. In the last days of his life, he made Usama, who was a youngster of eighteen years, the commander of the army which has been mobilized for battle against the emperor of Byzantium and which included such important figures as Abu Bakr and Umar. All these efforts were to insure that freed slaves would remain as equal in the sentiments of Muslims as they were legally equal within Muslim society.

The Prophet decided to ask a girl from the Arab nobility to be Zayd's wife. He did this so that both the abject feeling of foreigners, particularly freed slaves, would vanish and so that those family prejudices, which become more apparent especially concerning marriages, would be forgotten. He knew that no girl of a noble descent would consent to become the wife of such a person. Therefore he decided to betroth Zayd to a girl from his own kin so that he might mediate any discord between her and her relatives. For this reason he chose Zaynab, his cousin. But, as he had foreseen, Zaynab's brother, Abd Allah, although one of the purest and most self-sacrificing of the Emigrants, considered this proposal shameful to his family and refused it.

The Prophet made great efforts to dispel this entrenched, ignorant prejudice (which is still evident in the twentieth century in "civilized" European society), until Koranic revelation compelled Abd Allah and his sister to give in: *It is not for any believer, man or woman, when God and His Messenger hare decreed a matter, to have the choice in the affair. Whoever disobeys God and His Messenger has gone astray into manifest error."*

The Prophet paid the dowry of Zaynab himself. The wedding broke an ugly custom and replaced it with a new and humane one. Alas, although this union was a propitious event for society, it ended badly. Zaynab was never able to forget the "honor" of her family or the social inferiority of Zayd. She continuously harped on this subject making Zayd miserable. She complained to the Prophet who persuaded Zayd to be patient and called both of them to compromise. Although at the Prophet's order she had physically consented to the marriage with Zayd, Zaynab could not give her heart, for the heart is a separate realm and ruled only by love. Zaynab had no control over it.

The union which the Prophet had exerted effort to bring about daily weakened. Living with someone whose presence felt like a rock placed in her breast or as a knot tied in her throat, Zaynab became more impatient each day. Zayd, too, became continually more pained by his union with a woman whom he found to be increasingly distant. The wedlock of these two incompatible people become moment by moment darker and more bitter. It was not in the hands of anyone to change it.

Without doubt, as Shandel states, "A heart empty of love sends its owner after what has been lost. Until it gains what it seeks, the heart will not rest. God, freedom, knowledge, talent, beauty and friendship await him on the path through the wilderness of seeking until he fills his empty, dusty pitcher from the water of one such spring."

In one instant the Prophet read Zaynab's secret. A mysterious fire had taken hold of Zaynab and became apparent on her cheeks. A restlessness, pressing upon her heart, made her silence before the Prophet difficult and painful. Upon sensing this current of distress, the Prophet closed his eyes, immediately bowed his head and hastily retired. But where was Zaynab to return? She could no longer endure seeing Zayd. The heavens were pressing down upon her breast making breathing impossible. The patience demanded to look on any face or listen to any words seemed torture to her. In this cold house, two strangers sat next to each another, bitterly silent, waiting for nothing and witnessing only the meaningless coming and going of the sunrise and sunset. If suddenly a spark had entered through a crack, it would have made such a fire that neither Zayd nor Zaynab could have remained for a moment.

Zayd impatiently and painfully leapt from his house and took shelter with the Prophet. In complete sincerity he asked his adopted father to free him and Zaynab's from one another as there remained no forbearance in either of them. Zayd adored the Prophet who overflowed with magnanimity and kindness. Moreover, Zayd was a man of the sword, a man of loyalty and faith and "...he would not uselessly carry the body of a woman whose heart was not his." He could not simply, for the sake of becoming grafted to the Quraysh clan or for the pleasures of beauty, make himself and another person captives with nothing in common but the roof of their room. The Prophet gave a great deal of thought to this sad situation and hoped to find a solution, but he could not.

Many questions have been put and imaginative stories and delusive myths have been woven around this subject, but I see such questions as completely worthless. Any answer proposed is baseless. The hidden road of love is known neither by history nor by investigation, especially in a heart as deep, great and powerful as that of the Prophet. His heart was different from that of a singing poet who, like a harp at the soft beckoning of the tip of a little finger, begins to wail and rend asunder the collar of patience and silence. The heart is an ocean. What eye can see how a breeze dancing among the greenery of flowers suddenly rises in the morning and throws itself upon the ocean's surface, thereby disturbing the heart of the ocean; what eyes can view the ocean's depth from a distance of a thousand miles.

To speak of what was concealed in the depths of a heart is to wander far astray and to speak falsely. Such speech is like trying to measure bubbling soda in a glass for who can speak of the bubbling of hidden and unseen springs in the depths of a soul for whom creation was a tight, short garment.

We also know that the Prophet was not a stranger to love for God. This is obvious from a prophetic speech, overflowing with wonder and great beauty, which the leakcd have recorded and preserved: Whoever falls victim to love and keeps it hidden, remaining self-possessed, for him heaven is certain."

Love in the Prophet's life is a wondrous story—not at all like the story woven by the Christian priests or by orientalists or by popular exploiters. How ugly, perverted, hostile and ignorant are their views. These people have supposed the Prophet's love to be of that type which from time to time happens in the seclusion of monasteries or in the dark corners of churches between the holy sisters and holy fathers—that type which Victor Hugo might also disclose.

The Prophet was extremely depressed and distressed over Zaynab's unhappy marriage. He found himself in a very difficult situation with no way out. A continuation of marital life between Zaynab and Zayd was impossible. Salvation for both lay in separation. Because he had sacrificed his kinswoman for the sake of social harmony, the Prophet felt a great responsibility towards Zaynab. Furthermore, was it possible in the face of Zaynab's agony for the Prophet to remain indifferent? After her separation from Zayd should he abandon her, without hope, to a painful and wayward fate.

These are problems with which the Prophet was faced. The Prophet, the most pragmatic moral and social leader of mankind, could neither close his eyes to reality nor attempt to change it. One of the brightest, most correct qualities of Islam and its Prophet is the ability to acknowledge the realities of the human situation—such as war, wrath, revenge, the desire for pleasure, beauty and wealth—Islam provides for the breaking of a bond and the making of a new one. Islam knows that divergence from the institution of monogamy is a reality with which human beings and societies are constantly faced. Although many of the social philosophies, mystical orders and the majority of religions have attempted either to bypass all of these or to combat them, they have never been successful. Every reality which we attempt to bypass or to ignore will reveal itself in an uglier and more dangerous form. Should we fail to meet it head on, it will stab us in the back. This is a truth to which history has always borne witness.

Islam always faces volatile realities and acknowledges their existence. In this way it tames them and drives them on its road, thus averting insurgence, danger and corruption. The most dangerous internal enemies of a society are the realities which it does not officially recognize, to which it gives no countenance. Through its establishment of holy war, divorce, polygamy, repeated marriages, retaliation, ownership and permission to enjoy the wealth and pleasures of material life, in other words by admitting to and tolerating that which is everywhere and has always existed and from which there is no running away, Islam strives to bridle these unyielding and dangerous realities. Love is a reality—a reality as powerful as spite, revenge, and war. If the door is closed to it, as is the case with Christianity, love will jump over the wall!

At this juncture, he who does not understand the meaning of love and does not know the strange and mysterious power which calls two like souls together, will not understand what I am saying. Nor will he who sees the connection between two human beings as something illusory unless it is tied with the cord of name, bread, and physical pleasure. For such a person the relationship between man and God is unintelligible except as fear of the flaming scepter and the serpent of hell or as desire for the beautiful and handsome dwellers in paradise and for the dark-eyed girls with breasts like ripe pomegranates. How can he know what I am talking about here?

So then back to our problem. Why didn't the Prophet free Zaynab from the fetter which bound both she and Zayd? Zaynab, this injured bird, was trying desperately to open the door of the cage. She threw herself restlessly against its bars wanting to take shelter with the Prophet from a hopeless prison.

The Prophet was concerned about two things. One was his abhorrence of public interpretation. He was afraid that his pure and noble sentiments would be polluted by the unclean and base understanding of the people. For a beautiful and noble soul linked to the heavens, there is no enemy more wicked, uglier or more abominable than close-minded and short-sighted people who wriggle worm-like in the mire of their moral corruption.

How was it possible for the Arabs of Hijaz and Najd, whose feelings in love were equal to those of a camel, to see what even cultured writers of today's Europe have interpreted as the movie-like sentimental love which colors Western literature. With what filth would they contaminate a heart as pure as the heavens, a heart in which hundreds of hidden wondrous springs gush forth?

Moreover, there was a taboo blocking the Prophet's way, a taboo like those which make up the walls of every society and dam every escape. This taboo was an ancient and fixed custom which had taken root in the depth of people's feelings. Being an adopted son was an intermediate stage between slavehood and freedom. The adopted son was only half-free. One characteristic distinguishing him from other men was that his former master, (now called his step-father) could not marry any woman who was once his adopted son's mate. The Arabs viewed such a contingency as a great disgrace.

But why a disgrace? Why should a woman be deprived of a right which all other women possessed simply because she married a slave? Wasn't a freed human being free?

This custom, a superstitious and inhuman prohibition left over from slavery, was nothing more than a menacing reminder to the woman and her mate, as well as to the people with whom they associated, of the man's former slavehood and the shame of being wedded to him. This pernicious prejudice had to be removed and the freedman and his spouse liberated from any fetter which bound them to slavery and kept them separate from free people.

The decisive revelation which, as always, came down to answer society's needs removed it forever and destroyed this incorrect custom: "...*neither has He made your adopted sons your sons in fact. That is your own saying, the words of your mouths; but God speaks the truth and guides on the way...*"

Presently Zaynab was released from the trap of her marriage of convenience with Zayd, and he was freed from his painful union with Zaynab. Into this narrow and dark understanding could they not include the soul filled with the beauty and magnificence of the rising sun?

Dark days and life-sapping suffocating nights passed in this way while the Prophet kept hidden in his breast, veiled from the foolish distorted view of the people, a secret which like the flames of a fire was burning and restless His head bent down by pain, he became silent until suddenly an opening appeared in the overcast and heavy sky and the proclamation of a strong and reprimanding revelation descended into his heart: *"You hide in your heart what God would reveal, and you are afraid of the people!"*

God revealed the Prophet's hidden secret and proved that fear of men was illusory. The approval of people, people who are the products of ancient customs and irrational, ugly conventions, has no bearing on the truth. An act which allowed two incompatible people, ensnared in each other's traps and forced upon one another, to part from their mutual misfortune was a good act. Thus was destroyed an unbearable, illusory and ugly custom which was a reminder of the slavehood and shame of man and the deprivation and degradation of woman.

At that time marriage with one's step-son's former wife (whom people construed to be one's daughter-in-law), was a difficult task even though the law had recognized it as permissible. Nevertheless, the Prophet and Zaynab were married in 5 AH/627 CE when Zaynab was 38 and at last free to stand by the side of the man she truly loved. Thus was his secret wish fulfilled.

In such a society, who was the one to attempt such an action? Who had the courage to take the first step and trample upon this ancient custom? God picked His Prophet for the accomplishment of such an arduous responsibility: *"When you said to him whom God had blessed and you had favored, 'Keep your wife to yourself, and fear God,' and you were concealing within yourself what God should reveal, fearing other men and God has better right for you to fear Him. So when Zayd had accomplished what he would of her, then We gave her in marriage to you so that there should not be any fault in the believers, touching the wives of their adopted sons, when they have accomplished what they would of them and God's commandment must be performed. There is no fault in the Prophet, touching what God has ordained for him..."*

After studying the collection of various books of Traditions (*ahadith*) of the life of the Prophet and interpretations, this is what remains imprinted on a mind free of any prejudice or pre-judgment. Who can give an answer to questions concerning an event which took place in the depth of the souls and in the con-cealment of the hearts of Zaynab and Zayd? Even if we were liv-ing in their time in a house in Madinah, our discussion of the matter would be based on guesswork. However, scattered bits of information which we have in hand concerning the Prophet's life and matters not irrelevant to this story lead one to seek a door into the enclosure of history, which had hidden this reality in its inner darkness. From this distance we are able to look inside the enclosure and, with the help of our understanding and feeling, to gain an indirect comprehension of it. Our under-standing is aided by considering the following points:

* The interdiction of the modest dress came into being after this story [5 AH, after the Battle of the Trench]. Up until that time, every man was aware of the figure, stature, face and hair of the women of his city.

* Zaynab the Prophet's cousin, from her earliest childhood was continually before his eyes.

* The Prophet himself chose Zaynab for Zayd, and she, at the Prophet's insistence, consented to the marriage. If his heart had been effected with Zaynab's beauty, as orientalists say, he could have betrothed her to himself very easily while she was yet a virgin and more attractive and beautiful. There would have been no need for all this conflict, trouble, defamation, struggle and entanglement.

* Zayd's complaint of his spouse's lack of affection should come as no surprise. As we know, Zaynab and her family were opposed right from the beginning and even the Prophet's insis-tence could not make Zaynab surrender until a revelation com-pelled her to agree to such a forced and expedient marriage.

* After her marriage, Zaynab was in constant contact with the Prophet, for, besides being a close relative of the Prophet's, she had also become the wife of his adopted son. Zayd was one of the principle members of the Prophet's family and his wife, at that time, was viewed as the daughter-in-law of the Prophet.

*Wouldn't such behavior on the part of the Prophet (who in Zayd's opinion was his adopted father, the initiator of his mar-riage and his spouse's father-in-law), have an undesirable effect on Zayd's feelings? The love of Zayd and Usama for the Prophet and the faith and respect which they had for him until the end of their lives was astonishing to readers of the life of the Prophet.

*The story of Zaynab takes place at a time when the story of the Prophet's affection for Ayisha was on everyone's tongue. The Prophet was in the midst of Zaynab and Zayd's quarrel, their subsequent divorce and his own marriage to Zaynab. He had not yet forgotten his love for his rose (*humayra*), and Ayisha had not yet felt the sting of competition. How was it possible for the aware and sensitive, the jealous and audacious Ayisha to keep silent in the face of the Prophet's loss of heart to another woman? She did not tolerate even the small attention which, for the sake of his son Ibrahim, the Prophet paid to his wife Mariyah! How was it possible that she did not acknowledge or show the slightest reaction towards the Prophet's supposed sudden burning love for another woman, particularly when that woman was the wife of his step-son, and, therefore, considered socially off limits. Unless we assume the possibility that the Prophet's desire and love for his cousin Zaynab was secret, Ayisha did not get the slightest hint of it!!!

*The Prophet had not been concerned with love during the days of his youth and purity. So at age sixty such an electrifying love for his cousin is astonishing.

*A point which makes any researcher extremely prone to believe that the Prophet's marriage to Zaynab, like all of his other marriages, was based on love of faith is that after this marriage one cannot ascertain any special relationship between the two. As soon as Zaynab stepped into the Prophet's house, she took her place in the ranks of his other wives and disappeared in the face of Ayisha's radiance. Even the names of Hafsa and Umm Salama are mentioned more often that Zaynab in the life of the Prophet.

*Even if we can make ourselves believe that Ayisha remained unaware of the supposed burning and tumultuous love of the Prophet and Zaynab (to which orientalists allude) we cannot accept the story that, in his own house, the Prophet married a woman whom he had dragged from the house of his step-son with the noose of love, and still Ayisha did not find out! Moreover, the Prophet's sentiments and behavior towards his *humayra* changed, and still we are supposed to believe that Ayisha did not sense it!

In my opinion, the most sensitive mirror reflecting and magnifying one hundred-fold the smallest wave of love or the faintest color of affection which appeared in the hidden depths of the Prophet's heart was Ayisha's heart. Concerning this matter, Ayisha was absolutely silent. Indeed, one might say that the story of the Prophet and Zaynab had no connection with the story of the Prophet and his rose.

At the beginning of my investigation I did not have an opinion one way or the other. At the end of my investigation and after much reflection, I felt that the story of the Prophet and Zaynab, as written by orientalists, is simply cheap sensationalism. It is a story which overlooks the great soul of the Prophet and his model character. Many leaders have freely given their lives in the path of their beliefs and for the sake of their societies. In return, they have been rewarded with name and honor. To by-pass one's name and honor on the road of faith shows the height of character and philanthropy. Men who have not gone higher than the pinnacle of giving one's life are not able to see this peak of self-sacrifice and purity.

PLURALITY OF WIVES

As I previously pointed out, history changes the interpretation of many human ideals. Social and moral matters have a fate exactly the same as that of words: the spirit, meaning and even pronunciation of words changes according to the influence of time and the environment.

The word *shoukh* used to convey the grime and dirt of the body. Today it expresses the most subtle coquetry of a beautiful eye (in Arabic, Persian and Urdu) and the sweetest mannerism of the beloved which, because of their sensitivity and fragility, cannot be grasped by even the most poetic words.

The word *barakat* is the same. They used to call the camel's dry and wet excrement mixed with dirt and straw *barakat*. Today (in Arabic, Persian and Urdu) it refers to realities that human emotion and intelligence are unable to grasp. *Barakat* today means an increase of God's look of favor upon human beings and is even known to be one of the attributes of God!

Words are living beings and have a birth, youth and death. Words have a prime, an old age, a retirement and an anonymity. We see how our not-so-qualified literary people who have not consciously realized this important and vital principle and who , therefore, become helpless when confronted by these changes, transitions, and, especially, revolutions in the spirit, meaning and usage of words "eruditely" express themselves by stating that the correct pronunciation of these words is such and such and that their original and genuine meaning is so and so. These are distinguished mistakes! One must seek refuge! One must challenge! They do not know that a language is a living, moving, evolving society made up of words. You cannot force words to keep the same dress, behavior, relationships, soul and spirit that they innately possessed in the times of Bayhaqi, Ferdowsi and Nasrullah.

Many of the mores and customs of a society are similar. In every age they have assumed particular meanings, uses, and attributes which change in other times or environments—even to the extent of becoming contradictory. Polygamy is one such custom. If we study polygamy from today's perspective as an artifact, as something from a past tribal, primitive or patriarchal society which is still very far removed from bourgeois, complicated urban society and the monogamous family, prevalent in today's civilized European society, without doubt we shall believe it to be a thing worthy of condemnation and criticism. But such a method however suitable to propaganda, uproar and heckling is detrimental to knowledge and research. It blinds the eye of the researcher to accurate realities.

Generally speaking, in the past not only polygamy but marriage itself was not construed as it is today. It was looked upon less with the eyes of love and passion. It was considered more of a social ceremony which created new relationships and pacts. Political, social, economic and even moral factors involved were stronger than the element of love or even passion. In ancient Greece, although it had reached an advanced stage of urbanity, marriage was still construed as a vehicle for the continuation of lineage and the wife was viewed only as the mother of children. Passion was always outside of the home. In that age usually "...the woman was recognized only as a means of reproduction. A wife was wanted as a mistress for the house and not for the sake of enjoyment."

In regard to the plurality of wives of Prophet Muhammad

(ﷺ), does this make him a Don Juan as orientalists are suggesting? Those who wish to portray him as a loving individual will most naturally focus their attention on his youth, for desire and passion are the afflictions of youth. But history which has even revealed the fact that he joked with his wives, as well as the smallest details of his life, does not know of the slightest wave of passion in the youthful phase of the Prophet's life. Until the age of twenty-five, other than poverty, the orphan's lot, pain and shepherding, the Prophet had no experiences.

KHADIJA

The first woman, whom he met at the height of his youth and whom he married was Khadija, a widow aged forty, married twice previously and twice widowed, with children the same age as the Prophet. The Prophet spent his youth and even maturity with her. In the twenty-five years that he spent with her, no other woman entered his life. It should not be forgotten here that the Prophet during this interval was a young man. He, like the other youths of the Quraysh, was not constrained by social prestige, moral impediment, the burden of political and military responsibilities, old age, or the especially momentous responsibility of prophethood. All of these assailed him later on, tied him down, and made him a stranger to passion. It is astonishing that the son of Abd Allah who was a normal youth without responsibility, a man who until the age of fifty remained with a widow fifteen years his senior, did not even once during this span nourish the thought of another woman.

According to even the most zealous Christian missionaries, the Prophet was far from such accusations in Makkah. Then how could it be that as soon as he entered Madinah as an old man of fifty-three who had achieved the distinction of becoming God's Prophet, who bore harsh military and political responsibilities, and whose thoughts, soul, life, age and especially social and moral refinement inspired piety, pain and work with the people, should suddenly have become engulfed in the fire of desire and captivated by pleasure and passion?

Don Juan, as we know, having passed his youth forgot women and became a devout and moral man. How is it possible that a young Arab, who from the age of twenty-five until the age of fifty lived with a widow of forty to sixty-five years of age, suddenly became a Don Juan? Why when he became old and achieved the distinction of prophethood and carried the burden of war and politics should he become a Don Juan? How could a man overcome with the conflicts of war and politics, become a Don Juan? The fault which the missionaries have found in him and about which they have created such a great uproar pertains to the life of the Prophet in Madinah, where he married numerous women.

What they chiefly forget is that it is the beauty of a woman which quenches desire, not the number of women. A capricious man is in search of a coquettish and passion-provoking woman, not a widowed matured woman with children. Such women are either unattractive or, if they ever had any beauty, it faded in the homes of their former husbands. Such women have in place of the smooth lines of maidenhood, the emotions of youth and the playfulness of passion, the wrinkles of old age, cold self-possession and the heavy sobriety of chastity.

Fortunately it is history which records each of the wives of the Prophet and which also records why they had come to his house and how they lived. Without doubt, it knows the wives of the Prophet better than the missionaries and orientalists of Europe.

Khadija died at the age of sixty-five. The Prophet, at this time was more than fifty years of age and at the height of his disappointments and hardships in Makkah. Many of his adherents were living in Ethiopia. With a small group of his followers he was held captive in the grip of a city of enemies. Abu Talib, his only strong and loving protector, had died by this time, and he was left alone. Outside was animosity and torture, while within his home was only the small Fatima and the painful memory of her mother.

They took pity on him and coerced him to take a wife. But the love of Khadija which he never forgot his painful, extremely dangerous political life so consumed him that he was unable to think of any woman.

SAWDA

Sawda, the daughter of Zama and wife of her cousin, Sukran ibn Umru, was one of the first Muslims who in the dark and terrifying days of Islam became followers of the Prophet. She suffered greatly for her belief and, at the Prophet's order, migrated to Ethiopia with her husband. After returning, she lost her husband and became homeless. From then on no fate awaited her but humiliation and ill luck. She was obliged either to return to her family (difficult since she had stepped outside of their religious beliefs) to whom she must surrender and for whom she must return to pagan worship and the past; or to marry a man whom she did not love and who could not equal her lost husband's piety. The Prophet took into his shelter this pure, brave and honorable woman in 2BH/620 CE when she was about 30 years old. Her life, after much torment endured on his path, had become chaotic. By marrying her, he made her the successor to Khadija and the wife of the Prophet. He married her in Makkah before he married Ayisha.

AYISHA

Ayisha, the daughter of Abu Bakr, was the only girl among his wives who had been born in Islam. This uniqueness had made the intimates and followers of the Prophet come upon the idea that the first female who had been born in Islam, and who had no memory of the pagan state, should become the wife of the Prophet. Only emotion can discern the tenderness and beauty of such an action. The first flower to bloom in a newly planted garden or the first fruit to ripen in the orchard reminds the gardener whose heart bears witness that this new flower or fire is, fittingly, his.

Abu Bakr, who was of most tender sentiments and who besides having faith in the Prophet overflowed with love for him, suggested this marriage to him. But Ayisha was a girl of seven years while the Prophet was now over fifty. He was a man with a daughter in need of a mother. He was a man who had enemies like Abu Jahl and Abu Lahab and whose life was bitter, tumultuous, dangerous and painful throughout. He was in need of a sympathetic partner. It is obvious that Abu Bakr's seven year old daughter was not suitable for the job of being the Prophet's partner.

The Prophet betrothed her so that the first girl to be born in Islam, the first generation of the world's Muslims, would bear his name. He also wished to be related to his sympathetic friend Abu Bakr. In that time and surroundings, family ties were the most firm connection exiting between two human beings. The student of Bedouin tribes realizes this.

Ayisha was the only virgin he married and the only woman whose youth and beauty moved his heart. But her beauty was not the reason for the Prophet's marriage to her for the beauty of a six or seven year old child cannot effect the feelings of a man whose age was past fifty.

The wedding of the Prophet and Ayisha in 1 AH/623 CE was a symbolic wedding, mingled with sage advise. Here any talk of love or passion was out of place. He did not take Ayisha into his home while in Makkah. He married her three years later in Madinah. One should know that, in the words of Muhammad Husayn Haykal, a contemporary Egyptian author, "The love which he had for Ayisha came into existence after their marriage and did not exist at their wedding. It cannot be said that it was the demand of love which caused him to take a wife. It is impossible to believe that Muhammad was in love with her when she was seven. Therefore, even his marriage to the only beautiful young virgin to become his wife was not an amorous, sex-driven marriage."

HAFSA

Hafsa was the daughter of Umar. When her husband died at the Battle of Badr no one approached her for marriage even though she was the daughter of Umar until Umar himself felt obliged to do something. First he suggested the matter to Abu Bakr, in the hope that perhaps his friendship with him might be of some use. But Abu Bakr remained silent. Then he went to see Uthman and proposed he marry Hafsa, but Uthman also remained silent. Umar became dejected. His heart ached at the silent reply of his two dear friends. He complained about them to the Prophet. The Prophet, in order to soothe his mind, said, "Wed Hafsa to one who is better for her than Abu Bakr or Uthman." Thus the Prophet wed Hafsa, thereby strengthening his connection with Umar, one of the most influential and effective personalities of Islam. They were married in 3 AH/625 AH when she was 18.

One can discern the beauty of Hafsa through the efforts of Umar and the silence of Abu Bakr and Uthman. But it is preferable that on this matter, "We should also hear a word from the father of the bride." We may also become familiar with the

Prophet by listening to those women whom he had chosen while at the height of his power and influence.

UMM SALAMA

Umm Salama was the daughter of Abu Umaya. She was the wife of Abu Salama (Abd Allah Makhzumi), a great warrior in the cause of Islam who was wounded at Uhud. Later, when he returned victorious from the war with the Asad tribe, his wound re-opened and he died. The Prophet went to the bedside of his self-sacrificing Companion and prayed for him. He became so saddened at his death that he shed tears and wept profusely. Umm Salama, Abu Salama's widow, was left with several children, both young and old, from her martyred husband.

Four months after the the death of Abu Salama, Umm Salama, still mourning her beloved and great husband and grieving for her fatherless and homeless children, was living a hopeless and painful existence. The leaders of Islam knew themselves responsible for the fate of the family of their martyred brother.

For this reason, Abu Bakr proposed marriage to her, but Umm Salama excused herself saying, "My children are many and my youth has passed." Umar also proposed, but Umm Salama did not accept and repeated her answer. The Prophet himself went to see her and said, "Ask of God so that He will reward you in your affliction and give you something better in its place." Umm Salama replied painfully, "Who is better for me than Abu Salama?" The Prophet named himself, but she did not accept and again repeated the response she had given to Abu Bakr and Umar. The Prophet insisted, repeatedly proposed to her until her eldest child, Salama, wed her to the Prophet in 4 AH/626 CE when she was 29 years old. He took the wife and children of his martyred Companion into his home. He always held her very dear and worthy of respect. She was the only woman in the Prophet's life after Khadija who could have reminded him of her, for not only did she possess the moral character, wisdom and worthiness of Khadija but also resembled her greatly in behavior and mannerism.

ZAYNAB

The daughter of Khuzayma had been the wife of Abidah ibn

Harith who was martyred at the Battle of Badr. She had previously been divorced from his brother. The Prophet took this woman as his wife because he did not want the wife of a martyred Muslim warrior to end in a shelterless old age. She did not live for more than two years after the marriage.

Zaynab was a most devout, loving and beneficent woman. She had devoted her whole life to soothing orphans and aiding the poverty-stricken. She had striven so much in this work that she had been given the title, "The Mother of the Needy" [*umm al-masakin*].

JUWAYRIYYA

The daughter of Harith, the head of the Mustaliq clan, Juwayriyya had become the property of Sabet Ibn Qays at the end of the battle between the Muslims and the Mustaliq clan. Juwayriyya came to the Prophet and said, "Sabet wants an enormous amount for my freedom, and I do not have it. Will you help me pay my ransom?" The Prophet asked, "Do you want better than that?" She asked what that would be. He said, "I pay for your deed and marry you." She accepted.

The Prophet paid her ransom, freed her and made her his wife in 5 AH/627 CE when she was 20. Thus he tactfully placed love of himself in the hearts of the people of the Mustaliq tribe, especially the chief of the tribe, who previously had hated him. At the same time he persuaded the Muslims to release their captives. After the marriage of Muhammad and Juwayriyya, captives from the Mustaliq tribe became relatives of the Prophet rather than his enemies. It was not fitting for any Muslim to keep a relative of the Prophet as captive.

The captives were freed and all converted to Islam. The tribe of the Mustaliq, who had been dangerous enemies of the Prophet, became his relatives. The head of the tribe went to see his daughter and gave her the option of either returning with him or staying with the Prophet. She chooses the latter. She had previously been married to her cousin, Abd Allah.

MARIYAH

A Copt and slave-concubine presented to the Prophet by the ruler of Egypt in 6 AH/628CE or earlier. She bore him a son called Ibrahim who died when he was a small boy. She remained a concubine.

UMM HABIBA

Umm Habiba was the daughter of Abu Sufyan. She made great sacrifices at the height of the conflict between the Prophet and Abu Sufyan in Makkah. She became a follower of his and along with her husband, Ubayd Allah ibn Jahsh Asadi, migrated to Ethiopia. There her husband, influenced by the environment, became a Christian, but Ramla remained firm in her faith. She was, therefore, deserted by her husband and left alone in a foreign country. Neither could she remain shelterless in Ethiopia nor could she return to Makkah, as the Prophet and the other Muslims had already migrated to Madinah. Even if Abu Sufyan would have given her shelter, it would have been on no terms other than that she relinquish her convictions. She could not bear the shame of such a return to paganism. To reward such self-sacrifice, to make fortunate a respectable woman threatened with misfortune on his way, to wed the daughter of his sworn enemy Abu Sufyan was a most significant event. His proposal to her was very respectfully submitted. Najashi, the king of Ethiopia, personally concluded a marriage agreement as the Prophet's representative and gave Umm Habiba her dowry. They were married in 7 AH/627 CE when she was about 35 years old.

SAFIYA BINT HUYAYY

A Jewish woman from the an-Nadir tribe, she was captured at Khaybar in 7AH/628CE and assigned to the Prophet. She was 17 and perhaps a concubine at first, but apparently accepted Islam and was set free.

MAYMUNA

Maymuna was the sister of Umm Fadl, wife of Abbas ibn Abd al-Muttalib. One year after the Treaty of Hudaybiah, the Prophet entered Makkah to make the shorter pilgrimage. According to this agreement, he did not have the right to remain more than three days. During these three days, he tried to bring the hearts of the people closer to himself. Through kindness and generosity, goodness, flexibility, and friendly contacts, he wanted to lessen the animosity and prejudice which the pagan leaders carried in their souls. He was also searching for an excuse to prolong his own and his followers period of stay so that he might have a greater opportunity to endear the people to himself

In this interval, Abbas, who was still among the ranks of the polytheists, introduced Maymuna to him. During these few days the behavior of the Muslims had had a great impact on her, and she had been drawn to Islam. She was the sister of his wife and the aunt of Khalid ibn Walid, the famous champion of the Quraysh and the victor of the Battle of Uhud. Moreover the sight of the Prophet these three days—his charismatic look and behavior and his spiritual character—had greatly effected Maymuna's heart. She was so effected that the voice of her burning love echoed in the heavens and a revelation praises her pure feelings.

Abbas, whose wife had given him the authority to pick a husband for her sister, suggested the matter to the Prophet. Maymuna's inclination towards Islam, her kinship with Khalid, whose sword at the Battle of Uhud had assured the defeat of the Muslims and the victory of the Quraysh, and her family ties with the influential families of the Quraysh were elements which persuaded the Prophet to accept this proposal. He further hoped to gain more favorable notice by setting the date for the wedding on the last day of his stay, inviting all the Quraysh and offering food.

Since the conversion of Maymuna to Islam had not yet been revealed, she was still seen as an unbeliever. The Prophet's marriage to her and, particularly, the attendance of both Muslims and polytheists at the wedding feast where those who had fought one another at the battles of Badr and Uhud ate together at one table, had a profound effect on the feelings of the Arabs, warming the cold political air and lessening the distance and strangeness between them. It also provided an excuse to remain in the city. Additionally, this opportunity provided, besides the chance for propaganda and the conversion of souls, the milieu from which might spring more concessions than those in the Treaty of Hudaybiah.

The alert Quraysh leaders were aware of the Prophet's plan. For this reason they flatly rejected his suggestion. He was therefore forced to hold the wedding ceremony on the road back to Madinah in 7 AH/629 CE when Maymuna was 27 years old. Nevertheless, this marriage which related him to some of the prominent men of the Quraysh was not without effect on the souls of those men. In fact, a short while later, we see Khalid in companionship with Umar Aas and Uthman ibn Tacheh, taking the road towards Madinah.

RAYHANA BINT ZAYD

A Jewish woman from the an-Nadir tribe, she was captured with the Qurayzah tribe to which her husband had belonged in 10 AH/632 CE. She became a concubine of the Prophet and died before he did in the same year.

CONCLUSION

A few points should be mentioned at the end of this discussion. Islam did not bring about polygamy. Before Islam no limitation existed as to the number of wives an Arab could take. Islam limited the number to four. A close study of Koranic verses which speak of polygamy will clear up its philosophy and conditions.

The Koran firstly makes it incumbent upon men to act justly with their wives and then immediately confesses, *"....but if you fear you will not be equitable, then only one..." "You will not be able to be equitable between your wives, be you ever so eager...."*

Such a masterful and wondrous statement will make anyone who comprehends and is familiar with the spirit of the Koran understand this point. Anyone who is a stranger to the meandering of interpretation and the tricks and secrets of meaning—destroying discourse, and who does not have the passion for polygamy in his heart—must readily confess that the conditions are so arduous and the passage concerning permission so scrupulous that, except for individual and social cases where moral or spiritual exigency requires, it is impossible to pass them.

Individual cases can be judged from the content of the Koran. This commandment appears in the midst of verses which speak of the fate of orphans. It is obvious that in societies where an advanced form of government and social institutions are non-existent, women who have no guardian and fatherless children have an inauspicious and pitiful fate.

Fortunately the present generation lives in a century of civilization, in an advanced society, in an age of legal, economic and social independence for the individual. In particular the gain in character of woman and her equality with man has been pronounced.

Following W.W.II, as a result of the death of millions of men in Europe (especially in Germany, Austria and Poland) a crisis occurred. The waves of corruption and decadence and the psychological illnesses and mental distress which now torment husbands, women, and fatherless children have had a deep effect and created a grave deviation in the spirit and morals of European society.

In 1958 the Algerian National Liberation Front recommended to all its members that the *mujahidin* should be attentive to the families of their martyred brothers and marry the women who had lost their husbands in this struggle. This way martyrdom would not become a source of distress for children nor an affliction of women. This way the family of a martyr might not fall into the trap of poverty and corruption.

What I want to say is that the matter of polygamy in the past should not be viewed with that feeling which its meaning today engenders. We should see with the eyes of that former age.

Another point which should be known concerning the private life of the Prophet is that in Madinah he had no children from his wives although (apart from Ayisha) these women were all widows and most had children from their previous husbands. This is one of the wonders of the Prophet's life.

One of the points which naturally comes to mind concerning the Prophet's plurality of wives is that, without doubt, he as any other man, especially in the second half of his life, wanted to have children. It was only in the last year of his life that he had a boy, but he did not live. His captivation with this child and the extreme restlessness which he showed upon the death of the child reveal how deeply he would have loved to have a child. But fate had decided that from the greatest figure of Arab society in which children, particularly sons, bestowed honor and distinction, only one child, a daughter should remain. What a wise and beautiful decision—although it greatly pained the Prophet.

What did the house of the Prophet look like? It consisted of several rooms made of mud connected to the mosque, the roof of which was covered with the branches and leaves of date palms.

Ayisha's house was half carpeted with fur—half strewn with very fine gravel. The chandeliers were constructed of palm branches which burn! What of its kitchen and cuisine? Abu Hurayrah describes it: "Until his death, the Prophet never ate enough barley bread to fill his stomach. Sometimes two months would go by without any fire being lit in his home. During this time their food consisted of dates and water. Sometimes if extremely hungry, he would tie a rock to his stomach..."

Whenever I call to mind the house and life of the Prophet, the fact that he spent his youth and maturity with a widow from forty to sixty-five years old, his old age with well-matured widows who had children (like Umm Salama and Zaynab, daughter of Khuzayma, "Mother of the Needy" and especially Hafsa) and that his house was such and his food such, I cannot keep myself from feeling remorse that the Prophet did not have women more beautiful than these and a life more pleasant. Whenever I read the works of writers who speak of the carnality of the Prophet and of the Prophet's harem, I cannot but be distressed and shamed that a human being (even a writer) could, for expediency, defile with such lies the beautiful, truthful visage which was the glory of humanity and the wealth of history.

THE ISLAMIC
MODEST DRESS

That which all parents have in common is that they propagate religion as if they were blowing a horn from the wrong end. The advice they give to young people is just like a person who continuously says to someone whose face is full of pimples, "Don't grow pimples! Your skin will be ruined," —continuously putting pressure on the person, reproaching him and saying bad things. And even if what is being said is correct, what effect would it have? What do you want to happen? What do you think you will gain?

The situation should be approached from another angle. The factor that caused the "pimples" in the spiritual life of these young people and this generation should be examined. The roots must be found.

Initially when parents said to children, "Let's go on a pilgrimage," they would immediately jump up and get ready. They would really enjoy themselves. They would even ask, "When can we go back again?" The same was true when going to someone's house where there was a reading of the Koran or an activity relating to the prescribed fast or the prescribed prayer.

Then, little by little, children begin to lose interest. The parent speaks to the young person reproaching them with reasons, without reasons, or in anger. Parents continuously apply pressure: "You must perform your prescribed prayers like you used to do!" or "You must wear the modest dress when you go out like you used to do."

The advice parents give is like the advice given to the one who had pimples: "You must clear up your face." This advice is given without paying the least bit of attention to what is causing the pimples to appear.

I speak as a teacher and a person who has read and studied, as one who has spent his social life among people and the young generation, and as one whose work, thought, public and private life have been spent among people. I have seen scenes like this repeated hundreds of times. I have seen them at first hand which is worth more than a scientific opinion. And every time the result is the opposite of what the parents hoped to attain. There have been some very ugly scenes.

What has happened? Parents never understand what has caused the decline in their children's interest in religious matters. They never question why children no longer perform the prescribed prayer or wear the modest dress or lose their interest in attending religious gatherings. The father is authoritarian. The mother is authoritarian. What can be done? Should they force them to obey? If the force of the parents is strong enough to make the children outwardly obey them, inwardly the young people will become even more disgusted with religion. Their hatred for religious things will increase. The young people will stand in prescribed prayer, but instead of whispering the prescribed prayer, they will complain about their parents under their breath for forcing them to perform their religious duties.

Once I was in Madinah and I struck up a conversation with a shop keeper. I had gone in to buy something which I later forgot all about. We started to talk about Arabia, Islam and things of this nature. He was also an intellectual and knew some foreign language. When we first began to talk, he continuously referred to the kings. Little by little he dropped that, and I saw we felt the same way about things.

We became so involved in our conversation that he forgot his other customers. He preferred talking to me to selling a tape recorder to a pilgrim. Suddenly the call to prescribed prayer came. The moment we heard the call to prescribed prayer, he arose and said, "The prescribed prayer! The prescribed prayer." I said, "Good. Let us go together." He said, "We will talk as we go."

I was really surprised when I saw how rapidly he was moving. He was such an enlightened person who was familiar with issues in the Islamic world (at least in Arab countries), and still he was so precise about performing the prescribed prayer exactly on time. I followed him. I saw that without performing the ablution, he stood and said, "I will perform four cycles of the noon prescribed prayer in honor of King Faisal, may he grow close to God."

The prescribed prayer has taken on this form! How far from its real meaning, purpose and aim! Who will be satisfied with this prescribed prayer? The minute the guard left our area, the merchant made up for all those prayers by taking 90% profit on whatever he sold.

In an area I lived in several years ago, there was a woman who left her home everyday wearing a very strict interpretation of modest dress. She would hurry into a deserted house near my window and with the speed of lightening, she would change into another type. She would fold her previous modest clothes, put them in her bag and leave as a very modern woman. In the evening she would return to the deserted house and change back into being a Muslim woman. Acting thus is to live as two completely different types. It is hypocrisy, falsehood, a lying living. It essentially demolishes being human.

If the parents do not have enough authority over their children, when a young person returns home, he or she will resist parental influence and rebel. There is nothing the parent can do. Neither one obtains any solution or result.

What is to be done? The only solution I have found as a teacher and the way Islam teaches is to follow the method of the Prophet (ﷺ). We see that all of Islam, all of its practices and beliefs were not presented by the Prophet in the first year, but rather presented over a period of twenty-three years. He presented them in a gradual way.

First he presented the idea of monotheism. For three years he added nothing to the admonition, "Say: 'God is One,' and be saved." What is the prescribed fast? The prescribed pilgrimage? The poor-due? These had not as yet been presented. There were no constraints, limitations or practices. There was first only thought. It was just this thought which was used to negate the idols and promote belief in the One God.

Thus the people who accepted Islam in the first three years and came to believe in the oneness of God and died were possibly people who drank wine, did not perform the prescribed fast, had not performed the prescribed pilgrimage and had not participated in the struggle in God's way [*jihad*]. Some may even have been usurers because the Prophet announced the forbidding of the practice of usury only at his farewell pilgrimage. He said, "Whoever owes money to Abbas, do not pay it." When was this? Twenty-two years later.

His method was to gradually present Islam. He first presented an intellectual world view. When that thought grew and spread and took root in the minds of the people, a group became prepared. What for? For another type of practice. They were prepared to listen to something new. They themselves would ask to be taught, and he would answer their request. They would say, "Now that we are a group, prescribed prayer in congregation"—that is, "We have attained a level of understanding and preparedness so that we can now perform the prescribed prayer in congregation."

Prescribed prayer began with two cycles. Then it increased slowly. Little by little struggle in God's way was presented not "in order to attach the disbelievers [*kuffar*]," but "if someone has been oppressed, it is approved to cry out." What year was this? This was the twelfth or thirteenth year of the actualization [*bathat*], a few months before the migration to Madinah.

After the migration, sometime in 2 AH [624 CE], it became official to perform the struggle in God's Way against the enemy. In 3 AH [625 CE], the issue of taxes on the spoils of war was presented. It was accepted. That is, the Muslims' faith had so grown that they were prepared to pay taxes, to pay from their own pockets. Thus the Prophet told them to pay the poor due [*zakat*] on the spoils, whereas previously a person kept whatever spoils he could find for himself. This was because the thoughts of his followers had not grown to the point where they could accept the idea of paying out money.

In 7 or 8 AH [CE] the modest dress was presented as well as the issue of wine. How was the issue of wine presented? While still in Makkah, the Prophet did not say, "O people! O nation of Islam! O Arabs! Now that you have accepted monotheism, you must now do everything!" No. In the 7th or 8th year after his actualization, the issue of wine was presented in three phases. Look at this method of educating!

He was first directed to say, "*Do not perform the prescribed prayer when you are drunk*" [4:47]. What does this mean? It means you can drink wine but when you enter the mosque for prescribed prayer, do not stagger or appear to be drunk or have your breath smell of wine. Everyone accepted this. Even those who drank were prepared to accept this one limitation when it came to something sacred. In this way, God directed the Prophet to eliminate the social corruption of wine drinking without directly applying any pressure on the people.

Little by little came the second stage. *"There is a great sin as well as profit for some people drinking alcohol and gambling"* [2:219]. You see how delicately he discussed alcohol and did not entirely negate its profits. Its harm was greater. Who was presenting this issue to them? An enlightened person who is tolerant and who did not claim alcohol was taboo or an unclean monster or part of the unseen world. But because it had great social and individual harm (even though it did have profit), he negated it. People will listen to this kind of reasoning.

God says alcohol has some profit but because its harm is greater, do not drink it. Thus he prepared the groundwork. He criticized and limited alcohol.

Then when the movement reached its peak of struggles in God's way (martyrdoms, victories, etc.) suddenly it was revealed, *"Certainly wine, gambling...are impure and the actions of satan so avoid them"* [5:90].

He had worked on them for twenty years and prepared the ground. When he went to the street, he saw everyone had broken his jug. Historians have recorded that the streets were filled with broken jugs and wine holders without any force being applied.

Why had such a command been so readily accepted? Because it was issued in a scientific way. The manner and method was proper. Even now when we intend to enforce the prohibition of alcohol we say it is unclean, and anyone who uses it will become a disbeliever. The person drinking it will say, "That's fine by me! I want to be an infidel! What is the difference between you the believer and me the disbeliever? If I am impure, so what! I take a bath everyday, but you only take a bath when you do things you should not do!" Then you are left wondering what to say. You cannot say anything so you should not let things get to this point.

This is the scientific method and the conclusion that I as a teacher have reached. Over the years I have spoken about many things. Still you will not find one sentence in my work where I have advised the young generation how to dress. It is not possible that I will have said, "Wear the modest dress. Perform the prescribed prayer. Perform the prescribed fast. Pay the poor-due and religious tax." Why? Because experience has shown that this method is like blowing a horn from the wrong end.

In my experiences at the Husayniyah (which some of you here must be familiar with) some of the women who came to enroll for my classes were ultra modern in their dress. When they attempted to enroll, the person who was to write down their names and information about them was afraid or looked for excuses like, "The classes are full."

Among the board of directors at the Husayniyah there were some who were very religious and intolerant. They did not know what to do. They brought scarves and coverings. They would beg the women to put them on. But none of these solutions were proper solutions to encourage the women to dress modestly. After a few of the lectures without my saying one word on this issue, these very same women tended most readily to adopt the modest dress.

Why and how did this happen? Because clothes have two contradictory meanings just like having a beard does. If we want to stress the beard as a religious symbol all of the American hippies were religious par excellence. To which one of its meanings are we going to refer.

The modest dress is the same. We have to explain and analyze its meaning for people and then (without even telling them what they should do or not do) they know what they should do. The question of choice is important to them. Imposing or dictating what people should do causes them to offer resistance.

When these young women first came, they had no faith. They had accepted no ideology or else they had accepted an ideology which was anti-religious. At any rate, they were of the modern type. They knew Miss Universe who wore the latest style of clothes. They took their standard of dress from her.

Does this mean I should go to them and tell them, "You have to dress like Aunt Zaynab," Her model is Miss Universe who appears on TV, in the newspapers, on the radio, in every magazine and wherever she goes the values of this Miss Universe are presented throughout the world—in Holland, Paris and the London Sheraton Hotel. She has become her idol.

Someone may ask me, "What are you saying? Why should I lower myself? To what are you inviting us? What can be done to destroy this?"

You can destroy this when you uproot the psychological and

mental attachment and dependence on this type of person. Today no one basically worships Lat and Uzza. Today's idols are these things. How can we destroy idols? **When we present values which are higher then the values represented by Miss Universe, a woman may become attached to those better values. When she has formed an attachment to these elevated values, she will endure and incorporate all of those values herself. She will choose herself and will not sense any belittlement or abasement.**

This method does not only exist in Islam. Throughout human history, from 3000 years ago in India, China, Sind, and Samarqand, we have writings. A Chinese girl was regarded as an idol of colorful beauty to whom all women of the world bowed down in worship. Seven hundred years ago the poet Hafez said:

The icon-like Chinese woman is the enemy
of hearts and faiths.
O God protect my heart and faith
from temptation

This was what Hafez wrote at a time when there was no contact with the Far East, yet in Shiraz the beauty of a Chinese woman was worshiped. This shows that Chinese beauty and Chinese cosmetics were known throughout the world. There are books in Chinese which are 4800 years old. One whole book speaks of diets to keep bodies beautiful.

There are other books from 4000 years ago about coquetry, flirting and love about which Frenchmen have yet to write an equivalent. Philosophers wrote tomes about how a woman could become a coquette using cosmetics. They discovered a whole science and philosophy of beauty. Women had developed to this extent in regard to beauty in those days!

What has caused this same woman to wear coarse clothes [in 1968]? She wears coarse clothes and stands alongside a French woman, who in her twenty years has spent at least seventeen of them in front of her mirror, and feels no sense of abasement or inferiority. She even feels superior. What has happened? She knows herself to be a member of a revolutionary movement and the other to be a wind-up bourgeoisie look alike doll. She knows herself to be far superior!

Today we have to find out what caused this Chinese girl with 3000 years of experience of applying make-up to appear looking like this in the 20th century.

Evolution?

Evolution has a special meaning. What has evolved? China has been held-back and still is. Its culture is still not equivalent to French culture. Its civilization has not reached the same extent. Its economic system has not progressed to the same extent. Where is China and where is France?

The reason is a belief system and its values. This coat and pants, these coarse clothes, which the new Muslim woman wears are no longer her traditional dress. It is not something her parents have imposed upon her. They are not the clothes of poverty, not the clothes of one obliged to spend what she does not have in order to hide her state.

This is not traditional dress. It is not the dress of my class. It is the dress of my thoughts. These clothes show how I think and to what I am affiliated, how a *mujahid* thinks. What do your clothes represent? Your clothes are a reflection of how much money you or your father or husband earn. Thus they reflect money rather than a way of thought. One form of dress is an intellectual dress reflecting a belief system, while the other is monetary. All of one's values in the latter case terminates in families' money. All in the other case end in belief. Therefore the Muslim girl feels superior, not inferior.

Now let us return to the Muslim community. You are a member of this community. See how much values have changed. Fifteen or even seven or eight years ago, who were the girls in modest dress who attended the university? They were very fanatic. Also it was unclear whether it was just out of the family's social position or if they were so economically deprived that this modest dress was worn. These clothes were not right. They were not in style. Was there any other explanation? There is no third way. Little by little, the girl who did not wear the modest dress felt superior, while the girl who wore the modest dress felt inferior.

The values of the girl who did not wear the modest dress moved towards the newest luxury products and whatever hit the European market that very moment. After a while it became clear where one bought her clothing. It differed if one bought her clothes from the wealthy area or the poor area. Her type differed. The girl who dressed modestly was considered empty of new values and tied to a dying, deteriorating held-back culture.

This era has passed. An era came when Islam is no longer considered to be an out-dated tradition but rather a new perception in which a new human responsibility is present. Suddenly a reaction appears in the behavior of girls. Now these very girls who pretended to be living a life of luxury are transformed.

As a sociologist and teacher, I am involved in social problems. The parents of my students frequently refer to me to discuss their family problems. Some years ago, when parents would meet with me they would complain that their young people were showing a great tendency towards modern civilization, European models and styles had caused some problems for the parents. Nowadays the same parents tell me that their young people have turned away from modernization and towards their religious traditions, the values of which they even tend to exaggerate.

The young people have not changed. This person who enjoyed wearing modest clothes is the same person who enjoyed wearing hot pants. What has changed? **Values have changed.** The modest dress relates to national traditions and yet is the symbol of a new human perception. Both of these relate to religion.

One cannot impose a religion which is an out-dated, superstitious, inherited faith on young people. Our belief system is a religious one whereas the superstitious one is not. But what does each one mean? Both mean that (as experience has shown) one cannot impose the modest dress upon a girl because religion says so. She must first develop human consciousness and awareness, think differently about herself.

We usually suppose that the modest dress reflects a belief system, but to the older generations, it is a traditional cover. Only for the younger generation who have recently returned to Islam is the modest dress a symbol of Islamic belief.

Of course the modest dress is not limited to one form. The question is what is the nature of the young girl who now chooses to dress modestly? She has two profoundly different motives. One is that her mother wears this, and her aunt dresses like this. It is part of her environment. It is a traditional dress.

There is a related motive for dressing modestly, similar to the one mentioned above. The modest dress is the symbol of a religious belief. Such motives are based on a simple desire to imitate. Imitating the traditional dress shows that it is a public and generally accepted way of dress most women in this [Islamic] culture wear. It possesses no human value. It is simply the customary, habitual dress. It lacks meaning.

When imitation is the reason behind the modest dress, as a girl studies more and travels abroad, she sees that other women are not wearing it and nothing happens to them because of it. She had thought if she did not dress modestly, the earth would swallow her up. So she takes off the modest dress and, by rejecting it, becomes a pseudo-intellectual.

But there is a type of modest dress which is worn by intellectuals and the awakened generation who intentionally select the modest dress. This group says "no" with its selection. It says no to western colonialism and European styles. With this choice a woman negates the West's ill-intentioned efforts and clearly says, "You cannot change me! You cannot transform and negate my social, historical and cultural values."

Are these two types of modest dress in any way similar? We are speaking about the human and social manifestation of wearing the modest dress. The one who consciously selects to wear the modest dress manifests a special culture, school of thought, and intellectual group.

This is worth something. It has value. The girl who wears the modest dress with this type of inner belief does not feel herself to be inferior to the modern girl who wears the best of European fashions. She even believes herself to be superior to the latter.

Once after a lecture, someone asked me about the modest dress. I answered, "The modest dress is whatever you say it is. I am neither a religious jurisprudent nor a tailor. I am a sociologist." The person then asked, "What is it in the view of sociology?" I answered, "Well, a sociologist is not concerned with how it is sown. It has to do with the person who wears it." The person said, "Tell us about such a person." I answered, "This is what you should have asked me to begin with."

If you imagine Muslim society in the form of a pyramid, the bottom part, which is the widest, consists of the majority of our society, the women who wear the modest dress. Who are they? To what does their modest dress relate? It relates to the fact that they have been held-back. They are not educated. They have nothing to do with the modern age. They live at the beginning of time and are heirs of the core of 19th century Islam. If you give them a ticket and a passport, by the time they go and return, they will be wearing Christian Dior.

Above this group in the pyramid are a minority who have a modern education. Many have higher degrees. They know a bit of a foreign language. They know a bit about what is going on in the world. They have seen foreign magazines. They have themselves visited abroad. They know what the 20th century means. They can work in an office or a school and replace one foreigner. They receive a salary. They have set up a home. They do social work. They do not wear the modest dress and for the most part are educated.

The third group are at the very top, at the peak of the pyramid. They are a group who is rapidly increasing and growing in numbers. They are not the same as the common women. They belong to the new generation. They live among the highest ranks of our intellectual group. They have either received higher education or are in the middle of their studies. They have gone way beyond civilization and intellectual insight. They are far above one who attains a higher degree and becomes a PhD, MD or engineer. What stage have they reached?

They have attained the stage of faith and belief, responsibility, an ability to distinguish between good and evil, right and wrong Who are they? They are conscious, responsible human beings. This is a higher stage than obtaining a high school diploma, college or graduate degrees.

A woman who has attained the level of belief chooses her own life, her way of thinking, her very being and even her own form of adornment. She actualizes herself. She does not give herself over to television and passive consumption. She does not do whatever consumerism tells her to do. She is not afraid to choose the color of her dress because it may not be in style this year! She has returned and returned vigorously! To what? To the modest dress of Islam. As what? As a believer and committed human being.

Thus what tactic must parents use if they want their daughter to return to the modest dress? They must first distinguish for her what they mean by modest dress. Do they mean a traditional, inherited custom of dress? Do they intend through this

means to protect their own social and class interests by having
her wear such a dress? Or the contrary? Or are they referring
to a dress which is a symbol opposing Western colonialism
which has dominated us by force? Do they advise her to say,
"No," to fifty years of conspiracies, alienation and deceitful looking Europeans in an Islamic community? Are they saying that
they are willing to return to their own culture, identity, ideology and values? If this is the case, their daughter will not feel
embarrassed or humiliated or abased by wearing the modest
dress.

Why did Mrs. Ghandi not feel humiliated and inferior when
she met leaders from all over the world in a dress which was
3000 years old? When she entered the UN General Assembly to
speak, 500 representatives stood and applauded her. Her sari
was no longer a traditional dress that the old generation in
India wore. By wearing the sari she said: I have studied
Western women's journals (*Burda, Paris Match*) through which
the West propagates its mode of dress in an attempt to dominate and impose its culture, civilization, and style on us and I
have rejected it.

By wearing the sari and traveling all over the world, she
said: The West has been trying for 400 years to make us similar to themselves, to assimilate us into Western culture, to
alienate us, but by wearing the sari, I prove to you all that their
efforts and struggles have been in vain. I still maintain my own
identity and being in both my outer as well as inner self.

A distinction, then, should be made between the two cases.
And it is most interesting that the modernized, westernized girl
now feels humiliated before the girl who wears the modest dress
because of belief. The modernized girl begins to realize the modern dress is a style imported into her culture, assimilating her
into designs and styles made by those who are outside her culture and system of values.

Thus if you change the manner of thinking of your children,
they themselves will select their own way of dress. There is no
necessity in this case for you to push them. They themselves
will choose that which is most suitable. Create a loving relationship between them and their Creator and they themselves
will stand in prescribed prayer. There will be no need for force
or coercion.

The modest dress that the contemporary girl chooses to

wear is not returning to a past tradition but is doing something more progressive than even modernism. She has developed beyond education and formal knowledge. She has reached the stage of faith and commitment. She has moved from student to warrior. Here it is no longer a national, historical or customary dress.

Do you want to know how the modest dress developed in the age of the Prophet of Islam? It was not proposed by saying, "O women! Cover your bodies from those to whom you are not related." No. It was related to Islamic belief. It is now worn by women who select this party and school of thought with its orientation and arms. The Muslim woman is no longer a plaything in the hands of foreigners to be painted and dressed as they wish. And the same was true of the time of the Prophet.

EXPECTATIONS FROM THE MUSLIM WOMAN

Prior to beginning my lecture, I would like to propose some practical suggestions. Speaking about women's rights, women's personality and Islam's view of women differs a great deal from the realization of the actual value which Islam gives to human beings, and to women, in particular. Most often we are satisfied by pointing out that Islam gives great value to science or establishes progressive rights for women. Unfortunately we never actually use or benefit from these values or rights. We could benefit from these if we were to act according to the understanding which we acquire from them.

A great many people are acquainted with Islamic views of society, social relations, women's rights, children's rights and family rights, but these same people then actually follow non-Islamic, ancient cultural traditions and do not dare to base their lives upon Islamic values. That is, they do not practice what they preach. Thus we always remain at the level of talking.

We must complete Islamic views and intellectual discussions with practical solutions. We must find a way whereby we reach these values and rights in practice. After proposing my views, the question should be asked as to how we can actually put them into practice?[1]

Throughout history the problem of women's rights and their role has always been considered to be an intellectual problem. Thus, various religious, philosophical and social systems have reached varying views in this respect.

From the 18th through the 20th centuries (particularly after W.W.II) any attempt to address the special problem of the social rights of women and their specific characteristics has been seen as a mere by-product of a spiritual or psychic shock or the result of a revolutionary crisis in centers of learning or as a response to political currents and international movements. Thus, traditional societies, historical societies, religious societies, either in the East or in the West (be they tribal, Bedouin, civilized Muslim or non-Muslim societies in whatever social or cultural stage of civilization they may be) have all been directly or indirectly influenced by these thoughts, intellectual currents and even new social realities.

Unfortunately the crisis of the problem of women and their liberation which began in the West and has been strengthened by the ruling superpowers in the 20th century has influenced all human societies, even closed traditional and religious societies. There are only a few cultural, traditional and even religious societies which have been able to properly stand against this flood.

Such societies have frequently been confronted by a peculiar modernism which they have adopted, under the guise of liberation of women, either by rejecting old traditions or by undertaking blind struggles. None of them have succeeded in standing against this attack.

In such societies the newly educated class, the pseudo-intellectuals, who are in the majority, strongly and vigorously welcome this crisis. They themselves even act as one of the forces that strengthens this corrupting and destructive transformation.

In traditional religious societies, including Islamic communities, neither group could stand against the attack of the modern view of the liberation of women as announced by the West. The pseudo-intellectual and modern class of Islamic and non-Islamic societies in the East considered the modest dress to be the symbol of modern civilization, progress and awareness. The old, traditional group passed through and confronted this crisis with non-scientific and illogical tactics due to their lack of experience. It is a general law that when there is a fire resulting from a spill of oil, if someone tries to hurriedly and unskillfully put the fire out, it only spreads more rapidly and more vigorously!

Thus such unskilled struggles against the West have frequently been performed in a manner that has created complexes and various reactions inside such societies. In this way they have paved the way for acceptance of Western ideas and innovations. There are very few societies who have been able to stand against, to adequately resist, and to show an effective reaction to the modern West by consciously selecting their manner and form of lifestyle.

One of the most important factors that can assist Eastern societies in confronting and standing against the intellectual and cultural attack of the West (as it relates to the view of modern woman) is to have a rich culture and history full of experiences, values and ideas. It is important to have progressive human rights and, in particular, to have perfect and complete human models in the religious history of those societies and communities.

Fortunately from this point of view (although they have not been able to consciously stand against the colonial attack of the West), Islamic societies have cultural power and possibilities, have a very progressive history, value system and religion and are in this way very rich. Thus they can, by relying on these values and sources and by reviving and progressing towards the high humanitarian values existing in their culture and their past history encourage their new, young generation to stand and resist the West's attack.

The most effective weapon to confront Western values and the most important factor for creating a conscious struggle within the new generation of our Islamic societies against the West's seduction is to hold up very high, distinguished and characteristic symbols, real personalities of Islamic history.

If the lives of such personalities are known in detail, are shown precisely, are revived and introduced properly, scientifically, consciously, are scholastically recognized and presented to our societies, the young generation will sense that there is no need to accept the seductions of the West, no need to decline in the guise of modernism. Rather, they will sense that there are very high, elevated symbols in their own history and religion to be followed and to be considered as models for self-reconstruction.

It must be taken into consideration that all matters related to women, to science, to life-style, to class relationships, to scholastic understanding, to one's world view—all have been designed, described and discussed in Islam. We have only to solve our present difficulties, to answer the intellectual challenges, and to reduce our sensual needs. How can we understand our values? How can we use and obtain actual results from them? Our essential aim must be to solve the problem of proper understanding and recognition.

The members of the Prophet's family, in the view of all of the intellectuals of Islamic countries (who possess a more distinguished image of them) have always been the manifestation of the most elevating and liberating humanitarian and Islamic values. These values are not limited to a particular tribe—or even to all Muslims. Thus, all of the people of the world can easily see and understand these symbols and examples which have come out of a small house—which is greater than the whole of history.

Anyone who believes in the values and virtues of humanity will admit that the symbolic role of the members of this family—in various dimensions and fields—is beyond historical values of class or tribe. They are rather the highest, meta-historical, meta-tribal values. They are permanent symbols and examples of humanity.

Thus, anyone who is a human being respects them. Anyone who is aware of the values of humanity, any committed intellectual in the world, will admit the values and virtues which this small house created within the arena of human history.

Therefore, when we describe the biography of Fatima, as one of the members of the Prophet's family, we must learn lessons from her personality, her role, her social, mental, and political status and use them to guide our lives—in our groups and in our societies.

The problem of proper understanding is the most important and essential problem of our time. At the present time, the struggles of the committed Muslim intellectuals should be directed to a proper understanding and recognition of Islam's history and religion. This proper understanding, including the proper understanding of Fatima, is the key to our salvation.

After W.W.II, the problem of woman was designated as being the most important and sensitive problem in the West. The war itself was the main cause for family relations to be split and destroyed. Traditional religious values such as ethics, morals and spirituality collapsed. Also, due to the war, crimes, cruelty, aggression and plunder increased.

From the intellectual and ethical point of view, it had a very diverse effect, causing decline upon the post war generation. Its inauspicious effect after a quarter of a century [since W.W.II] can be seen in the spirit, thought, philosophy and even the art of the present time.

Those who have seen France, Germany, England and even the USA [the last of which was far from the actual field of battle], prior to the war and visited those countries after the war, can clearly see that, although it seems as if centuries have passed, actually the cultures collapsed within one generation. Therefore, the fall of ethical values was one of the natural results of the war, and woman was its bearer.

But the point must be noted that prior to the war, the West had already started a multi-dimensional fight—from the various philosophical, mental, social, productive and cultural points of view—with the Catholic religion, the ruling religion in the Middle Ages, and thus had unconsciously destroyed all of the ethical, intellectual and ideal values, as well as the restrictions and limits which the church had defended in the name of religion.

One of the values which the church defended in the name of religion was women's rights—women's values, both spiritual and social. This defense combined with the declining, anti-female traditions, bonds and limitations.

But after the Renaissance and the development of the bourgeoisie, the bourgeois revolution, the bourgeois culture—which is the culture of individual liberty—defeated the church and consequently, with this victory, the rule of the church over moral, spiritual, scholastic and legal values was abolished. Thus, all of the restrictions and values concerning women which the church had defended and supported in the name of religion, succumbed to the rise of the bourgeoisie and its culture.

Then suddenly the problem of sexual liberation appeared. Women realized that through the slogan of sexual liberation, all of the anti-human limits, restrictions, and bonds which restrained them could be destroyed. Women welcomed this change vigorously to the extent that sexual liberation entered the arena of science!

What is normally designated as scientific understanding of religion is not a pure scientific and scholastic understanding. It is rather a bourgeois cognition. After the Middle Ages, science which had been in the service of religion and the church, was made to serve the present ruling bourgeois system. If nowadays science appears to oppose religion and moral values, it is not really science that opposes these, but it is the ruling bourgeois which does so—just as in the Middle Ages, it was feudalism which defended aristocratic social-moral traditions in the name of religion. It was Christianity which was, in fact, defending feudalism, and now it is science which, in fact, defends the bourgeoisie. It is intellectuals—those who believe that economic and materialistic social foundations are the basis of all social transformations—who will more easily accept my argument and logic.

Up to the appearance of Freud (who is one of the agents of the bourgeoisie), it was through the liberal bourgeoisie spirit that scientific sexualism was manifested. It must be taken into consideration that the bourgeoisie is always an inferior class. Although feudalism was an anti-human system, it, nevertheless, relied on an aristocratic elite and their moral values even though these moral values led to a decline. Bourgeoisie mentality negates all of the high, ascending human values and believes in nothing except money.

Therefore, a scholar or scientist who lives, thinks and studies during the bourgeois age, measures collective cultural and spiritual values (the sacrifices of mankind, the martyrdoms, struggles, literature, art etc.), with only the scale of naked economy, with production and consumption and with nothing else. One who studies psychology or anthropology, looking at all the dimensions and manifestations of the mystic spirit of human beings—that which religion believes to be the spirit of God and the manifestation of metaphysical virtues sees only unsatisfied sexual appetites. Belief, culture, mental illnesses—all are related to the struggle to release an imprisoned and condemned sexual complex. The bourgeois social scientist looks at all of the delicate human sensations and feelings (even a mother caressing her child, the worship of the beloved by the lover and all other issues) in relationship to sex.

Freud, a modern bourgeoisie, armed himself against all moral and human values, against all high and ascending manifestations of the human soul and called it realism. Freud's "realism" was not that of the bourgeoisie, but rather of the scientist, scholar, philosopher, psychologist, and anthropologist who serve the bourgeoisie class—for all of these bring the human being down to the level of a sexual and economic animal!

Thus, the bourgeoisie, by alienating all values and virtues, made only one religion, one school, one temple and one messenger for all miserable men of this age for whom all must be sacrificed.

This messenger was named Freud. His religion was sex. His temple was Freudianism, and the first one who was sacrificed on the threshold of this temple was woman and her human values.

We who live in the East always speak about Western colonialization, but I would like to explain that this does not mean that Western colonialization only colonizes or exploits the East. It is a world-wide power and class that exploits and colonizes both the East and the West.

If I had the opportunity, I would explain that this power has alienated the European masses even more than the Eastern masses. The European has been captured by colonialization's legacy of unemployment and misery and will continue to be so in the future. They will continue as victims of anti-colonialism.

This ruling colonial power influences Eastern people in many ways—such as, emphasis upon unimportant, sensational and emotional matters; rumors, discrimination, and hypocrisy; and sowing discord and pessimism to keep Easterners occupied with mundane and unimportant issues. By these means Easterners are kept in a state whereby they are unaware of what Western colonialization is doing to them, unaware of their fate and destiny. These conspiracies, then cause young Europeans, likewise, to become alienated and destructive, and perform more tricks and crimes. All of these acts are performed in the name of colonialization in Eastern countries without the Easterners realizing it.

For example, we all know about the widespread international police network and the extensive intelligence services which observe even the minutest movement anywhere in the world. And yet, there are tons and tons of narcotics which are freely transferred from the East to the West. They are distributed and sold by huge international organizations and transferred through their factories, planes, ports, ships and offices.

Why is it that the international police cannot prevent the distribution of narcotics among the younger generation of Europe and the U.S.A. Why? Because ruling powers prevent the young generation from understanding what is going on in Europe and the U.S.A.? Ruling powers prevent them from car-ing about who rules the destiny and fate of humanity. This is the same ruling power which colonizes both West and East— only its methods and relations differ. At any rate, in both East and West, human beings are victims of this anti-human world-wide power.

One of the most important means that has been created by this ruling power from the intellectual, social, economic and moral point of view, is Freudian sexualism. This has become the common social spirit of our age and has become the substitute for all values, virtues and liberties.

It is not accidental that Freud's view of sexuality came to prominence after the second world war and became the funda-mental basis and foundation of art. Most motion pictures are based on only two elements: violence and sexuality. Both of these are legacies of the war. Motion pictures are one of the most important examples of the relationship of art to Western capitalism because film production is the only art which cannot exist and develop without the aid of capital. Thus it differs from the arts of painting, literature, poetry and music. A poor painter, writer, poet or musician can create the greatest work of art, but a film producer must have capital of millions of dollars to create a saleable film. Thus, this art is unconsciously sup-porting capitalism.

The pseudo-intellectuals and pseudo-scholars of the third and fourth worlds suppose that Freudism is really the science of the present age. Modern scholars research and record Freud's works in a special way.

It is interesting that in underdeveloped countries, under the guise of intellectuality and modern scientific psychology, schol-ars and scientists serve these universal powers free of charge. In the name of science, they freely propagate anti-human ideas among the intellectuals and younger generation. How miser-able are these thinkers and intellectuals who serve the capital-istic ruling powers! They really believe that they are serving humanity, freedom, liberty and science!

Thus, in order for the superpowers of bourgeois scientism to dominate, both the East and the West must be sacrificed. They must become the victims of narcotics as well as Freudianism. From scientism's point of view, every young person who is still human and who still shows sympathy and sensibility towards the destiny of his or her nation and other nations, must be caused to deviate, must be made indifferent to his or her destiny and the destiny of others. In order to accomplish this, any means is permissible and advisable—whether it takes the form of science, art, sports, literature, history, tradition, or religion. It does not make any difference. One must be amused by any form. One must be removed from the scene so that one takes notice of nothing. The best way is scientific and mental stupification and the strongest factor, particularly among the younger generation, is sex!

Why sex? Because it can be logically explained. It is new. It can easily and freely be accepted. It is the most important point that can attract the young generation, who, in turn, are the most important victim of Freudianism.

Thus all of intellectual, human, artistic, social, political and financial investments must strengthen this school. It is not strange to see how rapidly it progresses and develops.

It must be noted that there is another group who co-operates, albeit unconsciously, in a most effective way with this world-wide power to achieve the aim of attracting the younger generation, particularly women, to Freudianism, and to sex. This group unskillfully fights Freud's innovations by relying on old, strict, illogical and anti-human traditions create restrictions and complexes in the young generation, particularly, women. You may want to know how they co-operate in this inauspicious endeavor. They co-operate by pushing the young generation towards pessimism.

While Freudianism invites woman out of the house, this old group tries to hold her inside by creating bonds, obligations, and restrictions and depriving her of all her human and religious rights—thus unconsciously preparing the way for Freudianism. It is in this way that they co-operate with Freud.

Statistics show that the insidious invitation of Freudianism has been most successful in traditional societies and countries where women have been most deprived. Thus we cannot fight and confront this universal illness and danger only by relying on ancient traditions, customs, restrictions, bonds, etc. which deny rights to women. There is only one solution: to give human and Islamic rights back to women.

Yes! This is the only way! If the human and Islamic rights of women are given back to her, you have armed her with the weapon whereby she can personally resist and confront

Freudianism. But if you deprive her of her rights, you insure that this satanic invitation will capture her. You have pushed her towards it.

The essential and important problem which we have confused is the distinction between culture and religion. Culture and religion have mixed with each other throughout history. They make up the collection of ideas, tastes, behaviors, feelings, customs and legal relations which are sacred and honorable to a society.

For example, in Islamic societies, Islamic rights, values, precepts and laws relating to the economy, the family, the community and even the social system have been mixed with local and tribal traditions formed over the centuries. These are certainly not related to Islam. They are only ancient tribal and local traditions and customs supported and protected by society. Thus an intellectual wishing to be released from such ancient and local, tribal traditions must fight a combination of religion and custom in order to be free of both.

Thus both groups (whether they defend religion or do not) must defend the mixture of ancient customs. Those who fight against traditions also confront the living and ascending values of Islam. None of these groups—neither the progressive modern intellectuals nor the old traditional religious group—can distinguish between religion and culture. Why should they be separate and distinct from each other? Because we Muslims believe Islamic rights and laws are derived from the essence of humanity and the essence of nature and are made by the Will of the Creator of the laws of nature. The laws of nature are stable and never grow old. Thus laws which are based on the general dignity of creation never grow old. On the contrary, social traditions based on production and consumption (on cultural systems which are not fixed laws) have to change.

Religion, a living, permanent phenomenon which could be effective in the present age, can no longer play an effective role in the social life of a community, a society or a generation because religion has been captured by ancient, declining, solidified, deviated traditions and thus can no longer effectively confront the danger of the superpowers.

An aware intellectual is a historian, traditionalist, Islamologist, chronologist and sociologist whose most important cultural mission and responsibility is to distinguish Islam as a living faith from the old traditional moulds—which are not Islam but rather tribal customs—and to put the real Islamic ideas and faith into new moulds matching the necessities of the present age. The everlasting, living, moving, progressive Islamic contents must be protected and put into new moulds which meet the challenges of each age.

Based on my own experience I have to announce that even the most progressive, intellectual, rebellious and revolutionary thinker when confronted by pure Islamic values and virtues (once these values have been separated from inherited, tribal, ancient, ignorant customs) will be attracted and submit easily to them.

The visage of Fatima—the visage of the woman who existed, who spoke, who lived, who played a role in the mosque, in society, in the home training her children, in her family's social struggles and in Islam—a woman whose role should be made clear in all its dimensions to the present generations (not only to Muslims but to any human being, man or woman who has human feelings, who believes in human values and who is faithful to real freedom) should be accepted as the best and most effective model to be followed by the present generation.

I myself have experienced this. I have seen so-called religious histories which lack religious feelings, which have no idea about religion, which even negate and oppose religion. When a proper picture of the Prophet's family, all of whom showed humility and submission, emerges we feel that they are really living personalities.

When I say that Islam is living, I mean it is a collection of living thoughts and ideas. It is alive because of its living social laws and rights. It is alive because model, living personalities have been trained by it.

When the beautiful image of Husayn is presented, which no human society (no matter what form of production it may have, no matter what social system it may use, no matter at what cultural stage it may be) can deny his unique and exceptional personality. No one can deny he is an eternal human symbol who should be followed, admired and praised. All accept him.

Remember Zaynab at Karbala! She had withstood the difficult task of seeing martyrdom after martyrdom in her captivity in the Kufa bazaar and in the courts of Ibn Ziyad and Yazid.

What woman of whatever class, at whatever stage of life in whatever system of particular tribal, religious and social ideas, who believes in the eternal values of womanhood and ascending values of the feminine, does not accept Zaynab as a permanent, everlasting symbol of the social, human and progressive leadership of women?

Such people are living. They are symbols of Islam. To be alive means to be effective, to show the right way, to guide humanity in whatever stage it may be, in whatever land it may occupy, to whatever race it may belong.

But, unfortunately, customs and religion have been mixed together. This mixture of customs (which are changeable and vary from one social, tribal and local system to another and are related to and produced by economic and social relations and Islamic values—which are unchangeable, eternal and related to inspiration, revelation and the prophetic mission) is defended in the name of religion.

The intellectual, seeing the deprivations and abuse of women on one hand and the appearance of social freedom, class advantages and sexual liberty on the other hand, becomes confused.

When the religious group of a community (who are acquainted with religion and believe it), are unable to distinguish between the religion and the local, tribal, cultural customs, how can we expect young, modern intellectuals (willing to fight against ancient customs) to make a distinction between religion and customs?

If the distinguished scholastics of Islam, who are acquainted with Islamic truths, do not perform this task, what organization, what power will do so?

The Prophet of Islam—such an elevated personality—one before whom history is humiliated—when he entered his home, was kind, lenient and gentle. When his wives quarreled with him, he left his home and made a place for himself in the storage area without showing any harsh reaction against them.

This behavior of the Prophet of Islam must be considered as an Islamic criterion rather than the behavior of a supposedly religious but really abusive man. Such un-Islamic, abusive behavior was based on an ethnic, cultural tradition. Therefore, distinctions should be drawn between ethnic, cultural custom and an Islamic religious command.

The Prophet's behavior was so human that it amazes us. For example, some of the young girls of Madinah showed interest in participating in the Battle of Hunayn, a place between Makkah and Jeddah. There is a distance of more than 600 kilometers between Madinah and Makkah and then an additional distance from Makkah to Hunayn. This journey took several months. Nevertheless, the Prophet of Islam took a group of fifteen young girls along with the fighting caravan so that they could assist in the war effort.

In the Mosque of the Prophet in Madinah, there was a porch used for social affairs. Each corner of it was devoted to a social purpose. At one corner was the tent of Ruqiya who, according to the Prophet's command, had established a tent inside the Prophet's mosque—Islam's place of prayer—to hospitalize, care for, and nurse the war's wounded. Sad ibn Maaz (the Islamic chief officer wounded in the Battle of Khandaq with a spear) was hospitalized there. This tradition of looking after the sick patients and nursing them continued for many centuries afterwards in Islam.

I personally read about this in Ibn Yamin's book in which he praised Aladdin, the governor of Sabzevar, and mentioned that Aladdin built a hospital in a very large paradise-like garden in a village near Sabzevar. Describing the hospital, Ibn Yamin says that there were beautiful girls, like angels, who looked after the patients and nursed them.

When there was such a hospital, with such a staff in a remote village near Sabzevar in the 7th and 8th Islamic centuries, there must certainly have been more important and well-equipped hospitals in larger cities like Rey, Tus, Balkh, Bukhara and Baghdad. But we see that our ethnically-oriented intellectuals announce that a European or American woman serving in the first world war established nursing in the world. They negate and oppose the nurses who worked in the early stage of Islam, because it is a religious tradition.

Therefore, you see how problems are confused, how rights are abolished, how great talents are sacrificed in the name of religious traditions and how many great religious values and Islamic virtues are forgotten in the name of intellectualism and opposition to traditional, religious beliefs!

Thus the responsibility of those who understand both the present society and Islam (and who live in the present century) is very heavy. They must bear the burden of many centuries of emotions, ideas and faith. It is not an easy task to travel such a long distance and discover the truth which exists beyond it.

As mentioned, one of the most important factors that enables Islamic communities to stand against and resist the insidious invitation of pseudo-scientific Freudianism and its dreadful use of sexuality is the presence of an exemplary religious models in a humane culture. In the same way that Western world-wide colonialization stupefies the minds of its own youth through narcotics, Western colonialism designs and promotes Freudianism and sexual liberty for Eastern countries. Western colonialism exports sexual liberty into the Eastern countries in exchange for their raw materials. In place of the oil, diamonds, gold, rubber, etc. which the West takes from the East, it gives sexual liberty to them.

When a young man or woman is introduced to sexual liberty, he or she will become occupied by it and will not think about other things, such as problems of freedoms. And when such young people have matured, they will be so involved with installment payments, sexual obsessions, etc. that they will never come to look and think about other problems!

The most important weapon of Islamic youth against this insidious invitation of the West is the possession of symbols leading the mind to genuine spiritual experiences. The spiritual symbols made available to the present generation—which is unwilling to be captured either by hollow, conservative, anti-human, anti-Islamic ethnic traditions or by the stupefying culture of indecent Western modernism—are the best weapons against the West's attack.

The woman of the the Third World must be one who selects, who makes a choice. She is the woman who neither accepts the inherited mould nor the imported novelty. She recognizes both of them. She knows and is aware of both of them. The one which is imposed upon her in the name of tradition which she inherits, is not related to Islam at all but is related to ethnic customs of the period of paternalism and even slavery. And the one which is imported from the West is not science, not humanity, not freedom and not liberty. It is not based on sanctity and respect for women at all. Rather it is based on the low tricks of the bourgeoisie—stupefying consumerism and mindless self-indulgence.

She wants to select, to choose, but what model? She wants neither the model of the traditional, strict woman, nor the model of the modern degraded woman. She wants the face of a Muslim woman. Fortunately both material and history are available to build this third figure. And even more authentic than history, more logical than scientific arguments are the objective exemplary personalities who are symbols in our Islamic history.

All of them were gathered in a family. All lived in a small room—a family, each of whose members is a symbol, a model. Being Hasan-like means having patience and peace. Being Husayn-like means participating in spiritual and religious struggle in the way of God (*jihad*) and martyrdom. Being Zaynab-like means bearing the heavy social mission of justice and truth. Being Fatima-like means being a real woman. Being Ali-like means being virtuous.

I do not intend to once again repeat the life of Fatima as a model. All I knew in this respect I have already said and written. But I would like to mention once again that it is not sufficient only to understand and repeat the historical biographies. We must realize how to describe, how to understand, how to learn lessons from Fatima's life.

When the Prophet of Islam said that Fatima was one of the four greatest women of the world, when he consoled all the pains, miseries and disturbances of her life and implied she would be selected as the woman among women of the world, he was not intending to superficially greet her or to give her false consolation. He was quite serious in this respect. He recommended she be patient and bear the heavy burden and responsibility of being Fatima. Fatima's sisters did not have such a responsibility and were living with their husbands as ordinary Muslim women. But Fatima was exceptional. Thus the Prophet by calling her 'the woman among women of the world' was intending neither to make an idol for his followers to worship nor to praise her as a victim in order to mourn for her. He intended to introduce her as a model and a symbol, to learn lessons from the manner of her life and to act in accordance with it. This is the meaning of being the "woman among women of the world."

How can we learn from Fatima's life? You all know the various dimensions of her life and, thus, there is no necessity to repeat it here. The only point that I would like to make is that we should try to learn from this great personality .

For example, when we consider Fadak in Fatima's life, we must see what lesson we can learn from it. Fatima's insistence upon getting back Fadak was not for the sake of possessing a small farm. Her struggle must not be reduced to that level. Her struggles and efforts were to take what she thought was her right, even though the companions of the Prophet tried to show that their opposition was according to Islamic standards. Therefore, the real value of Fadak is as a symbol, an example, a reason and a manifestation—not as a farm.

Today Fadak does not exist. Some may say that such historical subjects must not be considered and discussed so much. But, quite the contrary, I believe these are living subjects which must be repeated and discussed—not as historical events which are taught in schools, but rather as subjects from which one can gain valuable lessons.

What lessons? A lesson to be learned about the highest manifestation of motherhood in Islamic history, about Fatima, about the edifying symbol of woman in the house, in marriage, in relationships, in motherhood, in training and nourishing children like Hasan, Husayn and Zaynab and in companionship with her husband Ali. She was a woman who throughout the whole of her life, from her childhood to her marriage, from her marriage to the end of her life, felt herself to be a responsible, committed person, a part of the destiny of the community, defending what was right, supporting justice in thought, idea and deed and confronting the usurpation, oppression and deviation, which existed in her society. She was ever present in all social problems and confrontations. She did not remain silent until her death even though she knew that she would not succeed in this fight. This is the meaning of social commitment and responsibility. This is the lesson that can be learned from Fatima's life.

When she was yet a small girl of around ten years, she went everywhere in Makkah with the Prophet of Islam, her father. No one expected a small girl to go hand in hand in such a social, political and ideological situation, together with her father. But Fatima felt herself responsible for the destination of the Islamic Revolution—although according to her age, she was not responsible. So she was present at any confrontation. She was present wherever the Prophet of Islam was alone against the enemy. She stood beside him. Numerous cases have been recorded. For example, once when the Prophet's enemies poured dust onto his head from a balcony, it was Fatima who cleaned the dust from the face of the Prophet with her small hands. It was she who gave consolation to him.

The Prophet and his family were exiled in the desolate valley for three years. Heroes such as Sad ibn Waqqas (the famous officer and commander) even after the passing of many years, when recalling those days, would tremble with terror. Throughout that time, when the whole responsibility for the blockade, imprisonment, humiliation, loneliness, hunger, and difficulties rested upon the shoulders of the Prophet, Fatima was present. She caressed her old mother, her hero father and even gave consolation to her older sisters! She was the only source of love, kindness and enthusiasm in this horrible valley and through those hard and difficult years.

When the Prophet migrated to Madinah, she bore the difficulties of the period of migration. Even in marrying Ali, she showed social commitment because everyone knew that Ali was not a man of the house but rather a man of battle. Thus he was not a desirable husband from the point of view which seeks only home, pleasures and comfort. Everyone knew that Ali possessed nothing except a sword and love. They knew he would not possess anything else up to the end of his life. Fatima knew that Ali would never return home with full hands. She knew that the hand of destiny had made Ali like an anvil which must bear all strokes, tortures and hardships. Thus by selecting a warrior like Ali as a husband, Fatima shouldered a great intellectual, human and social responsibility.

Thus Fatima consciously made her selection. She gloriously bore the heavy burden of this mission up to her death. She made a home which is unique in history, beyond human scale and standards. For everyone, whether Muslim or not, admits that her home was a paradigm of the human situation—a home in which Ali was the father, Fatima was the mother, Hasan and Husayn the sons and Zaynab the daughter. All of them were elevated symbols. All of them were gathered in one family—not dispersed throughout history in order to be collected and introduced separately. They were one generation inside one house.

It is really painful for Muslims who had such models, such

a religion and such a culture to have such a destiny. A great personality like Fatima was among the members of this family. She was such a distinct woman that Ayisha, the Prophet's wife, praised her saying, "I never saw anyone higher than Fatima, except her father, the Prophet."

Thus it is sufficient for any intellectual woman to read a book about Fatima (or about other distinguished Islamic women, like Khadija or Zaynab) to know these figures and compare them with figures who are introduced in the name of modernism.

When the Prophet migrated to Madinah, Fatima bore the difficulties of the period of migration. Even in marrying Ali, she showed social commitment. Any women comparing Fatima with women who are introduced through modern magazines will recognize significant differences and reach the proper and inevitable conclusion.

Therefore the most important duty of the aware, responsible writers and preachers is to introduce these figures clearly, brightly, consciously and accurately to the present generation thus holding up the most efficient, conscious, humane models to defend and resist the West's attack.

A real figure of a Muslim woman can be seen in the Battle of Siffin—the battle that took place between Ali and Muawiyah. In this battle, the women (who were in Ali's army) by singing epic poems, verses and by encouragement and enthusiastic lectures and speeches, inspired Ali's army against Muawiyah. After the Battle of Siffin and the death of Ali, Muawiyah ordered these women to be pursued in order to take revenge against their families. One of these women was captured and sent to Muawiyah's court in Damascus. Muawiyah told her that she had a very sinful past. She, in order to avoid Muawiyah's revenge, said, "God bless you. Overlook the past." But Muawiyah said, "Do you know that you shed the blood of our army when we fought by Ali's army in the Battle of Siffin?" She courageously answered, "God bless you that you gave me this blessed news [that I participated in that war against you and your army]."

This is the face of a Muslim woman! If we study the books which have been written about Muslim women, we will notice that wherever Islam ruled throughout history, Muslim women have shown the greatest talents in science, literature and social issues. But wherever Islamic societies have declined, women also declined. Our intellectuals have never found the opportunity to study the life and personality of Zaynab properly and to take note of her real figure and role.

When Zaynab saw that the revolution had begun, she left her family, her husband and her children, and joined the revolution. It was not for the sake of her brother Husayn, who was the leader of this revolution, that she joined it. She did so because of her own responsibility and commitment to her society, her religion and her God. When she saw that a struggle and revolution had begun against an oppressive system, she joined the revolution and was beside her brother Husayn in all stages in those difficult days. Even after the martyrdom of Husayn and his companions, she carried the flag of the continuation of Karbala's revolution. She performed her mission thoroughly, perfectly and fairly. She performed her mission with strength and courage. She expressed with words the truth that Husayn expressed with blood. She shouted out against tyranny in any land. She distributed the seeds of revolution in any land that she entered, either free or as a captive. It is no accident that Muslims, wherever they are, show a great and deep sympathy towards the Prophet's family and love them.

It was Zaynab, the Prophet's grand daughter, who stood against and confronted the ruling oppressive power and who destroyed all resistance. She accomplished all this against a tyrannical caliphate which had conquered Iran and Byzantium. She spread the thoughts and ideas of Husayn's school of revolution and martyrdom everywhere and in every land. She took the drops of the blood of Karbala as a symbol of courage and justice to all places and all times.

Yes! All of these miracles belonged to a woman! Thus when a woman—a conscious and responsible, committed woman— sees such heroics from a woman who belonged to Fatima's family, she understands where she must look, how she must be. She realizes that a woman of any age and any century can emulate this model.

These are the values that will not change or grow old nor do they depend upon the customs of the social, cultural or economic systems. These are stable and permanent values which will be destroyed only when there is no longer any humanity in existence. Thus, the present day woman must know Fatima was a

woman who was a warrior during her childhood, a woman who
showed patience and tolerance in the hard days of the economic blockade, a woman who endured three years of imprisonment
in the desolate valley in Makkah, a woman who co-operated and
showed great sympathy to the Prophet of Islam after the death
of her mother. She was the woman who acted 'as his mother'
and, therefore, was entitled to be addressed by the Prophet as
'her father's mother'. She was the woman who, in Madinah, was
the wife of Ali, the great warrior, the man whom she herself had
selected. When she married Ali, she entered a home which
lacked everything—except poverty and love. Then as Ali's wife,
she showed the highest example of companionship, fellowship,
and the most ascending spirit. She was always beside Ali as a
wife, a friend, a companion and a confidant who kept his secrets
and bore his hardships.

And finally, she was the nourisher and trainer of Hasan,
Husayn and Zaynab. Her part in training Zaynab was even
more important than Husayn, the symbol of humanity, because
Husayn had grown up inside the Prophet's mosque and among
the companions of the Prophet. He had grown up in Madinah at
the center and peak of the confrontations and great social
events. But Fatima had trained Zaynab inside her home and in
her lap. The role of Zaynab in the revolution of Karbala and its
continuation and progress, resulted from Fatima's teaching
and from the high spirit of Zaynab.

From every corner of Fatima's house, a symbol and a manifestation of humanity appears. The Prophet's family was considered to be the benchmark of Islamic understanding in all
ages and at all times. Even after the victory of the Prophet in
Madinah, Fatima still was the emblem of the bearer of poverty,
harshness and difficulties outside the home and was the highest calibre mother inside.

At the peak of victory and the glory of Islam, when her
father was the leader of Islam, Fatima was still the example of
a woman who lived as your sister and my sister. She bore
hunger as a slave. She bore hardships and tolerated deprivation
for the glory of her husband and the leadership of her father.
And after the death of her father, when those difficult days were
renewed, she once again started the struggle. Throughout the
crises (when all the companions of the Prophet and all warriors
from the battles of Badr, Hunayn and Uhud were silent in

Madinah) this solitary mother did not cease her resistance. She actively continued her struggle.

Even at nights she visited the companions of the Prophet and influential political personalities. She spoke with the great friends of the Prophet and important personalities. She brought awareness to all. She criticized all of them. She analyzed and foresaw the calamity. This was her social role at that stage until she died. But even with her death, she created a political event! She asked to be buried at night. After her death, her memories, actions, and struggles created a revival in Islamic history.

She became the manifestation of the search for justice and truth in all the revolutionary uprisings of the 2nd through the 8th centuries in all countries from Egypt to Iran. Even at the present time, she acts as a model for Muslim women: as a daughter of God's Prophet; as a mother who trained a girl like Zaynab and sons like Hasan and Husayn; as a wife, a high, ascending and exemplary wife to her husband; and as the companion of Ali's solitude, hardships and difficulties. She was beside him everywhere as a committed social woman, a woman who from the early stages of her life never left her father and fought beside him and struggled with him. She was the woman who fought against tyranny on the external front and who fought against deviation, usurpation and oppression on the internal front.

She died in solitude and silence. She asked Ali to bury her in secret, at night. Here was a woman who even used her death and burial ceremony as a means for struggle in the way of truth. This is how it is to be a Muslim woman in the present age.

FATIMA IS FATIMA

PART ONE

FOR THE READER

T he words you are about to read are from a lecture I gave at the Husayniyah Irshad. To begin with, I had wanted to comment upon the research of Professor Louis Massignon concerning the personality and complicated life of Fatima. I had wished to refer to the deep and revolutionary influence her memory evokes in Muslim societies and the role she has played in the breadth of Islamic transformations. These remarks were intended particularly for my university students participating in 'History and Knowledge of Religions', 'The Sociology of Religions', and 'Islamology'.

As I entered the gathering, I saw that, in addition to the university students, many others had come. This spoke of the need for a more urgent response to the problem. I agreed to answer the pertinent question of womanhood so extremely important today for our society.

Women who have remained in the 'traditional mould' do not face the problem of identity while women who have accepted the 'new imported mould' have adopted a foreign identity. But in the midst of these two types of 'molded women', there are those who can neither accept their hereditary, traditional forms nor surrender to this imposed new form. What should they do?

They want to decide for themselves. They want to develop themselves. They need a model, an ideal example, a heroine. For them, the problem of 'Who am I? and who do I become?' are urgent. Fatima, through her own 'being', answers these questions.

I would have been satisfied with giving an analytical description of the personality of Fatima. I found that book shops had no books about her and thus, our intellectuals know nothing about her life. I was obliged to compensate for this lack to a certain extent. Thus this present essay is the same lecture—but

expanded to include a biography based upon documented, traditional sources—about this beloved person, who has remained
unknown or misinterpreted. In this biography, I particularly
drew from historical documents. Whenever I reached a problem
of faith and explicitly Jafari views, I chose Hanafi, Hanbali,
Maliki and Shafii sources. From the scholar's point of view, they
are irrefutable.

I cannot say that this lecture is without need of criticism.
Rather, the reverse is true. It is in great need—waiting for those
with pure hearts, those who like to guide, those who are willing
to serve, rather than those who use hostility, abuse and slander.

INTRODUCTION

ı was greatly influenced by her blessed life as well as her effect upon the history of Islam. Even after her death, she kept alive the spirit of those who seek justice and oppose oppression and discrimination in Islamic society. She was a manifestation and a symbol of the Way and essential direction of 'Islamic thought'.

As a student, I played a small role in the preparation of the great work of Massignon especially at the beginning of the research stage. The documents and information which existed had been recorded over a period of fourteen hundred years. They were written in all languages and local Islamic dialects. The historic implications of various documents and even of local odes and folk songs were studied. I have been asked to summarize this work here.

I said to myself, "I will offer this work here today because it has yet to be published, and the great man who began it, has left this world with this work uncompleted." People unfortunately do not know about this work. Even Europeans, who are familiar with Islam, do not know about this study. This has also affected our own scholars, who are familiar with Islam through the writings of Europeans, and, therefore, remain uninformed about this work.

I accepted this invitation and I said to myself, "I will describe the manuscripts to my students, in particular, those who participate in my classes at the Husayniyah Irshad. I will give them the scientific and historic results of the deep research of this great man."

But now I see and sense that this gathering differs. It is not a group gathered for a sermon or a discourse. The women and men who are now here are all intellectuals and educated representatives of the needy of today's generation in this society. They have not come to hear me speak of Fatima in order to gain spiritual reward from this gathering tonight. They have not come to hear a dry, scientific, historic lecture. They have a newer, more urgent, more alive need to answer the most sensitive question for those who are affected by our contemporary fate: Who am I?

CHAPTER ONE
WHO AM I?

In our society, women change rapidly. The tyranny of our times and the influence of institutions take women away from 'what she is'. All her traditional characteristics and values are taken away from her until she is made into a creature 'they want', 'they build'. We see that 'they have built'! This is why the most important and relevant question for the awakened woman at this time is, 'Who am 1?' She knows full well that she cannot remain what she is. Actually, she does not want to accept modern masks to replace the traditional ones. She wants to decide for herself. Her contemporaries choose for themselves. They consciously adorn their personalities with awareness and independence. They dress themselves. They manifest an essence. They reflect a sketch. But they do not know how. They do not know the design of the real human aspect of their personality which is neither a reflection of their ethnic heritage nor an artificially imposed imitative mask. With which of these do they identify??

The second question which arises from this, stems from the following: we are Muslims, women of a society, who wish to make decisions through reason and choice and to relate them to a history, religion and society which received its spirit and basis from Islam. A woman in this society wants to be herself. She wants to build herself, 'herself'. She wants to be reborn. In this re-birth, she wants to be her own midwife. She neither wants to be a product of her ethnic heritage nor to adopt a superficial facade. She cannot remain heedless of Islam, and she cannot remain indifferent to it.

Thus, it is natural that this question should arise for the Muslim woman. Our people continue to speak about Fatima.

Every year, hundreds of thousands of Muslims cry for her. There are hundreds of thousands of gatherings, prayer meetings, festivals and mourning ceremonies in her memory. There are ceremonies of praise, joy, honor and majesty for her in which her generosity is remembered through unusual customs. They hold rituals of lamentation where they re-create her sorrows and speak ill of and damn those who offended her. In spite of all of this, her real personality is not known.

Yet, in spite of the little Muslims know about her, they accept Fatima, her majesty and power, with their whole hearts. They offer her their hearts with all the spiritual strength, faith and will that a people can have or a human community build.

WISDOM AND LOVE

Each religion, school of thought, movement or revolution is made up of two elements: wisdom and love. One is light and the other is motion. One gives common sense and understanding, the other, strength, enthusiasm and movement. In the words of Alexis Carrel, 'Wisdom is like the lights of a car which show the way. Love is like the motor which makes it move.' Each is nothing without the other. A motor, without lights, is blind love—dangerous, tragic and potentially fatal.

In a society, in a movement of thought or in a revolutionary school of thought, men of letters (who are clear thinkers, who are aware and responsible) show, through their works, that there is a way to come to know a school of thought or a religion. They show that there is a way to give awareness to people. The responsibility of the people, on the other hand, is to give their spirits and their strength to a movement. They are responsible for giving the starting push.

A movement is like a living body. It thinks with the brain of scholars and loves through the hearts of its people. If faith, sincerity, love and sacrifice seldom found in a society, people are responsible. But where correct understanding of a school of thought is at a low level (where vision, awareness, logical consciousness and deep familiarity with the goals of a school of thought are lacking, where the meaning, purpose and truths of a school of thought are missing) the scholars are responsible. Religion, in particular, needs both. In religion, knowledge and feelings are not treated as separate entities. They are transformed into understanding and faith by means of common sense and knowledge.

This is Islam. More than any other religion, it is a religion of the recitation of the book, a religion of struggle in God's Way (*jihad*), a religion of thought and love. In the Koran, one cannot find the boundaries between love and faith. The Koran considers martyrdom to be eternal life. It blinds one to the pen and writing. If Muslims are unaware of this, who is responsible?

CHAPTER TWO
WHO IS RESPONSIBLE?

R eligious scholars! It is they who do not perform their responsibilities in respect to the people. They should give awareness, consciousness and direction to the people. They do not.

All our geniuses and great talents occupy themselves with philosophy, theology, Sufism, jurisprudence, conjugation and syntax. Through all the years of research, thought and their own scholarly anguish, they write nothing other than 'practical treatises' on such subjects as purity for the prescribed prayer, types of ritual impurities, rules of menstruation, and doubts which arise in prescribed prayer.

They leave aside writing treatises on how to speak with people, treatises on how to communicate the religious truths and the philosophy of the pillars of the religion, treatises on how to communicate consciousness and awareness to people, treatises on the understanding of the traditions of the Prophet and the personalities of the Companions, treatises on the revolutionary purpose behind Karbala, treatises on the family of the Prophet, and treatises on the faith of the people. All of these treatises are written, but all of them are written without responsibility, without the role of a commander. They pass their responsibilities on to the ordinary speakers in the mosques, not to the religious leaders whose directions for the practice of the faith are followed (*mujtahids*).

This is why the task of introducing the Prophet's family, the task of understanding religion and the task of studying the truths of Islam fall prone to the 'failures of the old schools of religion'. It is for this reason that a group of young people, in order to study Islamic sciences and to carry jurisprudence forward, enter the schools. If talented, through great efforts, they become jurisprudents or *mujtahids* or *faqihs* [theologians]. This group is imprisoned as teachers and removed from the community. Those who do not succeed in studying properly, because they do not have the ability, talent or spiritual strength but rather have warm, often artistic, voices, are obliged to propagate and advertise the truths of the religion. The third group, who have neither this nor that, neither the science nor at least a voice, take the third way. They become dumb and speechless. They take themselves to the 'sacred door' and move ahead of both *mujtahids* and speakers in the mosques.

In the midst of this, be just! What will the fate of the people be? What is the fate of their religion? It is not necessary to think very hard. No. Just look.

We know a dream appeared to Joan of Arc, a sensitive and imaginative girl, commanding her to fight in order to have her king returned. For centuries, her dream has given a vision of freedom, of sacrifice and of revolutionary courage to enlightened, aware and progressive French people. Compare Joan to Zaynab, the sister of Imam Husayn, who carried a heavier mandate. Zaynab's mandate was to continue the movement of Karbala. She opposed murders, terror and hysterics. She continued the movement at a time when all the heroes of the revolution were dead, when the heroism and wisdom of the commanders of Islam at the time of the Prophet were gone. But she has been turned into only a 'sister who mourns'.

I hear reproachful cries towards the scholars who are responsible for these beliefs, ideas and thoughts of the people. I do not know whether these cries come from the throats of people or from the depths of their consciences.

With what are you busy? From where do you speak? Throughout all of these years, where is one book for people telling them what is in the Koran? In place of praise, eulogy, prayer, poetry, song, lamentation and the love of Rumi, why have you sealed your lips among people? An English speaking person cannot easily understand what the Prophet has said, but can he read all of the works of La Martine, the French lover. What do you say? All the songs of the ancient Greek woman, Bilitis, of dubious morals, can be read, but the words of the Prophet, one saying of the Prophet, cannot be read.

You speak so much about the generosity and miracles of the

Prophet's family but where are the books about them? You recount their miracles on their birthdays and days of their deaths. You have festivals and mourning ceremonies. Where are the treatises for Muslims, enamored of the Prophet, which say who he was and who Fatima was, which say how their children lived and how they thought, which say what they did and what they said?

Our people, who spend their lives in love with the Companions and who cry over the difficulties they faced, who serve them for months and years, who glorify their name, spend money and give sincerity and patience to them, deserve to know the real lives of each one of them. Their lives, thoughts, words, silences, freedoms, imprisonments, and martyrdoms should give awareness, chastity and humaness to people.

If an ordinary person mourns for Husayn and on the anniversary of his death [ashura] strikes his head with his dagger and bears the pain—even with pleasure—and still knows Husayn only in an oblique way and misunderstands Karbala, who is responsible? If a woman cries with her whole being, if the recollection of the name of Fatima and Zaynab burns her to her bones and if she would, with complete love, give her life for them, and yet, if she does not thoroughly know Fatima and Zaynab, who is responsible?

Neither this man nor this woman knows one line of their heroine's words. None of them have read one line about their lives. They can only recall Fatima standing beside her father when someone threw dust on him. They only knew Zaynab from the moment when she left the tents to go to gather the bodies of the martyrs. They only knew her from the morning of the day of Ashura up until noon; from then on they lost her. Their awareness of Zaynab ends the day when her great mandate, the legacy of Husayn, just began. Their knowledge about Zaynab ends here. Then, who is responsible?

And, thus, educated and open minded boys and girls judge the situation and say, 'What is the use of this religion? What can such a religion do? What knots do all this excitement, lamentation and cries for Husayn, Fatima and Zaynab untie for our backwards, imprisoned people who need awareness and commitment to negate oppression and to seek freedom.

'What pain does this religion of remorse, these ancient wounds, historic lamentations and curses create for our deprived, illiterate women who want their freedom and clear vision. Does one reach the heart of the problem by doing away with love and hatred? People are busy with feelings which passed centuries ago in foreign lands. They relate to lives passed among strangers. They do not know persecution. They have not sensed the chains of oppression around their necks, nor the pain when falling upon their human shadow. They have never burst in anger nor boiled under the remembrance of the chains which a caliphate one day hung around the neck of a sick person.

They have not thrown up their hands and struck their daggers upon their heads until they leave their senses. They have not seen them when their consciousness returns, when their heart grows quiet, when their sins become pure, when all responsibility falls from their shoulders, when they cheat the scales of divine justice and when they tamper with their deeds for the after life.

As a result, when they have performed enough dirty deeds to compare with stars in the sky, with foam of the sea and with the sands of the desert, when with a small amount of surgery performed by striking their daggers upon their heads, they imagine that they have completely changed their situation and become as innocent as the moment they were born from their mother's womb. They fed that then even God owes them something.

If people believe that the advantage of following Prophet Muhammad (ﷺ) will result in a chemical reaction which accords with the Koran, "God will change their evil deeds into good deeds" [25:71]; if people believe that the soul of this treason which they commit in this world will change its essence in the other world and will take the form of good deeds, then who is responsible?

If this belief in Prophet Muhammad (ﷺ), which has for centuries had the strength of a movement desiring justice, seeking freedom and fighting oppression and despotic institutions; if this movement can free awakened and aware people and give them liberty, justice, chastity and independence; if it can change them both socially and individually; and if the movement can bring about an intellectual, revolutionary leadership fighting class distinctions and giving life and consciousness to a society and if they have not shown this to the people, then who is responsible?

If the value, influence and effect of remembering the family of Prophet Muhammad (ﷺ) is transferred from this world to another world and if its effect is only measured after death, then who is responsible? If the promises and covenants of our ancestors to this family have had no effect upon their thoughts, their time, their society; and if their sons and daughters (seeing this ineffectiveness) remain cut-off from these promises and links with this religion and this family, then, who is responsible?

CHAPTER THREE
WHAT DID THEY MISS?

THE FAMILY OF MUHAMMAD:
INTELLECTUALS VS. THE PEOPLE

Is it that this family is without effect or is it that our young generation and our intellectuals are in error? Or have our mothers and fathers failed in their responsibilities? Prophet Muhammad (ﷺ) is the clearest of truth. He represents the most progressive school of thought which has ever taken human form. It is not a myth. It is a human reality (or should be). It is what could be but isn't.

And his daughter, Fatima is a perfect example of an ideal woman whom no one has yet become. His grandchildren—Husayn and Zaynab—the sister and the brother, who brought deep revolution to mankind and who fought for honor and freedom and who opposed despotism and oppression.

The house of Prophet Muhammad (ﷺ) is like the Kabah in which the children and the inheritors of Abraham (ﷺ) reside. It is a sign and a symbol. It is Real. It is made of stone whereas they are human beings. The Kabah is the place of circumambulation for Muslims; whereas, the house of Prophet Muhammad (ﷺ) is the destination of every heart which understands beauty, majesty, freedom, justice, love, sincerity, and strength. It is the destination of those who encourage jihad and sacrifice to preserve the lives and freedom of the people.

From another point of view, the palaces of the caesars (from which, historians say, waft culture, civilization, religion, thought, discipline and art) are turned around. Our intelligent, loyal, lovers of virtue who have known this household—luckless and quiet—have always been sacrificed. Our people have tied eternal links to them. All their faith, longing, thought and feelings have been devoted to them. Their hearts beat for them. Their eyes cry with their sorrow. They sacrifice themselves and their possessions in their way. They withhold nothing.

Look at these poverty-stricken, starving people who show their feelings and the faith which they have in each individual member of this beloved family. What things have they not done and what things will they not do for them?

The spending of money often shows with much clarity the power of faith and sincerity. Let us examine all the time, endowments and money which people have spent for this family. We see that the poverty among people is so advanced that the problems of bread and water, children's milk and medicine for the hospitals are the most important things in life. Still, any time and under any circumstances which relate to this family, we see that over one million ceremonies are held in their honor.

Over 150,000 clergy and speakers exist for reciting the congregational ritual prayers. There are more than 700,000 descendants of the Prophet's family who speak at the lamentation ceremonies where eulogists restore the memory of this family. How much is spent for construction of the   buildings for the ceremonies related to Husayn [husayniyahs], on places where the passion plays are performed [takiyahs], on neighborhood clubs where young men form groups which participate in religious ceremonies [hayats], on dastahs [the generic name of the groups]. How much is spent for lamentation ceremonies and food, for that which is held in the name of taxes [khums], for the religious leaders' share, for that spent in good works and feeding poor people. It is above and beyond counting. This is particularly important when we consider that this country is one of the most economically backward countries. Income, according to head count, is minimal.

If we pay attention, in particular, to the great differences in classes which exists in Islamic societies, we see that half of the capital of the country is in the hands of a few thousand people. We see that two-thirds of whatever there is, is at the disposal of only 10% of the population. We see that, as opposed to the past, capital has been taken from the former landlords and the former merchants of the bazaar and has been put into the hands of new capitalists, new industrialists, modern bourgeois companies and middle men who sell foreign goods or produce new products themselves.

We see that the money has moved from village storage areas, from the shops of the old merchants under the old roofs of the bazaar, from the hands of local handicrafts workers, from the hands of money changers and indigenous professional guilds, from traditional industries and classical professions to the banks, to stock exchange, to foreign companies, to agencies, to distributors, to contractors and to factories. A new class is created. It is characterized by foreignness and modernization. It adores the West. It is not religious. If it had a memory of or inclination towards religion, it has long since been stamped out. Luxury, transience, pretentiousness and foreignness prevail among this class. And their Islam, in the words of Sayyid Qutb, is an American Islam.

People who follow religion without responsibility and without effort, most often give their opinions without acting or investing anything. Intellectuals spend no money. Our young girls and boys have for years given dancing parties in Switzerland, France, England, America and Austria. They have been most generous in their expenditure on such parties.

Men and women of this materialist class go abroad with their money bags overflowing. In the stores and casinos, they put money into the pockets of the capitalists, the milkers of money. They are no more than cash-cows, seen by deceiving Westerners as donkeys with money, donkeys coming out of a backward country. They squander their wealth on expensive dancers. They go slumming and then return to their country— until once again they gather up enough money to go back to be milked. They do all this very naturally and without any understanding of their mistake or error—even holding their heads high. With lies, people are turned in circles. They call this progress, modern living and a sign of civilization.

At the same time, a small merchant or villager gets ready for his pilgrimage (*hajj*) to Makkah or Karbala after a lifetime of work and anguish. He goes on the principle that this is the only thing in his life which will be both a time of rest as well as pleasure—a journey, a tour, traveling abroad and coming to know other countries. He will see the world and renew his faith, his beliefs and his union with his history. He makes the pilgrimage to his beloved people. He comes to know the remains of his civilization. He sees art which relates to him. Because of his love, the longing of his spirit, and finally, the duty of his religious faith, once in a lifetime, he intends to make the pilgrimage. He takes a minimum amount of money. He pays for his plane ticket and the rest he uses for his expenses there and to buy gifts which he takes back home. What he spends there is the money to rent a tent or to take a bus or to buy a few days of food. The total of all this does not reach the cost of one night of Mr. and Mrs. so and so's champagne in the Lido or one of their caviar breakfasts in the George V Hotel.

These pseudo-intellectuals who supposedly understand the subtle points of things, who are recently reborn (financially), look down upon a little merchant or a villager who lacks sophistication. All the feelings of such 'gentlemen', their knowledge, their class prejudice produce such hatred for the worker and the peasant that even Che Guevara could not stem it.

We see this new moneyed class side by side with our general poverty. Town dwellers and village dwellers have become poorer, more afflicted and more hungry while the class of minor landowners and merchants has become weak and dispersed by the growth of new capitalist classes. The majority have remained in the same class. A minority of people change classes, moving either up or down.

We see only two groups, modern types and traditional types. Those loyal to their beliefs and religious rites in a sense are part of these two groups. The strength of religion and the great expenses incurred in respect to rites and the inaugurating of places for gatherings or buildings for religious purposes—all are a sign that the binding of our peoples' spirit with the Prophet's family is unbelievably deep and strong. It shows to what extent faith and sincerity are strong and pure.

It is after considering these things that the question, 'Who is responsible?' suddenly drops upon our head like a sledge hammer. A person who has until now followed the problem logically and clearly uncovering all sides of the issue, studying it phase by phase, concludes that all is correct. Take a good look at Islam!

ISLAM

Islam is the last historical, religious school of thought possessing the most perfect Prophet, the Koran, the Companions and their histories as models of life, chastity and civilization.

Islam brings law, progress, strength and culture to society. Islam has had a history full of struggle in God's Way. Its believers show perseverance. They are inspired by freedom and justice. They are an avenging fire for despots and for the prejudiced. They have submitted to the way. Linked to the wrath of Truth, its followers are enemies of anything which conceals the Truth. They are enemies of a politics which reduces one to slavery. They are enemies of economic exploitation and spiritual despotism.

We can see the issue from another point of view. Our people, warm with faith, melting with love, with more than religious belief, with truth in thought, give their love to the Prophet's family. Their names raise their spirits. The mere mention of them makes blood boil in their veins. In their longing for sacrifice, their zeal flows. They are ready to be martyred out of their love for them. They cry in pain from their sorrow. They are full of sorrow because they were not present on that bloody day of Ashura. Then bloodied tears run. Sometimes, nearly insane, they draw their daggers and strike their heads. They lament all year long. Their sorrow is real. All year they think about those who went before them. Then—full of praise for their positions and titles—united as lovers, dressed in black from head to toe, drowned in tears and pain, they long with their whole being to pay with their lives. Their love brings on thirst, restlessness, anguish and it finally consumes them.

From yet another point of view, our enlightened thinkers are sensitive people, awakened, aware of the fate of the world and the fate of their society. They are familiar with the spirit and movement of time. Their timely demands need a boiling faith. They seek out revolutionary thought. They think about freedom, equality and justice for people. They attempt to bring about awareness, and responsibility among their people. They see their people and the religion of Husayn and Zaynab. They see justice, strength, struggle in God's Way, torture, martyrdom, Karbala...and they wonder...

Why are there no results when each member of that blessed family can inspire life, awareness, and enthusiasm in those who are faithful to these ideas, overflowing with life and liberty? Why do these perfect forms, whose origins lie in the majesty of humanity, not bear fruit?

Then, who is responsible? In one word, the religious scholars. It is they who should have made Prophet Muhammad (ﷺ)

understandable. It is they who should have taught his thoughts.

In Islam, the scholars are not wise people. They guarantee nothing. They do not have a handful or a bucketful or a truckful of knowledge. Science does not consist of hundreds of pieces of information and knowledge. In their hearts is a ray of light, the light of God. It is not a question of divine science, illumination or gnosticism. It is also not chemistry, physics, history, geography, jurisprudence, principles of jurisprudence, philosophy or logic, which are all types of scientific knowledge.

A science becomes illuminated with light when its knowledge brings about responsibility, guiding knowledge, and organization of ideas. This is called jurisprudence in the Koran, but today it is known as 'the science of rules of the divine Law and things related to it'. This science should not remain in or with darkness. Rather, it lightens space and breaks the night apart. It shows the way.

The learned Jafari religious scholar is the vice-gerent of the Mahdi. He takes the religious taxes on his behalf. The most evident of his responsibilities is to have people come to know who the Mahdi is. If a good translation of the Prophet's prayers is not available, religious scholars are to blame. If people only know a little of the virtues, good deeds and miracles of our Prophet and his Companions, then religious scholars are to blame.

CHAPTER FOUR
WHAT SHOULD BE DONE?

Islam distributes freedom. People are in love with Islam and yet, the young intellectuals realize the weakness and decline of Islam's followers. The main reason for this contradiction is 'not having come to know'. It is coming to know which has value. Love and faith have no value if they precede coming to know and precede chose or commitment. If the Koran is read but not understood, it is no different from a blank book. The Prophet gave his followers awareness, greatness, chastity and freedom when they came to know who he was. When one reads a book mis-stating the Prophet's character or when a book of his sayings is not given to his longing people, what effect can loving him, praising and eulogizing him have?

Love and faith follow coming to know something. It is that which moves the spirit and brings up the nation. This is why the face of Fatima has remained unknown behind the constant praise, eulogies, and lamentations of her followers.

In Muslim societies there are three faces of woman. One is the face of the traditional woman. Another is the face of the new woman, European-like, who has just begun to grow and introduce herself. The third is the face of Fatima which has no resemblance whatsoever to that of the ethnically Muslim woman. The face of the ethnically Muslim woman, which has taken form in the minds of those loyal to religion in our society, is as far away from the face of Fatima as Fatima's face is from the modern woman's.

The crises which we are facing in the world today, in the East, and in particular in Islamic society, the contradictions which have appeared are all the result of the break-down of human qualities. It has come from the agitation which affects the way a society behaves and thinks. Principally, the changing human form has produced a particular type of intellectually educated man and woman, modernists, who contradict the religious man or woman. No power could have prevented the appearance of this contradiction.

This is neither to confirm this change nor to deny it. That is not within the scope of this discussion. Rather, we refer to the change in society, the change in the dress of man, his thoughts, his lifestyle and his direction in life. Woman also follow this change. It is not possible that she remain in her same mould.

In previous generations a son was inclined to fit exactly into his father's mould. His father had no fear that his son might be other than him. There was no difference between them. There were such strong feelings and ties between them that no doubt or indecisiveness could be heard in their words. But today it is not like this. One of the peculiarities of our generation, whether in the East or in the West, is the distance between the older and younger generations. From the point of view of 'calender time', their distance is 30 years, but from the point of view of society's time, 30 centuries.

Yesterday, society was permanent. Values and social characteristics seemed unchangeable. In a period of 100, 200, 300 years, nothing changed. The foundation of society, the forms of production and distribution, the type of consumption, the social relationships, the government, the religious ceremonies, the negative and positive values, the art, the literature, the language—and all other things—were the same during the lifetime of a grandfather and of his grandchild.

THE WORTHY AND THE UNWORTHY

In such fixed worlds and closed societies, where society's time stands still, men and women are of a permanent type. It is perfectly natural that a daughter be an exact copy of her mother. If there is a difference of opinion between a mother and her daughter, it only relates to extraneous things or it arises from daily conflicts. In the world today, a girl, without having gone astray, without having fallen into corruption, creates a distance between herself and her mother. They are strangers to each other. An age difference of 15, 20 or 30 years separates them into two distinct people, two different human beings attached to two different social cycles, attached to two different histories, two different cultures, two different languages, two different visions and two different lives. Their relationship is such that only their home addresses are the same.

In the external forms of society, we see this same contradiction and historic distance between two generations, two types of visions. For example, we see flocks of sheep grazing on the asphalt streets of Tehran, and being milked in front of the consumer-resident of the capital at the same time that pasteurized milk is available in the stores. Or, we see a camel standing next to a Jaguar sports car. The distance is the same as that which separated Cain and Abel from the electronic age and automobiles.

We see a mother and daughter, with this distance between them, walking shoulder to shoulder down the street, one eating bakhlava and the other chewing gum. When you add these two together, you do not get a natural, permanent sum. It is obvious that the mother is beginning the last years of her life. She is pulled and preserved by habit. The daughter, on the other hand, is just beginning the first days of her life's journey. It is clear that the daughter will never become the type who eats bakhlava with relish.

Yet the mother and daughter will eventually become identical. The mother will have the same relationship to her daughter that she had to her own mother.

The change from this type of mother to the new type of daughter is inevitable. Only beginners write about this phenomenon of change. They have not sensed the abusive language, accusations, anger, punishments, and deprivations. They have not sensed the chains and irons around the necks. They have never kicked and screamed or cried out in pain. They have never fainted from loss of strength.

These observers of change in society are just beginning to touch upon these issues, but the work has already been done. They are wasting their efforts. Their results are worth less than zero. The opposition is strengthened.

Those who act as guides, who give explanations, in the name of faith, religion and charity are also mistaken in trying to save forms inherited from the past. They try to preserve old customs and habits. They are referred to in the Koran as 'tales of the ancients', 'the ancients,' 'legends of the ancients', 'fathers of old', 'fables of the ancients', and 'stories of yore'.

These words all refer to the first myths and first fathers. But those who act as guides see old as synonymous with traditional. As a result, they call every change, including even change in dress or hair-do, infidelity. They mistakenly believe that the spiritual source and the belief in submission to God (*islam*) can only be preserved through the worship of anything which is old. They turn away from anything new, from any change and from any re-birth .

Woman, in their view, must also remain as she is today because, simply enough, her form existed in the past and has become part of social traditions. It may be 19th century, 17th century or even pre-lslamic, but it is considered to be religious and Islamic. It must, therefore, be preserved. Those who seek to guide accept this view because it has become part of their way of life and because it suits their interests. They try to remain the same and hold onto things of the past forever. They say, "Islam wanted it to be this way. Religion has taken this form. It should remain like this until Judgment Day."

But the world changes. Everything changes. Mr. X and his son change. But a woman must retain her permanent form. In general terms, their point of view is that the Prophet sealed woman into her traditional form and that she must retain the characteristics which Haji Agha, [her husband], inscribed in her.

This type of thinking tends to lead us astray. If we wish to keep the forms because of our own inexperience, time itself will outrun us. We must realize that destruction is also a reality. Insistence upon keeping these forms will bear no fruit as society will never listen. It cannot listen because these are mortal transient customs.

Those who seek to guide try to explain social traditions ,which have come into being through habit, in religious terms. When we equate religion with social or cultural traditions, we make Islam the guardian of declining forms of life and society. We confuse cultural and historical phenomena with inherited, superstitious beliefs. Time changes habits, social relationships, indigenous, historical phenomena and ancient, cultural signs. We mistakenly believe the Islamic religion to be only these social traditions. Aren't these great errors committed today? Aren't we seeing them with our own eyes?

THREE CLEAR METHODS
OF PROBLEM SOLVING

There are three well-known methods of problem-solving.

Conservatism is the method used by the guardians of Traditions—as interpreted by culture. It is used by leaders who guard and preserve society so that the guardians have something to guard.

The logic of the conservative is this: If we change the customs of the past, it is as if we had separated the roots from the trunk of a tree. The cultural relationships which are preserved in custom are connected to the body of society like a hierarchy of nerves. If the roots are destroyed, so is the rest of the tree.

It is exactly because of this that after a great revolution, anguish, confusion and/or dictators come into being. Hastily digging out the roots of social and cultural phenomena in a quick, revolutionary manner will cause society to face a sudden void. The unfortunate results of this void will be made apparent after the revolution subsides.

Revolutionism is a method used by leaders who tear out things by the roots, believing that all custom is based only on old superstitions and, is, therefore, reactionary and rotten. The reasoning of the revolutionary runs like this: by retaining outdated cultural customs, we keep society outdated and living in the past. We stagnate. Thus a revolutionary leader says that all forms inherited from the past should be eliminated because these forms are like chains around our wrists, feet, spirit, thoughts, will and vision. All of our relationships to the past should be done away with. New rules should replace old. Otherwise society remains behind, fanatic, stagnant, and bound to the past.

Reformism is a method used by people who believe in gradual change. These people lay the groundwork for gradual change in social conditions. Reformism is the middle way between the other two. The reasoning of the returner is just as weak as that of the other two methods. He takes a third way, believing change should be quiet and gradual so that the different factions do not oppose each other. If change is gradual, reformers reason, the foundation of society will not take on a revolutionary form but rather change over a long period of time. Thus, programs should be graduated to reach this end.

But the method of reformism or gradual evolution usually faces negative, strong reactions from internal and external enemies during the long time period this method requires. These forces either stop it or destroy it.

If, for instance, we wished to change the ethics of our youth, or if we wanted to enlighten the thoughts of all people, we would be destroyed before we could reach our goal. Or, perhaps, corrupt, circumstances would dominate and deceive society and paralyze us. A leader who tries to gradually bring about change in society over a relatively long period of time believes that he used logic in calculating his programs. But such a leader does not take into account the powers seeking to neutralize change. One does not always have the time necessary to neutralize powers which are against change. Reactionary elements do not always give the time necessary to leisurely implement gradual changes. Factors considered minor make themselves manifest.

THE PARTICULAR METHOD OF THE PROPHET STEMMING FROM HIS TRADITIONS

The Traditions of the Prophet (*ahadith*), so important in Islam, consist of the words which he spoke, the laws he brought, the deeds he performed, things he remained silent about or did not disagree with and deeds he actually performed in his lifetime without telling others that they should themselves perform them. The Traditions of the Prophet, then, are his words and his conduct. These become the rules of Islam which are divided into two groups: first, those which existed before Islam but were confirmed by the Prophet (signed rules); second, those which had not existed previously but were established by Islam (created rules). Besides these signed and created rules and the words and deeds of the Prophet, a third principle can also be perceived. It is my belief that it is the most sensitive. It is the method that the Prophet used.

The Prophet preserved the form, the container of a custom which had deep roots in society, one which people had gotten used to from generation to generation and one which was practiced in a natural manner, but he changed the contents, the spirit, the direction and the practical application of customs in a revolutionary, decisive and immediate manner.

He was inspired by a particular method which he uses in social combat. Without producing negative results, without containing any of the weak points of the other methods, his method contained the positive characteristics of the others. Through the customs of society which apply the brakes, he quickly attained his social goals. His revolutionary method was this: he maintained the container of a social tradition but inwardly changed the contents.

He used this method in reconciling social phenomena. He adopted a process and method which is a model for all problem solving. This method can be applied to two problems or two phenomena which in no way resemble each other. Recognizing how important this method is, we cannot fully explore it here. We can only clarify it by a few examples.

Before Islam, there was a custom of total ablution which was both a belief and a superstition. The pre-lslamic Arabs believed that when a person had sexual intercourse, he or she incarnated *jinn* [spirits which inhabit the earth], thereby rendering both body and soul unclean. Until he or she found water and performed a total ablution, the *jinn* could not be exorcised.

Another example is the pilgrimage to Makkah. Before Islam, it was an Arab custom, full of superstitious ancestor worship. It was a glorified type of idol worship, holding economic advantage for the Quraysh tribe. It had gradually come to assume this form from the time of Abraham. Islam kept the pre-lslamic custom of pilgrimage, believing that Abraham, the Friend of God, had built the Kabah which (after a period of decline) had been purified of its idols and renewed.

The basis of the pilgrimage had been twofold: to protect the economic interests of the Quraysh merchants in Makkah and to create an artificial need among the Arab tribes for the Quraysh nobility. It was revealed to the Prophet of Islam to take this form and change it into a most beautiful and deep rite founded upon the unity of God and the oneness of humanity.

The Prophet, with his revolutionary stand, took the pilgrimage of the idol-worshipping tribes and changed it into a completely opposite rite. It was a revolutionary leap. As a result, the Arab people underwent no anguish, no loss of values or beliefs, but rather, revived the truth and cleansed an ancient custom. They moved easily from idol worship to unity. Suddenly, they had left the past. Their society was not aware that the foundations of idol worship had been torn down. This leap, this revolutionary social method found within the Traditions of the Prophet preserved the outer form but changed its content. It maintained the container as a permanent element but changed and transformed the content.

The conservative, at whatever cost, tries, to the last bit of his strength, to keep his customs—even if it means sacrificing himself and others. (The revolutionary, on the other hand, wants to change everything into another form all at once. He wants to annihilate everything, to suddenly jump—whether or not society is prepared to leap in that direction.) When the conservative senses the possibility of revolution, he turns to anger, dictatorship, and extensive public murders not only against his enemies but also against the people themselves. A reformer, on the other hand, always gives a corrupter the opportunity to destroy. The Prophet, through the inspired method of his work, showed us that if we understand and can put his method into action, we can behave in a most enlightened and correct way.

A clear-visioned intellectual, confronted by outdated customs, ancient traditions, a dead culture and a stagnant religious and social order, takes up the mandate of the Prophet rather than submit to prejudices from the past. By this method one can reach revolutionary goals without the danger of revolution, on one hand, and without opposing the basis of faith and ancient social values on the other. By doing so, one does not remove oneself from people, nor does one become a stranger on whom people may turn and condemn. This method works because the Prophet received knowledge from the divine Infinite, because he asked for the help of revelation and because he made use of what he received.

REALISM: A MEANS OF SERVING IDEALISM

One of the peculiarities of Islam is that it accepts both beliefs which are identical to it as well as coercive beliefs of society. It admits to the existence of both. Here the perception of Islam is special.

The idealistic schools of thought embrace the highest values, the absolute and most desirable ideologies. Each and every fact is categorically rejected if it does not suit them. They have no patience. They deny unpleasant realities and dig out the roots of anger. Anger, violence, pleasure-seeking and greed are realities which do exist. Moral idealism or religious idealism (i.e. Christianity) ignores these vices and denies their existence.

On the other hand, schools of thought which are based on realism accept all things as the basis of reality. For instance, sodomy is not accepted in England or in Christianity due to religious idealism, not reality. Divorce among Catholics is prohibited to preserve the family and to re-inforce the sacred nature of marriage.

But reality is other than this. Some human beings cannot preserve the first, sacred marriage and remain loyal to each other. It so often happens that human beings grow apart during their lifetime. They become strangers. They live together like two pitiful people. That which has joined them is not love; it is only the ties of law. They are afflicted. One might even become lucky with someone else. This reality has existed in the past, exists in the present and will exist in the future. Civilized and uncivilized people, the religious and the nonreligious, have felt it and continue to feel it. Statistics show it, but some Christian groups deny this reality. They bind marriage to the sacred. They force a family to stay together even when a real hell is behind the doors, and the family has become a center of murder, adultery and corruption. The door of divorce has been closed, but thousands of windows of swindle and illegality have been opened.

CONCUBINES

Social realities are such that if we do not open doors to them, they will spring out from the windows. Forbidding divorce brings about a type of concubinage. That is, a man who cannot live with his legal wife separates from her without being able to get a divorce. The same is true for a woman. She cannot get a divorce, so she lives separately. They each live for years separated from each other. Perhaps each finds another man or woman. The children born out of such a situation are natural but illegal. Such people often have sick beliefs and complexes. Their spirit is anti-social.

Suppose a woman and her legal husband become strangers. They begin opposing each other. They both reach the conclusion that the relationship of husband and wife is not just sleeping together. It cannot continue. They cannot even live as neighbors. It is natural that they separate. The man leaves the household and goes looking for the type of woman he always wanted. Love, the need for a family life, and the pull of sex (one way or the other) helps him to find a natural tie. The man and his new partner find a place and live together. The wife's life follows exactly the same pattern and the same fate. As a result, we see that nature and reality build two new families, two incompatible types find compatible partners.

But some Christian ideologies do not accept this reality. Therefore, no one, including that man and woman, is responsible. People close their eyes so as not to see it. As a result, they accepts, in legal terms, a decomposed house which has no external existence. Its materials have all been used to make another house. It is the former empty marriage which is acknowledged as official, while these two natural families are denied.

Here we see the distance between common law, civil law and religious law, and we see how natural forces, realities and oppositions arise. As a result, families which are Christian, do not actually exist, while families which are real and natural are considered to be corrupt and sinful Christianity, by denying this reality, causes the family which comes into being to be illegal. The children which are born of concubinage are also illegal. From the point of view of a religious society, they are criminals. They do not have a share in the kindness of the family nor the purity of society. Society looks upon them as sinners. Complexes arise within them. They suffer anger and anguish which is beyond imagination. They take their revenge on society.

Crimes which occur in Europe and, in particular, in America, do not exist in backward and underdeveloped countries. The reason is that in these Western societies (even though they have civilizations in the sense that they have culture, ethics, nourished minds, freedom of thought, etc.), there is something born into this generation which makes them take revenge upon society in the worst of forms.

An Englishman had built something which resembled a very small bow and arrow. He had attached this to a box upon which he had displayed cigarettes, selling them along the streets and at movie houses. With this device, he shot a tiny poison tipped arrow into a group of people blinding or killing them. The police could not find the killer. They were looking for a motive connecting the murderer and the murdered. But the murderer had no particular reason for murdering those people. He murdered simply because other people were accepted by society and he was not.

Such a murder can be explained as the result of complexes which the church refuses to accept. It thus has had a hand in bringing misfortune about. Fortunately, we have not yet seen such complexes here. Because there is divorce in our society, there are no illegal families. Because there is divorce there is no family which is a non-entity forced to live with each other under common law. We do not bind people together through the force of law.

A child wanted to go out of a room, but a samavar, a teapot and various dishes were in the way. He closed his eyes and tried to pass through. He thought all the obstacles were gone. Idealism is like a child who does not see reality. It does not want to see reality. It closes its eyes to that which it does not want to see. Because it does not see obstacles, it thinks they do not exist.

The opposite of idealism is realism. Its followers see everything, no matter how ugly or unpleasant, simply because it has an external existence. They accept a thing, attach their hearts to it and find faith. They oppose and reject, however, all beauty, truth and correctness simply because these do not record with existing realities. Through this rejection, they become unbelievers.

One of my students, who was among the pseudo enlightened of this country, drew only one conclusion from our conversations. As he was a supporter of dialectical materialism and I was religious, a believer in Islam, he rejected whatever I said because of his pre-conceived notions. Even if I said something which agreed with Marxism (with which he should have agreed) without attributing the idea, he rejected it.

One day I was speaking about the murders committed by the Umayyids and the disagreements which existed between the classes. The Umayyids had a political dictatorship which dominated religion in order to justify their situation. They wanted people to believe that whatever happened was God's will. This, they said, was particularly true about their own government. I spoke about the people who opposed them and resisted the situation. I saw how my student suddenly became unhappy. I was opposing the Umayyids. I was praising the Prophet, the Companions, Fatima, Abu Dharr, Hujr and Husayn as leaders of a movement for justice and human freedom against prejudice, oppression and ignorance. What could this first class enlightened thinker do? He yelled out, 'The despot is history!'

According to the Marxist philosophy of history, society must move through historic phases in a certain predictable sequence. Ali, Husayn and Abu Dharr were ideologists who opposed the despotism of history. I said, 'The Mercy of God be upon this enlightened one.'

I see that I was right in re-iterating the fact that when the level of thought and vision of a society is transformed, the religious, non-religious, enlightened, reactionary and ignorant scholar are all the same. When a religious view prevails, all unknown and uncomprehended facts are called it calls it fate and destiny. Such a view believes that whatever occurs is the Will of God.

When a society becomes Marxist, it believes in the despotism of history. It believes that whatever happens is beyond human will. Whatever exists is accepted because it is a reality resulting inevitably from the processes of history. I said, 'No, look my friend, the sword is the despot here, not history.'

We see that realists believe that whatever exists should be as it is! The members of the Parliament in England defend the laws of homosexuality because homosexuality is an objective reality which exists in society. Therefore, it must be made legal.

To oppose this realism is to worship idealized fantasies which form the outlook of politicians and pseudo-intellectuals. You do not hear them argue that Israel is a reality. The settlement of the Palestinian people in lands occupied by Israel is a manifestation of someone who worshiped the ideal. Even though it is wrong, it is a reality which a realist must accept. Although it goes against the grain of humanity, although it is murder, it exists. Politicians and intellectuals accept it, and officially recognize it.

A magazine entitled 'This Week' has recently been published for young people. All the articles, translations, news items and photographs are the output of only two or three well-known writers using pen names. These writers visit whore houses and then, damn them. They write for our young people giving them a point by point description of events which take place. One of the top writers (who is too knowledgeable) is a politician who officially represents Islamic culture! He advises women who are overweight and unhappy because of it to find an illicit lover as a solution to their obesity. This is all a reality. Most probably the writers of "This Week" had first scientifically experienced this form of weight loss.

Abuse of the weak by the strong is also a reality. Oppression and suppression of certain classes are also realities. Reality seekers are completely objective viewers. They see the external form which is a scientific and sensible reality. Then they judge. They face no difficulties with imagination, ideology and ideas which are not translated into real forms.

We see that an idealist, a thinker, a reformer tends towards mental desires, ideals and sacred values, but denies or rejects the realities which deviate from his beliefs. It is impossible to negate them. He turns his back on them, or else, through inexperience, rejects them. He pulls. himself away from realities. He thinks in terms of imagery. He occupies a sacred place but does not realize that he is in an idealistic environment.

A realist, on the other hand, kills flights of thought, visions, efforts, mental longings of perfection. A realist keeps everything as it is. He builds walls around the framework of existing values and within the existing situation. He paralyzes creative thought, rebellion and the deep changes of life. His needs and desires tend only towards the present, external purposes of mankind. He surrenders to realities and nourishes that which exists.

NEITHER IDEALISM NOR REALISM: BOTH

Islam is a pure tree which belongs neither to the East nor the West but has its roots in the heavens and its branches reaching towards the earth. Contrary to idealism, Islam recognizes the realities of life (in both body and spirit) of the individual, as well as the realities of community relationships and of the depths of a society seen only in the motion of history.

Islam like realism only admits to the existence of life's harsher realities, but unlike realism, Islam does not accept the *status quo* but seeks to change. It changes essence in a revolutionary way. It carries the common idea of 'reality' along with its ideals. It uses such realities as a means to reach its idealistic goals, its real desires, which are without form by themselves. Unlike realism, Islam does not submit to realities, but rather, it causes the realities to submit to it. Islam does not turn away from realities as idealists do. It seeks them out. It tames them. Through this means, Islam uses that which hinders the idealists as raw material for its own ideals.

For example, Islam accepts divorce, a new marriage contract and temporary marriage (in certain very exceptional cases). Islam accepts divorce in certain social circumstances. If it did not accept divorce, divorce would still exist, but it would be outside its control. By accepting an unavoidable, natural reality, it makes it into a legal form. As a result, one can conquer the sense of guilt one has in the eyes of God and society. Thus, divorce is based upon ethical principles and religion is preserved. Such people can nourish their environment. Society does not look upon them as sinners or on their children as illegal and impure.

Islam succeeded the day it admitted the existence of these social and human realities. Because of this, it can control its results. It can give realities a corrected legal form. It can bestow an ethical and religiously accepted form upon amorphous 'facts'. By confirming and admitting the existence of reality, Islam gains strength. It can then control, guide and dominate any reality within its framework.

If we deny realities, they will dominate us. Without knowing it, we will be pulled wherever they want us to go, and we, like the realists, will be drowned in existing realities, whether good or bad. On the other hand, idealists make the mistake of imprisoning themselves in the chains of useless customs. Realists move along with realities and accept them. Idealists who do not recognize such realities, deny them through their ignorance and their attachment to imaginary ideals. Idealists are then attacked by realities. The idealists fall on their knees because they are defenseless, inexperienced and weak. They are destroyed.

We don't see the form that girls who are raised in very strict religious homes take. We don't see how she covers her face so that, God forbid, the fish in the courtyard pool do not see her. What happens when she enters the ocean of society? She vigorously swims, but she is so afraid that she loses control of herself and drowns. In order to make up for what she lacks now, she pays her fine a thousand times over.

The same is true for young men who grow up in a pious society. The *nouveau riche* have just moved from the former world of their idealistic pseudo-religious environment in which they were prohibited from learning physics or chemistry, and in which women were forbidden to have a high school or college education. The men did not shave their beards. They sat in coaches instead of in buses or in taxis. They wore no neck-tie. They did not let their hair grow long. They did not change the form of their clothes or their hair-style. They neither bought radios nor did they spread the word of the Koran through a microphone! Suddenly, these young people faced the new world of realities, full of twists and turns.

You see what confusion it has caused. The newly rich young person sees the pretense. He has learned certain airs through watching Western films and TV. He has learned about showing off luxury and being silly. He has seen the exaggeration of it all. It is so exaggerated that even foreigners laugh about it. Why? Because these pretenses exist side by side with reality whereas we deny the realities before we even come to know them. This is why we have been captured by our imagination.

This new civilization has attacked all boundaries toppled all the watchtowers of the world. The new generation has been caught in the whirling wind of the Renaissance, the 17th century intellectual movements, the French revolution and the industrialized life style. These historical events changed the weather of the world. The change of atmosphere of our country is also a reality. It is a most certain reality. It is clear that sooner or later lightening will strike. When it does, machines, printing presses, books, newspapers, democracy, electronic media, movies, schools, women's education, new industrial techniques, new sciences, and many other new things will come and will change us.

The leaders of the people, those responsible for ethics, those who have been given the responsibility of guiding lives and thoughts, those who stand face to face with unavoidable realities have closed their eyes. They have given their hearts to mental ideologies and to their ancient thoughts. They have tried to preserve their horse drawn carriages side by side with taxis.

They still light lamps when they have electricity. They correctly predict the rush to the inferior world. They know it will bring about the decline of much belief, faith, piety, health and independence. They know that corruption will find a home deep within people's brains. But face to face with this rush towards modernity (and knowing the relationship which it imposes on the furthermost points and on the most backward tribes of society—even those in the depths of the desert) they only say one thing and one thing only: Forbidden! Radio? Don't buy one. Movies? Don't see them. Television? Don't watch. Loudspeaker? Don't listen. University? Don't go. The new science? Don't study it. Newspapers? Don't read them. Vote? Don't do it. Office work? Don't do it and..woman? Shhh...Don't mention that word!

Face to face with the flood of new technology covering the globe, face to face with civilization which sells refrigerators to the Eskimos, they attempt to completely defend the past. Their total army and strategy consists of only two words: 'Forbidden!' and 'No!'.

What is the result? What we see is what happens. Contemporary events and realities break the barriers and tear down the watch-towers. Realities tears down the bricks of the walls and destroys the defenders of the past who hide with their eyes closed and faces averted in disapproval..

The force of these modern consumerist realities ruins everything at once. They attack the city's inhabited areas, its bazaars, mosques and even our homes like wild bulls, wolves or chained dogs. They plunder everything. But they do not leave. They come, they kill, they burn and they take, but they do not leave as the army of Ghengis Khan left. Why?

Because no one even sees them. Our border guards, our watchmen, don't like them. They are so exasperated that they don't even bother to look at them. They don't want to go and separate the good from the bad and correct them. They don't want to adapt them to the climate and the people of our country. They don't want to choose among them. They don't want to shame, control and dominate them. They stand in the middle of the road facing a driverless car. They are run over and crushed.

This is why the veiled woman who wants to give birth to her children, screams, "Why men physicians? Why should women not be treated by women physicians?" She wants her child to go to school and to the university. Her cries increase—is this the faculty of literature or a fashion show? Is this an Islamic university? Is this an Islamic society? Does this school smell just a bit of Islam? Does it contain a bit of ethics and meaning? Is this the radio of a religious country or just a noise box? What kind of a translation is this of one culture by another—this full-scale importation of television, publications, laws, and banks? What film is this? What theater? What art? What craft? Really, what kind of a civilization is this? But then again, as Hafez [the great poet] has said,

As our destiny has been shaped in our absence
If only a little fails to accord with our wishes, don't
    worry
And, in our case, we have to say:

If all of this is not according to our wishes, don't worry!

When modernism came and found a place for itself, when it begin to work, you were absent. You ran away. When you, a pious man, a religious, ethical Muslim (sensitive to people's feelings, responsible for the spirits and thoughts of society, preserver of the Islamic culture) sulk and retire into a corner, you allow a Reza Khan to bring a new civilization into effect and to employ a new industry and science.

It takes great effort to effectively interfere in events which unfold. Yet it is only through this effort that one can guide the determined motion of society. People who believe we should preserve that which is incapable of being preserved which is dying (and who are in a position to advise those who inspire, those who appease and those who give condolences) do not recognize the dangers. They create believers from among those who accept the unacceptable. They delude the majority of society. They keep them in an unholy state of prostration—silent, weak and submissive.

Those who seek a flowing, active society and want a better human life, acknowledge realities. They know pain. They take their strength from pain in order to heal their wounds. This group does not include those who, as demigods, defend that which is incapable of being defended, or those who take the public into their own hands, or those who follow the styles of the day, or those who praise according to what is fashionable, or those who try to attach themselves to something.

Those who acknowledge realities are people who know time moves. They know that society has a skin which it sheds. They feel that the strong forces of the world have turned to us to make us change. Neither are they sufficiently without pain to sit down and watch, nor are they, without shame, able to take whatever job is handed to them. They are not so stupid as one who sees a flood covering his town but protects only his wife and children, pulls only his own carpet from the water. They know that today is not like the past when families were living in a closed society. Now, even if you hide your daughter in the back room of your house, national and international television will follow her, find her and show her the attractions of the outside world.

CHAPTER FIVE
WHICH MOLD DO THEY FILL?

TRADITIONAL OR ABSURD

In reality, in our society, those who ask, 'Who am I?' 'Who should I be?' or 'What is my identity?' are of two types. One type is a person attached to out-dated, existing traditions which are called religion and ethics and which that person wants to impose upon others. He can't. Even though he knows he can't, he still adheres to outdated customs. He still retains them. He tries to impose them upon young people .

There is another type afraid to act even under the pseudo-name of intellectual, modernist or freedom-seeker because he thinks, "If I interfere or negate or agree or control the 'ifs', I will be condemned as being old-fashioned, eastern, backward and religious." So against the social changes, the changes in the types of young men and women, he plays the role of a dead person. In other words, his child acts while the mother and father create possibilities for him. They are called intellectual parents. But their silence and surrender does not stem from their intellectual abilities. Nor does it come from their beliefs, but rather from their impotency and weakness. He says to himself, "If I interfere, I will give up my outer, external strength to this show and my inner emptiness." He shouts out, "Prestige, Papa!"

These are two types, two types of people who can be molded. One is attached to the traditions of the Chahar Bagh in Isfahan—huge, ugly, crooked and decayed. The second is a product of European brick kilns—straight, subtle, without endurance, hollow and absurd.

These are two types and two ways, both of which are lost. Why? One stands against the roaring flood of realities which is about to ruin everything. He tries to turn back the waters with his hands. He tries to stop the flow. He cries out, laments, sobs, and swears at the flood, but the flood just builds up, flows out and sinks everything in its way.

The other one stretches himself out next to the flood waters, like a dead person, like a useless observer. This dear man who has no personality of his own, is quiet and works from morning until night, committing murder, ripping people off, pickpocketing, and performing a thousand dirty deeds. He tricks people and then fills his pockets which he, in turn, empties into the pockets of the foreign companies.

WOMEN WE CANNOT KNOW

There are only some European women whom we have the right to recognize. It is they to whom we always have to refer. They are the women introduced through magazines, television and sexy movies. They are women made sexy by writers. They are introduced to us as a universal type of European woman.

Let me tell you about the European girl we have no right to know. At the age of sixteen she went to the deserts of Africa, to the deserts of Algeria and Australia. She spent all of her life in wild places. She lived with the threat of sickness, death and wild tribes. Throughout her youth and old age she studied the waves emitted from the antennae of ants. When she grew old, her daughter carried on her work. The second generation of this European woman returned to France at the age of fifty. At the university she said, "I discovered the language of the ants and I learned some of their signs of communication."

Also, we have no right to know Madame Gushan who spent her whole life finding the roots of philosophical ideas and the studying the wisdom of Avicenna, ibn Rushd, Mulla Sadra and Haji Mulla Hadi Sabzevari. She also studied Greek philosophy and many of the works of Aristotle and compared them with Islamic material. She showed what our philosophers received from them. She corrected that which had been badly translated and incorrectly understood for a 1000 years of Islamic civilization.

We have no right to know the Italian Mme. De la Vida. She edited and completed the 'Science of the Soul' of Avicenna itself based on the ancient Greek manuscript on the soul written by

Aristotle. We have no right to know Mme. Curie who discovered radioactivity.

And what about Resass Du La Chappelle who knew more about the sanctity of Ali than all the Islamic scientists. Resass Du La Chappelle was a young, beautiful, free Swedish girl, born far from Islamic culture. She was distant from Muslim behavior and beliefs. From the beginning of her youth, she devoted her life to knowing that unknown spirit in the structure of Islam. She followed a man covered by the hatred of his enemies, caught in traps laid by hypocrites and meaningless friends. She discovered the most correct manuscripts about Ali. She came to know the most subtle waves of his spirit, the depth of his feelings and the highest peaks of his ideas. For the first time, she felt his anger, pain, loneliness, brokenness, fear and needs. Not only did she 'see' Ali in the Battles of Uhud, Badr and Hunayn, but she found Ali praying in the *mihrab* of the mosque in Kufa. She discovered his nights of complaining at the wells of Madinah. She gathered together the *Nahj al-balaqah* to which the Arab Muslims had access through the literary edition of Muhammad Abduh, the great Sunni religious leader, but about which the Jafaris had only lectures of Javad Fazel which had to be read with the help of the Arabic text!

This girl—a disbeliever destined for hell—gathered all of the writings of Ali from books, notebooks or manuscripts, hidden here and there. She read all of them and translated them and interpreted them. The most beautiful and deepest writings ever written about someone flowed from her pen. For forty-two years she has continued to study, think, work and research Ali.

We have no right to know Angela, the American girl in prison who is not only the hope of two countries, but of all the free people of the world, of all the wounded, of all those condemned through racial discrimination—in other words, all the oppressed.

We should not know that foreign women are not just toys of the Don Juans who take money and jewels—female slaves serving men as long as they want them, as long as they are interested. We should believe that they are worthy only of man's desires and lusts.

The foreign woman has progressed to the point of becoming the embodiment of an ideology, of a country, of salvation and of the honor of a generation. But we have no right to know her.

We only have the right to know fashion models and beauty queens. We have only the right to know movie sex goddesses in cheap exploitation films, the Queen of Monaco and all of the seven female guards around James Bond. Such women are the sacrifices made to European production. of Europe. They are the toys and wind-up dolls of the wealthy. They are the slaves of the houses of the new merchants.

We Muslims only have the right to know these examples of the women of European civilization. I have never seen photographs from Cambridge, the Sorbonne or Harvard University telling about female university students who go to the library to work on 14th and 15th century manuscripts and to research artifacts from 2500-3000 years ago in China. I have not seen pictures of those who bend over Koranic manuscripts based upon Latin. I have not seen pictures of those studying Greek, Cuneiform and Sanskrit texts without moving and without allowing their eyes to rove. They don't take their heads out of their books until the librarian takes their books away or asks them to leave.

You—men and women, seekers of knowledge, scholars, researchers—have you ever heard of the famous German scholar, Frau Hunekeh? Have you heard that she has recently written a very comprehensive study of Islam and its influence upon European civilization which has been translated into Arabic and is entitled, *The Arab's Sun Spreads over the West.*

These are not today's women and they should not be known. Why? Because one group is made up of old fashioned, ethnic cultural-bound seekers. The other is superstitious, newly rich and hidden, but at the same time known and apparent. If they join hands, they will awaken us. They will destroy everything we have. So people are obliged to take the form of tamed consumers and quiet slaves.

These two groups, old-fashioned and newly wealthy, for all practical purposes, work together to produce a new type. One does this under the name of ethics and religion while the other does this under the name of freedom and progress. The old-fashioned woman is abused by prejudice and fanaticism. They push her, leaving her without bread and water. They show her anger. They have no compassion. They treat her so badly that the woman, half crazy with her eyes and ears closed, throws herself into the skirts of those with goat-like beards, who welcome her, take off their hats respectfully and with correct manners, bend forward politely, smiling, and treating her gently.

The European woman about whom I was speaking, is a woman of today. She delivered herself, but she is the progeny of the Middle Ages. She is reacting to the inhuman treatment and fanaticism of the priests of the Middle Ages, who, in the name of Christianity and religion, misguided women and cursed and enslaved them. They even said woman was hated by God and was the main cause of Adam's fall from Paradise to the earth!

In the Middle Ages, people asked priests, "If there is a woman in a house, should a man, who is not related, enter?"

The priests said, "Never. Because if the man is not related and he enters the house where there is a woman—even if he does not see the woman—still he has sinned."

In other words, if an unrelated man goes to the second floor of the house and a woman is in the basement, sin occurs. It seems that the sins of women spread through the air.

St. Thomas Dakin said, "If God should see the love for a woman upon a man's face—even if the woman is his wife—he becomes angry because no love, other than the love of God, should sit upon his heart. Christ lived without a wife. A man can be a Christian without having touched a woman. This is why Christian brothers and spiritual fathers—and even Christian sisters—never marry. They believe marriage is a tie which arouses God's anger. We should only join with God through Jesus Christ because two loves cannot fit into one heart. Only those who remain unmarried can carry the Holy Ghost."

In Christianity, the first sin was the sin of woman. Every man, as the child of Adam, who turns towards a woman, even if that woman be his wife, as Eve was the wife of Adam, repeats the first, primordial sin. The sin and disobedience of Adam is renewed in the memory of God!

Thus one must do something so that God will forget Adam and his sin! This is why a woman in the thoughts of the people of the Middle Ages was hated, weakened and held back from the ownership of anything. Such hatred even extended to the point that if a woman, owning property, went to her husband's house, she lost the rights to her own property. Her ownership was itself transferred to her husband. A woman had no legal status. The effects of this can still be found in European civilization, which is completely unacceptable to us.

Even today, if a woman marries, she changes her name. This is not just for use in her home or unofficially. Her education certificates, her identification, her passport—everything is changed from carrying her father's name to her husband's name. This means that a woman herself is nothing. She has no essential existence. A name is significant. A creature who lacks significance stands through others. In her parent's home, she uses her father's name. She lives with her first owner. When she goes to her husband's home, the name of another man (her new owner) distinguishes her. She does not possess sufficient value or credit to have a name of her own. Modern Muslims believe that European tradition has also influenced Muslim countries. They believe European traditions are better than ours. Even if it is a tradition from the slave age, even if it is a detested and ugly action, the very fact that it has a foreign mark upon it is sufficient for our modernists to attempt to imitate it. This is just an example which our pseudo-foreigners take from the foreign 'better' race. Whatever that race does is copied without even knowing its reason, purpose or value. Our modernists have no common sense.

In imitating, whether by a modernist or by an old-fashionist, choice is impossible. There is no questioning or judgment about good or bad, no distinction between the useful and the useless. The basis of all imitation is the principle that "Whatever defect the king accepts is art." They confirm him until it reaches the point where if he says, "Day is night," they add, "Yes. I see the moon and the stars."

In the official European marriage forms, the two people to be married are asked, "Name?" Secondly, girl's family name. In answering the first question, the family name which will be taken after marriage, that is, the family name of the husband-to-be is recorded. In answer to the second question, her unmarried family name, the name of her father, is recorded.

In other words, a woman belongs to the owner of the house. Even if a house had originally belonged to her, she could not continue to own it because she was a woman. In her father's house, it was her father's name and in her husband's house, it is her husband's name which is used. This is why she officially changes her name through marriage.

Only an idiot ridiculously and unconsciously acts and thinks like a foreigner because he or she cannot distinguish values. This is why we say pseudo-foreigners have been born into our modern society who do not resemble foreigners. Pseudo-Europeans have come into existence for which no example in Europe exists.

In Islam, from the very beginning, the purest form of Islam, (not the present composite form of Islam), a woman is completely independent in respect to woman's rights. She can even seek payment from her husband for nursing her child. She can carry on her own businesses without any interference from her husband. She can work. As to production she can independently and directly put her capital into effect. She has the most economic independence of any member of society.

All of the anti-human and pseudo-religious pressures committed against European women in the name of religion have caused a reaction. This reaction is directed against the Middle Ages. The memory of it has remained with her. In Italy and Spain where religion is still strong, women are denied many of their human rights in spite of the signs of freedom and the emphasis upon human rights.

We are talking about human freedom and social rights, not sexual freedom and sexual rights. We see with what speed the latter becomes prevalent. In return for the second world's (the previous third world's oil, diamonds, rubber gum, copper, coffee and uranium which inexpensively enter Europe, Europe exports freedom, ethics, techniques, culture, art, literature and, in particular, sex, to our hungry, plundered world. All the means of advertisement, all the means of social, technical, artistic and educational expertise of an underdeveloped country are employed to serve propaganda, promotion and distribution. These things are all other than freedoms and human rights!

Sexual freedom is deceiving. It is part of a new exploitation, a type of limitless deception, which the impure system of Western capitalism produces. It causes both the East and West innocently to reach out towards it—until things get to the point that the influencing West and the influenced East form a continuous culture.

The young generation (in particular, those who are rebellious, audacious and have not been stupefied by religious stipulations and the hereditary chains of traditions falls into the Western trap. At any moment it is possible that, based upon rebellion, they take up a notion contrary to their interests and as a result put their heads into a cheap foreign lover's grasp and thereby, become so drowned and giddy in the artificial freedom presented by capitalists that they no longer know what the world is about. They so completely saturate themselves with materialism that they no longer sense their poverty and slavery. We see to what extent the internal conditions of despotism in Asia, Africa and Latin America have resulted in an insane emphasis upon the rights and freedom of sex as advertised by the Western capitalists. Sexual freedom is emphasized and strengthened so that the groundwork is laid for its daily increase.

We can, with a little bit of caution and discernment, come to know what is behind these attractive forms of thunder-struck, sexuality. It is none other than the denial of the modern world. We have to come to know these great idols and the three faces of the contemporary religious trinity: exploitation, colonialization and despotism. This trinity makes Freud a prophet. From Freudism they build a supposedly scientific and human religion. From sexuality they build an ethical conscience. Finally, from lust, a blessed temple is built. They build their place of worship and create a powerful servant class. The first sacrifice recorded on the threshold of this temple is woman.

WHO IS THE CONTEMPORARY WOMAN? SERVING ONESELF VS. SERVING OTHERS

In the 15th and 16th centuries (following the Renaissance and the passing away of customs and ancient religion) the thought of Descartes and the logic of analytical science replaced natural sensitivities and religious feelings. According to Durkheim, individual autonomy in one's dealings with one's society (family, tribe or country) and serving oneself as an independent entity replaced the unity of society and the serving of others. Utility replaces values. Realism replaces idealism. Instincts replace spiritual efforts. Welfare and the problems of life replace the search for perfection, consciousness of God and self-sufficiency. Intelligent logic is consciously chosen to substitute for the sacred and spiritual which, through an unacceptable materialist analysis are related to a kind of eternal pleasure.

Finally, known phenomena, capable of analysis and synthesis, are considered to be relative and materialistic. They form the people, life, culture, all of the dimensions of the earth, the elements of society and the unlimited attractions of the new spirit. They replace the essence of inspiration and the composite truths which are above one's individual will. They do away with anything which is only understood by the supra-intellectual (spiritual faculty)—that is, everything which is beyond logical science, such as the eternal, hidden Platonic dimensions.

The roots of these dimensions exist in the depths of being. Since the beginning of humanity, they have poked their heads through. They are enigmatic attractions from another world. They are from the essence of fate. They are absolute Their source is divine destiny. Alas, nature has replaced metaphysics; science has replaced inspiration; pleasure has replaced chastity; happiness has replaced perfection; and tranquility has replaced piety. As Francis Bacon said, "Power has replaced Truth."

This spiritual and intellectual change in the deep evolution of human values has changed the main direction of culture, knowledge and feelings. New means of earning a livelihood, new view of love and the relationship between men and women, the place of women in society and their relationship to men have had revolutionary effects upon the roots of the fabric of our life, literature, art and sensitivities.

All things are analyzed according to the science and positivist vision of Descartes. This includes the sacred and ethical principles always viewed as values above human knowledge—that is, divine virtues. These are now analyzed as material things. Among these values are women and love, which had previously existed together in a halo of sanctity. They were hidden in the imagination, spirit, and inspiration where they remained untouched. Now they place them upon the blackboard and the billboard.

One of the people responsible for this is Claude Bernard who saw human beings as corpses without a spirit. Freud considered the spirit to be a sick animal. For the bourgeoisie, life is money. The result is what we see now.

Opposed to these were the Christian priests. Next to their laboratories were churches. They had nothing to offer other than 'excommunication'. They were club wielders whom no one feared. Compared to materialists who at least reasoned and gave examples, they simply cried out, 'Religion is dying!' They issued unreasonable cannon laws. They constantly threw the fire of hell into the faces of their parishioners but to no avail.

A woman, as far as her life was concerned, was part of a family. Even though she had no independent human personality, at least she could easily be dissolved in the family, which was one spirit. Little by little she became economically independent. She began working outside of the home. With industrialization in full swing, with daily progress and improvement in social occupations, women went to work.

From society's point of view, economic independence has also made her socially independent. Thereafter she found individual existence beside her husband and children. Today, before marriage and setting up a household, she has individual independence. Because she has developed intellectually and logically, this has of itself altered her relationship with others (her lover, her father and her family). Family life is no longer based on sensitive feelings or intuitive attractions or deep, unconscious, spiritual efforts but, rather, upon the linear principles of intellectual accounting and detailed calculation. She has been freed from many social, family and religious chains through her accountant's vision of the situation. She is now capable of seeing reality, of being able to analyze and intellectualize, of seeking herself, of finding her own interests and individual profits and spending for herself. She authentically seeks pleasure, encounters things, and looks for tranquility, intelligence and happiness. At the same time, however, many of her deep feelings have been taken away from her. Her hereditary feelings, which are other than the intellectual, have been removed. Her humaness has suffered (and has left her lonely). But it has made her independent.

Durkheim has shown that in the past, the social spirit of command responsibility was strong. Whenever economics and individuality grew individuals lost family roots, sensitivities, traditional ideas and spirit. They became autonomous. This independence gave them multiple possibilities. The very fact that an eighteen year old girl can very easily get her own apartment and live alone without any supervision is one of them.

A woman is allowed many freedoms in her home for economic reasons. Whenever she becomes angry over life, she can flee from her situation, as she has individual rights. In her view, bearing the sorrow of another does not fit with a healthy intelligence; therefore, whenever she must make a sacrifice, or give in abundance, she closes her eyes.

For peace of mind, pleasure, freedom, and for anything which affects her own well-being, she opens her eyes. This is because things like loyalty, sacrifice, generosity, gratitude, and love are all spiritual and ethical things. They are not capable of intellectual and logical demonstration.

"Sacrifice your life so that others may live," or "bear sorrow so that others may have peace," are transactions which do not pay off, no matter how you account for them.

Then who can answer her question, "Why should I sacrifice myself for he who needs me? Why should I remain loyal to him? Why should I remain with this ugly, weak man because of a promise, an agreement, made when he was handsome, strong, and the only creature around at that time? I bore him patiently. Why should I now close my eyes to the handsome, strong man who is available and who understands my spirit and my goals?"

Sartre presents an example. A woman is the wife of a man who has no attractive qualities. In comparison to him, there is an attractive man who loves her. The intelligent way is clear. Both men need her. One needs her as a wife, the other as a lover. The woman does not need the first man but rather the second.

By remaining loyal to her husband, two needs are sacrificed (those of herself and her lover) and one is satisfied (that of her husband). In fleeing from him and letting him go, two needs are satisfied and one is sacrificed. The duty of this woman is clear. Her intelligence makes the decision a clear mathematical formula. The reason behind why a woman would sacrifice two needs for one is not simply an intellectual, logical Cartesian or Freudian one. An intelligent woman thinks and acts logically. Economic freedom and social rights present her with the possibility of doing it. She does it.

Children come into the world. A child restricts the freedom of its mother and father. Intelligence cannot accept the fact that the peace of mind and freedom of two people be sacrificed for one person. They either do not bring children into the world or they leave them with a nurse or in an institution. Among all of these illogical feelings and ethical and traditional bounds, there is a conscience, a spirit which a woman holds onto. She finds it by immersing herself into the fabric of the spiritual depths of her family.

There are a hundred irrational, impractical rationalizations which encourage her to choose forgiveness, suffering, sacrifice for her husband and children, home, family, and the sensitive values of life which had been disconnected. Because of economic and social independence, she had developed an individual spirit and independence instead of gaining a social spirit through which the individual is dissolved.

LONELINESS

Loneliness is the greatest tragedy of the century. Durkheim has analyzed the situation in his book, *Suicide*. Suicide in the East is an exception. It is not a common event. In Europe it is looked upon as a social phenomenon. It is not an accident; it is a reality. Its incidence grows higher and higher everyday in developed societies. The rate of suicide in Spain, which is an underdeveloped country, is less than in other European countries. In Northern Europe the suicide rate is higher. This same pattern exists between villages and urban centers, between the developed areas and the more underdeveloped areas and between the nonreligious, modern group and the old-fashioned religious group. Why? Because people are lonely.

Religion ties people together. It causes a common spirit which is born in its followers to be shared. It nourishes a sympathy between each individual and God. In the past, each individual was linked through hundreds of connections with others-family, friends and tribes. Social and economic self-sufficiency makes people needless of each other.

It used to be society which gathered individuals together. Now instead of gathering individuals, the family defends the individual and his or her material needs. Intellectual studies and logic attack the spiritual and traditional religious connections. Intellectual growth, the logic of mathematics, the spirit of materialism, cause the spiritual connections to become unstable.

The individual becomes autonomous. Individual reasoning of necessity becomes self-seeking. It becomes needless of others. It stands alone. Because people no longer need each other, they uproot themselves, and each person then seeks out his or her own interests. Individuals are alone on their islands. Then the thought of suicide attacks them, for suicide is the neighbor of loneliness.

Women choose their men and men their women. But the very fact that men and women are both independent, powerful and without needs, causes them to move towards each other only because of sex. Other factors such as love, kindness, social and traditional roots, friendship, and sympathy, are not taken into consideration. Today, these sorts of attractions have died. Then what remains? A frail intellectual calculation without light, a logical necessity, or a force.

Sexual freedom in men and women's thoughts (although officially beginning at puberty) for all practical purposes begins whenever one wants. A new idea appears—namely, that in order to satisfy a sexual urge the only requirement is the sexual urge. It can be eliminated with money. Only money is necessary. At different levels or with different amounts of money, the sexual urge can be satisfied. One can at any time and under any government be a Don Juan or an Onassis. The First Lady of America can also be bought for a price. The difference between her and those who stand on the street is one of rate. Since boys and girls both enjoy sexual freedom, neither one wants to restrict him or herself for the whole of their lives. It is not to their interest to restrict the power of their sexual urges.

In such circumstances none of the answers of logic or wisdom justify an individual choosing one person for one's whole life—thereby restricting all future availability of pleasure and beauty in life.

FORMING A FAMILY

At the present time, men and women freely satisfy their sexual urges in universities, restaurants, outings, and various gatherings of this kind. This continues until a woman comes to herself and sees that it is empty around her.

No one any longer seeks her out or if they do, it is to review, to revise a memory of the past. When a man has passed the freedom of his sexual cycle, when he has picked a flower from every garden and from each flower, taken its perfume, there is nothing any longer for him which is interesting or new. His sexual urge has subsided. It has been replaced by attachment to his position and his money. He seeks fame and worships position. His inclinations are now towards getting a house and forming a family. These feelings then appear in his being.

A woman, face to face with the reality that no one seeks her out, and, a man, exhausted from his freedoms and indeed by sexual experiences which have finally turned his heart, confront each other. They reach out towards each other at the end of a long and tiring road. They want to form a family.

A family is formed but that which draws these two together, that which causes them to join hands, is fear and fatigue. On the part of the woman it is fear of bankruptcy and no longer being noticed. The man is tired and no longer interested in anything. A family has been formed but in place of love and the intensity of an ideal, instead of creative happiness and imagination, exhaustion and ennui set in so that nothing is new. They know what is there. Nothing!

There is nothing for which their hearts beat. They know why they have found each other. They know what needs they have from each other. Both, completely conscious, calculating, aware, seek each other out. Each knows what the other meant by the words, 'be my divine sacrifice'. Each has achieved their wishes. Both sacrifice for the other. Both die for the other. But in the opposite way from which we normally understand it.

On the day of weddings, city hall is filled. Someone from city hall, with a medal on his coat, looking like a beauracrat attends to them, not a clergyman who is a symbol of spirit, faith, reverence and sainthood. Each couple is called forward exactly like molded sugar cones. Their names are read from a list. They answer, "Yes." Often several children standing behind the bride and groom also answer yes. It shows their existences have influenced the yes of their mothers and fathers. They pay their money. They sign the register. The ceremony is over. Each returns to his mould, his home. From among the 200-300 brides only 20-30 wear a bridal gown. Most of them say, "What, at my age, in my condition, it would be degrading to wear a bridal gown. It is not right."

Then the wife goes to work and the man as well. They have a *rendez-vous* with their friends to meet at noon in a restaurant and eat lunch together. This, of course, only happens when the wedding to some extent has been full of happiness and excitement. Otherwise they forget what had happened and what event had occurred. Most often, outside city hall—after the civil ceremony, the bride and groom (who have been living together for years and each one has probably spent a year or more living with someone else), give each other a cold look as if to say, "So what? Where should we go? Fun? We've gone out a thousand times together. Embrace each other? We've tasted each other a thousand times and we've fled from the taste. Home? We came from home." What appeals to them? Do they excite each other's imagination and feelings? Not at all. Then its best if each continues his work each day like always.

Families are formed in this way. Both the man and the woman have schemed to find each other and form an economic union. Or else, they were married because of the other pressures. Perhaps a child was born causing the father and mother of the child to become a bride and groom. They show no understanding, feelings and desires towards each other. They do not sense any secrets in each other, no paradox in their union. Nothing begins. Nothing changes. No imaginary flights, no heart beats—not even a smile upon their lips. This is why the foundation of a family becomes frail. Once the foundations have weakened, the children in that family no longer see understanding, warmth and attractions. Because the mother and father will not sacrifice all of their freedoms for their children, they put the child in a school or boarding school and they only give it money so that they can continue their free life.

Afterwards, having formed a logical but deceitful partnership according to the laws and having created a family, they then separate from each other. The possibilities continue for the man who has experienced thousands of warm and young embraces. How can this woman who is tired and fallen in spirit and whose masculine actions cause disgust in the man, satisfy his needs? And visa versa? A woman who can make a thousand comparisons, takes the worn out man into her arms. Through her comparisons, his number is up. In such a situation, within a household which lacks understanding, he turns to bars, fraternities, new experiences, official and unofficial centers. Once again, contrary to the original invitation, the factor which keeps these two within the same household is an illogical one.

WOMEN IN THE CONSUMER SYSTEM: SEX INSTEAD OF LOVE

Societies which only authenticate things in the economic

terms of production and consumption only understand economics. Women are no longer creature who excite the imagination
nor speakers of pure feelings. Neither are they the beloveds of
the great lovers nor do they have sacred roots. They are no
longer spoken of in terms of mother, companion, center of inspiration and mirror of life and fidelity. Rather, as an economic
product, women are bought and sold according to the value of
their sexual attraction.

Capitalism, as a result of producing leisure time, has
shaped a woman to serve two purposes. In the first, she fills the
time between two jobs which is part of the fate of society. The
bourgeoisie exploit her and create a dry and absurd future for
her without any purpose whatsoever. Should she not ask, "Why
am I working? Why am I living? 'For whom am I suffering?"

Secondly, women are used as an instrument of entertainment. As the only creature who has both sex and sexuality, has
been put to work, office employees and intellectuals can think
about ways of spending their capital during their leisure time
(instead of thinking about the ideas of classlessness, for
instance). Women have been put to work to fill every empty
moment of the life of society. Art quickly joins the market so
that they can meet the orders of the capitalists and the bourgeoisie. The main purpose of art has always been beauty, spirit,
feelings and love. This has now been changed into sex. The market of Freudism, the worship of the most vile and wretched sex
has been made into an intellectual philosophy. Sex has been
introduced as the virtue behind contemporary art. This is why
we find instant paintings, poetry, films, theater, stories, novels
etc. all concerned with sex in some form.

Capitalism encourages people to consume more in order to
make people more dependent upon it. It also wishes to increase
the amount consumed and the products produced. Women are
presented only as creatures who are sexy and, other than this,
nothing. In other words, woman is used as a one dimensional
creature. She is placed in advertisements and used as propaganda for creating new values, new feelings and drawing attention to new consumer products. This causes artificial feelings in
people. To protect the profits of capitalism, women are thrown
in. In order to kill the great and spiritual feelings which destroy
capitalism, woman works to prevent capitalism's death.

Sexuality replaces love. Woman, the imprisoned creatures of
the Middle Ages, has taken the form of a wage-slave in the new

age. It is in great civilizations with progressive religions that woman has held a high place through the love she can give in and through the arts—even though she may not have had a direct relationship with art. But, she was looked upon as the source of inspiration, feelings and spiritual characteristics. Now she has taken the form of an instrument employed for serving social and economic purposes. She is used to change the form of society. She is used to destroy the highest values of the traditional societies. She is used to change ethics. She is used to change a traditional, spiritual, ethical or religious society into an empty, absurd, consuming society. She is used to pollute art which had been the theophany of the divine spirit of humanity. She is changed into an instrument for sexuality in order to change humanity.

BUT IN THE EAST

Now consumer society approaches the East. It is our turn. Here its work is very easy. Young eastern boys reach the age of puberty early. It is this early sexual awakening which causes eastern sociologists and psychologists to face many problems. Where is the owner of this generation? Who thought about them? There is a war between two groups. Conversations center on type of clothes, habits and tastes. Human problems, whether they are new or old, do not concern either side. The war is between being old-fashioned and modern. Winning is to the advantage of neither. One is called civilized and the other, is called pious, religious. Neither one relates in the least to either civilization or religion. One, the pious type, calls out for Fatima and Zaynab and the other calls out for the European woman. Both are insulting to each other.

Europeans want to change eastern societies to plunder our property and to ride upon our thoughts and our feelings. They want to take the food from our mouths as well as to destroy our common sense values. Without destroying these things, they cannot take the food from our mouths or our property.

First the West must break our moulds. We must be made to forget all of our human values and all of our traditions which were the very things which kept us upon our own feet. We must give these up and break them within ourselves. Once, empty-headed, with an impotent spirit, crippled and without content, we must become exactly like garbage cans which are filled with dirty and useless things and then are emptied.

This is what the West is doing to the brain and spirit of the
East. They are emptying them of their contents. When we have
no faith in anything, we have no intelligence or awareness so
that we have no hero, we think the past is completely without
value. When we believe our religion to be empty and full of
myths, we feel spiritual meanings to be old-fashioned, reactionary and that way of life to be ugly and detestable. We either
do not know ourselves, our children and our spirituality or else
we know it badly. So what form does Western values change?
They empty out our brain and heart so that we begin to thirst
for exploiters. Whatever the plundering exploiters then want to
pour into our interior, in whatever order they choose, they are
free to do so.

It is because of this that the exploiters assign permanent
slogans to plundering the East, emptying the minds of Muslims,
Buddhists, Hindus, Iranians, Turks, Arabs, Blacks and others.
All must take one form. All must have only one dimension. They
must be consumers of Western economic products and have
thoughts, but not think for themselves.

Insistence upon old values, traditions and religions, which
are full of meaning, close the way to the West and guard the
East. Insistence upon traditional values stands like a watch-
tower with a strong spirit against the West. They defend Islam
and independence. Foreignness does not penetrate. Muslims
are overflowing with honor, spiritual meaning, values and
pride. Their history, people, culture, faith and religious characteristics give them independence, greatness a reason for which
to hold their heads up high.

They see the Westerners as *nouveau riche* and newly civilized. They criticize them, humiliate them and confront them.
But the West falls upon the soul of the Easterners like termites.
Little by little the head is emptied out of its contents. The West
even destroys the forces of resistance which remain. In place of
the brave guardians of the watch-towers, full of spirit and pride,
it builds a people empty of common sense, perseverance and
pride. The Easterners go forward to meet the enemy. They take
whatever the West gives and do whatever it wants them to do.
They become exactly as Westerners will them to be .

CHAPTER SIX
WHAT ROLE DID WOMEN PLAY IN THE ATTACK?

Women in Islamic countries held a power whereby they could have changed the traditions, social relationships, ethics, spiritual values and, most important of all, the pattern of consumption in the same way that they held a power to preserve all this. Why? Because of the sensitive spirit of the East. It tends to accept the luxuries of civilized life and new products quickly more easily. This is especially true when confronted by bright, new, eye-catching things of beauty—especially when opposed to these, they find nothing but ugliness.

During the time of the exploitation of Africa, European imposters would move among the black tribes offering glass beads and fake jewelry (which are usually even brighter than the natural stone). In all of the ceremonies, the better-off among the tribes, the kings, the large farmers and the feudal lords could all be pointed out. This was particularly true of the local ceremonies and weddings because their actions were based one hundred percent upon psychological laws. Those who liked the fake things the most were the most primitive.

We see that today, those who worship luxurious ornaments are the Arab shaykhs, the heads of some African nations, the movie stars and the newly wealthy people. A few of fake lights and glass beads were given to the heads of African tribes and in return the colonialists received a herd of sheep or a great pasture land or the rights to mine diamonds or permission to plant coffee. It is obvious from this how important the role of the newly modernized African woman is.

135

It is also apparent how sheltered, Eastern women suffer from social rules presented to them in the name of religion and tradition as is done by present day Islam. They are presently denied learning, literacy, human rights, social possibilities and freedom to develop. They are not able to explore and nourish their spirit and their thoughts. Even the rights and possibilities which Islam itself has given to women, have been taken away from them in the name of Islam. Present day Islam has placed woman in the same category as a washing machine. Her human values have been lowered to 'mother of the child'. She no longer even has a name but is called by the name of her child even if her child happens to be a boy. She is called Hasan's mother. This is exactly like paralyzing her and then saying that because she is paralyzed, she is deprived of everything. The sorrow lies here.

OPPRESSORS AND THE OPPRESSED

Ali said two parties are required in order to bring about oppression. One is the oppressor and the other is the one who accepts the oppression. It is the co-operation of these two which brings about oppression. Oppression cannot be one-sided. An oppressor cannot perform oppression on the air. Oppression is like a piece of iron which is formed by the striking of the hammer of the oppressor upon the anvil of the oppressed.

Not only is oppression a result of corruption, deviation and misery, but it requires two sides working together to come into being. In the defeat of a society, it is not just the victor who breaks. Society must allow itself to be broken. For instance, in the 7th century AH it was not Chengis Khan who defeated us. It was we ourselves who were corrupted from within. From the 5th to the 6th century AH, we were preparing ourselves to be defeated. It was because of this that Chengis defeated us. He only kicked the corrupted states once and they fell down and were defeated. The termites (who had built their homes inside our tree and had begun eating away the body from the inside) left it empty, dry and without roots. These termites caused the tree to fall to the earth and not the strong wind which blew upon the tree. Strong winds always blow in the forest. Why is it that just this tree or that one falls down?

The creation of superstitions, the spreading of ignorant backward beliefs, the inherited systems of cultural servitude, the tradition of 'father power' in the community, the lack of psy-

chology, all weave themselves together like a spider's web. And
it is this very web which impoverishes the woman within itself.
She becomes known as 'someone who is behind the curtain'. All
of this occurs in the name of Islam, in the name of religion, in
the name of tradition and worst of all, in the name of 'similarity to Fatima'.

It is explained to her in terms of chastity and the necessity
to nourish her children. I don't know how a person who is herself incomplete and useless, who is missing a part of her brain
and who is excluded from literacy, books, education, discipline,
thought, culture, civilization and social manners could possibly
be worthy of being the nourisher of tomorrow's generation.

Most probably they mean fattening their bodies when they
say nourishing their children. What can this weak creature of
the house, (born to sit behind a curtain without thought or culture), who has not been educated do for the development of her
child? How can she develop her child's sense of completeness?
How can she awaken the depths of the spirit within anyone?
How can she learn to accept the complicated ideas and feelings
of her child?

What can she do other than nurse her child and change her
baby's diapers? In disciplining her child she can only swear at
it or use lewd language or cry or curse her fate. If none of these
has any effect, she implants the fear of an older brother or the
father in the child. If this doesn't work, she calls upon the *jinn*
and the angel of death or threatens the basement or the well.

And if this bad child with a roguish father should die young,
if he should be burned in the fire of brawls, there is nothing this
hidden creature can do when news of the death of her child is
brought to her. She in some measure created this situation. She
had unintentionally called forth the dead, dark monsters.

Yes! These are the ways and means of educating and disciplining a child in a system where the only duty of a woman is to
nourish her children. It is perfectly natural to think that if she
spent her time making use of her cultural and social abilities, if
she were to become part of civilization, she would not be able to
perform her special mandate which is to bring up children. If
she were to develop and nourish her thoughts and her spirit
and become aware of the system she is part of, some would obviously conclude that her mandate would suffer.

Thus we see the fate of woman in our conservative society

which has had false undertones of religion added to it. She grows up in her father's home without breathing any free air. She goes to her husband's home (her second lord and master) in accordance with an agreement which is made between a buyer and a seller. She is transferred to her husband's house where the marriage license or ownership papers shows both her role and her price. She becomes a respectable servant. A married man means someone who has a servant who works in his house. She cooks food, nurses babies, watches the children and sees to the cleaning and ordering of the house. She manages the inside of the house.

She is a household laborer and a nurse but because she works without any wages, she has no rights. She does the work of a servant in the name of common, ritual, or civil law, but since she cannot be a servant, she is called a lady. Because her lord is her husband, she is called wife. As she acts as a nurse to the children, she is also called mother.

At any rate, she is working for herself. She is an expert at her work, even though the level of work she does is equivalent to the work of a servant or a nurse. It is no more than this because she has not been trained to do more than this. She is uneducated.

We must point out here that our objection is to the well-established fathers and wealthy husbands who condemn their daughters or wives and who do so because they are women. They keep them from an education and from self-completion in the name of religion and faith. There are many women in Islam who reached the level of authorized theologians, established centers of learning and wrote important texts on science and ethics and spirituality.

But girls who do not have the economic means to pursue education and those who work hard in their father's or husband's houses, are most worthy of praise. Such a girl is the woman of the tribe or the farm who helps her husband, who shares in production (either by taking care of the animals or by helping in the fields) who brings in an income as well as doing the household work. She weeds, gathers spades the earth, gathers grain, grapes and cotton. She gives water to the animals and milks them. She then makes butter, yogurt or cheese for her family's consumption or for selling at the market. She beats cotton and wool. She spins thread. She weaves cloth. She sews clothes. At the same time, she nurses her child, cooks food, and cleans the house. Often she produces handicrafts within the home as well. She is a wife, a nurse, a mother, a worker, and an artist. She grows as freely as the trees of the gardens. She gives her love with the purity of a turtledove. Like the deer of the plains, she gives loving, motherly birth. She remains faithful in this free house even though no force is applied. She gives freely of her love to her family. Yes! She has the freedom to give—and she has something to give, as well. Her freedom has not been taken from her so that she can no longer move. It is not as if she would want to run away if she were permitted to do so. Finally, she pushes her fingers into the earth of the fields to cultivate it. She plays with her child in her home. In the bedroom of her husband, she removes his tiredness. She creates the most beautiful and colorful handicrafts for the bazaar. She is the woman we praise.

The most bizarre woman, on the other hand, who must be called 'absurd', is the lady of the house. She is a frightening creature. This absurd woman is neither traditional nor European. She is not like the European woman who is a member of a household of two partners where the husband and wife are equal, where both work outside of the home and where both do the household duties inside the house. When the European is a girl, she is free exactly like a boy. She is free to grow amidst everything society has to offer. She is experienced from her encounters. She has seen everything. She has come to know all types. She has seen corruption and the correct way. She has seen the right way and the wrong way, the bad way and the good way, treacheries and kindnesses. Finally, she has seen all of the colors, designs and architecture of life and society. She has seen all the things in her own environment. She has sensed them. She has received an education like any boy. Like a boy she has specialized. She has achieved social independence. She has her own economic income. She makes her own choice of husband or partner in life.

But the absurd woman is the woman who sits at home and is good for nothing. As she can afford it, she has a maid, a cook, a nurse, and it is they who actually do the work. She is a woman who stays at home to take care of it, but others actually do the work for her. As she is not a village woman, she does not work and co-operate with her husband in the fields. As she is not literate, she does not read books, nor does she write books. Because she has no artistic talents, she is not productive. Because she has a wet nurse, she does not nurse her children. Because she has a man servant, she does not do the shopping for the house. Because she has baby sitters, she does not care for her children. Because she has a cook, she does not cook. Because she has an F.F. system, she does not even open the door of her house!

What does this living creature do? Nothing. What role does she play in the world? None! Can it be that a woman does not fit into either an eastern or a western mould, is neither modern or old-fashioned? Neither a woman of the office nor of the factory? Neither a woman of a school nor of a hospital? Neither a woman of art not one of science, not of the pen nor of the book? Neither a woman looking after the home nor a woman looking after the children? She is not even the most common-place woman of women's magazines.

Really, what is her work? Who is this person? She is the lady of the house, Daddy's lady of the old days. What is her profession? Consuming and only consuming. How does she pass her time? Her time? As a matter of fact, she is very busy. She is busy night and day. She is a thousand times busier than the village woman. For instance, what does she do? She gossips, she develops jealousies, objections, affectations, ornamentation, rivalries, pride, false friendship. She complains, grumbles, ogles, has a mincing air, full of coquetry and falsity. This lady of the house is always busy. In her type of society, and in her social relationships, she fills her frighteningly empty life.

The public woman's bath was a weekly seminar where all of the chaste women, who had nothing to do, who suffered no pain, went. They gathered together and each one recounted the biggest and most important event of her life that week, either honestly or dishonestly through insufficient explanation. They sold each other on their pride; they told their stories one after the other; their imaginations took flight; their sweet ignorance implemented their lack of intelligence. Surprisingly, all of them were also aware of these groundless pretentions.

Each one had such a scenerio. Each one listened to the lies and exaggerations of the other one with relish, amazement, deep understanding and faked feelings. Each would believe the other until it was her turn to be indebted to the others for listening to her. Thus, the others gave her a free chance to speak of all her bruised beliefs, lack of excitement, uselessness and ineffectiveness. Her existence, her inner emptiness and hollow life were spread out to show off her ability, her current price, her fantasies and her revenge.

Now the public womens' bath has been closed to women of this class. Modern living has prevented these women from such social halls of forty columns and forty windows, where one full day a week would be spent. To replace them, they have opened women's clubs under various names. Absurd women leave their homes and enter these cold women's clubs—which even lack the steam and water of the previous establishment.

If our women today are crazy and look like foreign dolls (not foreign women), and if we look at the other side of the border, we may see the innocent economics of exploitation, whereas on this side of the border, we will see ourselves working hand in hand with them. We cause our women to run away. We call her the weak one', 'broken legged', 'servant of her husband', 'mother of the child', and even 'lacking manners' and 'goat'.

We separate her from humanity. We thought that if she had beautiful handwriting, she would write to her lover. With this type of thinking, it would have been better if we had blinded her so she would never see a 'forbidden' person. In this way, Mr. Jealous, who feels the weaknesses of his own personality, would not have to worry about the disloyalty of his wife. He would be safe to the end of his life.

The virtue and chastity of woman is preserved by walls and chains. She is not a human being who thinks and who nourishes common sense and comes to know things. We present her as a wild animal, incapable of being disciplined. She will never be tamed. The only thing to do is to keep her in a cage. Whenever you leave the cage doors open, she will slip away. Her chastity is like dew. When it sees the sun, it is gone. Women are placed in a prison which neither leads to a school nor a library nor to society. Like an unclean creature, like the untouchables of India, she is not counted as a human being by society. People who are called human beings are men, social animals. Women are kept apart from society and given no credit for self-control.

It was the Prophet who said, "Education is necessary for Muslims, both men and women." But it is always men who have had the right to be educated, and women (other than those wealthy women who are educated with private tutors) are denied education. They cannot take advantage of this important Tradition.

Parties centering on old religious traditions are no longer open to today's young woman. Ceremonies for gaining favor and seasonal lamentations are not interesting to her—nor are the special animal sacrifices, nor the cooking of a special stew on the third day after someone departs on a journey. Wedding activities prepared without the groom and parties hunting for a groom don't interest her.

The young women sense the loneliness and nothing-to-do-ness of their mothers, a loneliness barely covered over by religion and tradition. This, they know, gives their mothers a feeling of positive action. It gives them a sense of responsibility. They are busy with comings and goings, designs and false plans. But to the young women, these channels have all been closed.

The opportunities which their mothers had to show their beauty and make-up skills are now gone. Younger women no longer force themselves into the falsity of these sessions. If they go, they take on an unattractive, cool, strange appearance, and it is obvious that they are looking for a way out.

The daughter of this woman, who belongs to another generation and another season lives in an intermediate world of two meanings. The world of the grandmother is for her a complex of stupidity and structured rites, full of ugly men and restrictions. The grandmothers want to keep their gathering, their circle of friends, their lamentation ceremonies as they were in the olden times. While for the young woman, books, translations, novels and art are important. She has more or less sensed the cultural spirit of the world. She has caught the scents of learning, knowledge and progress in school.

The sermons given for women at their ceremonies—mostly ceremonies of praise or lamentation—are usually given by illiterate lamenters. The exhausting continuation of this is unbearable to the young woman. She wants to fly away. But to where? There are hundreds of invitations for parties. There are dancing parties, night clubs and dirty bars which look upon her as easy prey. They pull her to themselves.

But she wants to retain her human characteristics of faith, ethics and loyalty. She sees that what her mother, father, uncle and other members of her family, offer her (in the name of religion, ethics, character, chastity and strength) is a collection of, "No, don't go, don't do that, don't sing, don't see, don't say, don't know, don't write, don't want, don't understand!"

We see that the mother lives in a type of comfortable, empty wasteland. She has no direction, no responsibility, no philosophy of life and no meaning to her existence. She has money and no problems and no reason for living. Day and night she turns her house around but there is nothing to fill her life. Out of boredom, she leaves the house to go shopping and then, under a veil, she tries to fill her empty life with amusement, jewelry, make up, and redecorating. She makes expensive purchases of strange things so that she can induce wonder and amazement in others.

But her daughter is not moved by these wonders. She breathes a different air. She is like a doll caught between two children who understand nothing. Each one pulls her towards himself until the doll is torn to shreds. She becomes crushed and steamrolled.

Now, her heart experiences romantic thoughts, the attractions of freedom and love, the whisperings of her budding sexuality, the blossoming of intellectual endeavors and the attractive images of a new world outside her wall. Sometimes she looks through a peep hole or turns to the windows like a thief. Her body is under the influence of the commands of her mother and the advice of her father. She is like a fly caught in the spider's web of no! no! She remains imprisoned. She feels that the only crime she can be convicted of is being a young girl. She is an illegal, dangerous entity who must remain hidden in a corner of the house until an authorized thief comes and takes her as his mate to his harem. And there, the whole range of her existence will be the space between the kitchen and the bed. It is only the man's stomach and that which is under his stomach that give her existence meaning! The man doesn't even allow her to attend religious meetings or entertain religious feelings. Even religion is separated in this system of thinking.

Speaking, chanting, the lamentation ceremony and table offerings for gaining favor—these are the religion of women, whereas centers, schools, libraries, lessons, discussions and lectures constitute the religion of men.

THE CRIES OF EXPLOITATION

What has prepared the groundwork for exploitation which cries out, "Free yourself!" From what? It is no longer important to know from what. You should be freed. Your breath is cut-off. You have nothing. Free yourself! Be free of all things.

The one who is burdened under the heaviest of loads and is drifting off only thinks about awakening, getting free and rising above her burdens. She does not think, 'How should I arise?'

They said, "Women will be freed—not by books or knowledge or the formation of a culture or clear-sighted vision or by raising the standard of living, or by common sense or by a new level of vision of the world—but rather with a pair of scissors. Yes. Putting scissors to the modest dress!" This is how they think that women will all at once become enlightened!

The complexes of Muslim and Eastern women have become the playthings of psychologists and sociologists in the service of exploitation and world economics. They say of her: "A woman is a creature who shops!"

The description such as, "A human being is a rational animal," is transformed when it relates to women. It becomes, "A human being is an animal who shops." She knows nothing other than this. She has no feelings and essentially, plays no role. She has no spirituality, no beliefs. She is valueless.

In one of these magazines devoted to Eastern women the amount of cosmetics and beauty ads increased 500 times. 500 times is a very great quantity. It is a miracle. It has never happened before in the whole history of humanity. The consumption of economic goods usually increases 8%, 9%, 10%, 20% but not 500%! This is a symbolic consumption.

In present day society, the desire to consume one new item is followed by the desire for more. For instance, as soon as the traditional coat changes, a new coat and trousers replaces it. The old type of shoes are replaced by leather shoes. Traditional styles of hats are replaced by new ones. In homes, carpets are replaced by modern furniture and old houses are replaced by new ones.

Thus, when Europe sends a new product to our society, it paves the way for consumption of further new products. When consumption changes, it is a sign that people are changing because there is a very sensitive relationship between a consumer and the product consumed.

Women in Islamic societies must not only be transformed

into consumers of goods exported from Europe and America but they must also become active participants within their households. They must learn to relate according to today and tomorrow's generations. They must change the form of society. They must have an effect upon ethics, values, literature and art. They must have a deep revolutionary effect upon everything. They should be put to work upon this way.

Time, culture, social possibilities, new economics, changes in social relationships, new thoughts—all of these conditions in an Islamic society, themselves, change the types and traditions. Women become obliged to change internal and external conditions because past modes are no longer practical nor sufficient.

Now that things must be changed, isn't it logical that capitalists should get busy and prepare their moulds so that as soon as a woman puts aside her traditional mould, their mould can be forced upon her? They make her into a form they want and then place her, instead of themselves, in a position to corrupt society.

WHAT SHOULD WE DO?

In the midst of this disruption—which has been imposed upon us and will continue to impose itself upon us what can we do? Who is it that can take up the mandate?

The one who can do something, and, in saving us plays an active role, is not the traditional woman asleep in her quiet, tame, ancient mould nor is it the new woman, the modern doll who has assumed the mould of the enemy. Rather, she is the one who can choose the new human characteristics, who can break old traditions (presented as religion, but in fact, only national and tribal traditions ruling the spirit, thoughts and behavior of society). She is a person who is not satisfied with old advice. Slogans which are given by doubtful sources do not interest her. Behind the prepackaged slogans of freedom [of the monarchy], she sees ugly, frightening faces which act against the spiritual, and which oppose the human. She sees that they contradict the spiritual, the rational, the human. They are against women and the human reverence of women.

It is such people who know where those things which are forced upon us come from. They know from where they get their orders. What creatures they have sent to the market place! Creatures without sensitivities, without knowledge, without pain, without understanding, without responsibility and, even, without human feelings. Fresh, clean dolls—'worthy ones'. It is obvious what their worthiness is in and for. Their means of support and its derivation are also obvious. This is tossed to our women and they know why.

It is because of them that "Who am I? Who should I be?" is pertinent, since they neither want to remain this nor become that. They cannot surrender themselves to whatever was and is without their own will and choice playing a role.

They want a model.

Who?

Fatima.

PART TWO

CHAPTER SEVEN
THE SOCIAL CUSTOMS
OF THE HEJAZ

Fatima was the fourth and youngest daughter of the Prophet of Islam. She was the youngest daughter of a household in which no sons survived. She was a girl born into a society in which special value was placed upon a son.

Centuries before Islam, the social order of the Arabs had passed beyond the Age of the Matriarch. During the Age of Ignorance, prior to the mission of the Prophet, the Arabs had established the Age of the Patriarch. Their gods had become masculine whereas their idols and their angels were feminine (that is, daughters of the great god, *al-lah*). The tribes were governed by 'white beards,' and the family was ruled by the grandfathers. Essentially, their religion was a kind of ancestor worship. They adhered to whatever beliefs and practices their fathers had maintained.

It was against the religion of ancestral fathers that the great prophets, mentioned in the Koran, revolted. When confronted with these prophetic revolts against ancestor worship and myths of the first fathers, the Arab tribes preserved their masculine traditions. It was a kind of inherited, imitative worship based upon the principle of father worship.

The Prophets brought a revolutionary message. They tried to awaken thought based on the principle of worshipping God. Beyond this, the difficult life of the tribes of the dry desert was filled with mutual hostilities. The basic principles were 'defend and attack' and 'keep your promises'. In this society, the son played a special role based upon the 'uses and needs' of the society's social and military principles.

According to a universal principle of sociology, where profit is substituted for value, being a son is by and of itself of the highest essence. A son embodies virtues, meaningful social and ethical values and human nobility. For this very reason, being a girl or having a daughter, is humbling. A girl's frailness is 'being weak'. Her 'being weak' pushes her towards slavery, which lessens her human values.

She becomes a creature who is a disgrace to her father, the toy of a man's sexual urges and slave of the home of her husband. Finally, this creature always threatens her kinsman's sense of honor, as she is considered the highest form of shame and disgrace. For the betterment of society and the relief of one's mind, how much better to kill her while still a baby! Thus, the honor of her fathers, brothers and ancestors, of all men for that matter, was not stained. As Ferdowsi tells us in the *Shahnameh*:

It is better to bury women and dragons in the earth.
The world will be better off if cleansed of their existence.

An Arab poet tells us, "If a father has a daughter and thinks of her future, he should think about three different sons-in-law: one, the house which will hide her; two, the husband who will keep her; and, three, the grave which will cover her! And the last one, the grave, is the best."

The saying which refers to the grave as being the best son-in-law has existed in all languages of the wealthiest and most honorable men. All of the honorable fathers and brothers who are bound to and place emphasis upon their male ancestors, all who understand the ideals of name and honor live in anticipation of ridding themselves of their sister or daughter through marriage. A poet reminds his daughter of the most beloved of sons-in-law, "The most beloved son-in-law is the grave."

This is that very same poet who says women and dragons are both better covered by the earth. "Covering the girls with earth is a way of preserving honor." This is why the Koran, in the strongest terms, warns of the dangers of this frightening 'highest honor' when it says: *He hides himself from the people of evil for the tidings given him. Should he keep her with disgrace or bury her alive in the dust? Behold, evil is what they decide"* [16.59]. As an Islamic commentator on the Koran has shown, this tragedy essentially has economic roots. Society's fear of poverty was prevalent in the Arab Age of Ignorance.

Girls have been buried alive because of the fear that they might bring dishonor in the future by marrying an unsuitable husband or fall into the hands of an enemy during a war thus becoming slaves in a strange land. All of these are secondary phenomena. But the basic reason is an economic one.

As we previously indicated, in the old Arabic tribal system, people were faced with the hardships of life (particularly in the deserts of Arabia) and the constant difficult relations among the tribes. Such a life required strong and powerful support. Automatically, a son became an important factor in economic and social life as well as in the defense of his family or tribe. He was a necessary social element of the family and the tribe. A son brought bread, but a daughter ate it. It was natural that the sexual differences caused class differences. Men fell into the class of ruling and owning, and women fell into that of the ruled and the owned.

The relationship between a man and a woman was like that between a landowner and a peasant. A man and a woman, as economic entities, had different human and spiritual values placed upon them. A landlord, for example, might embody a noble blood-line and possess inherited wealth and princely virtues. The opposite might be true of a peasant or a woman.

Poverty sends all the male gains or can gain to the four winds. Through poverty, a woman may become the cause of the family losing self respect. The possibility always exists that she will "disgrace" the family by marrying someone who is her social inferior. In my opinion, this fear (although disguised as an ethical phenomenon) is related to economic factors of inheritance law whereby the son preserves the ownership of land and assures the continuation of centralized wealth for the next generation of the family.

In patriarchal societies, when the father dies, the oldest son inherits everything—not only the land, but also the wives of his father, including his own mother! So, if daughters did not inherit, the wealth of the father would not be divided up and distributed to other families through the daughters. This is the reason why in our old wealthy families, there is still a very strong emphasis placed upon the daughter marrying within the family. They pledge an uncle's daughter to an uncles' son 'in heaven'.

Thus the uncle's daughter cannot take her inheritance out of the family as she would if she were to marry a stranger.

This is why ancient historians and modern scholars who write the history of religion have different explanations for the burying alive of female children in the Age of Ignorance. Some of the scholars say, in primitive religions, girls were sacrificed to the gods. But the Koran most strictly and clearly says that the reason for their murder was the fear of poverty. In other words, it was an economic factor. The other explanations are just words. In my opinion, this clear interpretation and description is not only scientifically correct but also emphatically rebuts those who talk about the ethical, chaste and noble responsibility a tribe had in burying new born females alive. This crude, cruel action resulted from baseness, vileness, fear of poverty and love of wealth. It was a direct result of their fear greed, and weakness, although they tried to hide their deed by explaining it with noble words of honor, integrity, chastity, respect. The Koran emphasizes, *"Do not kill them from fear of poverty for We will provide for you and your children"* [6:151]. It expresses the main reason for the tragedy. It awakens people. It directly and straight-forwardly says that this practice is neither ethical nor noble but rather is one hundred percent economically motivated. It stems from greed and wealth, from weakness and fear.

Before Islam, the public was not aware. The majority of the people believed female infanticide to be a reaction of the public conscience. They believed it showed a brave spirit. and that it protected the family honor. Arab tribal society gave all the human values to a son, whereas a daughter was considered to lack all virtues and human authenticity.

A boy was not only capable of earning his livelihood, but he was also a help to his father, a protector of his family, a tribal hero, the bearer of his heritage, the continuer of society, the spirit of his family, and the flame which lights the family lamp upon the death of his father.

A daughter was a living piece of furniture. After she married, her personality dissolved in a stranger's house. She became the furniture in another house where she could not even retain her family name. Her children belonged to a stranger. They carried his name and were inheritors of his heritage.

A boy had the material power to generate capital, aides society and perpetuate the patriarchal system. He had prestige, fame, value and spiritual credit. He supported the authenticity of the family. He was the giver of security and subsistence and the future authority of that family. But a girl was nothing. She was considered to be so weak that she must always be protected.

Like a bird whose foot is tied to a stone that prevents it from flying freely, she prevented a warrior from freely attacking the tents and castles of his enemies. And when defending his tribe, the warrior was always anxious that she not be taken as a slave. His slightest negligence could put her into the hands of the enemy. Then the entire tribe would suffer the shame of her enslavement.

During times of peace, the family must be careful that she didn't cause them shame by marrying an outsider. After all of these efforts, expenses, and anxieties, a stranger might come and take her away. She was like a field that one cultivates and whose crops another bears off. This was why the best solution was naturally to kill her at an early age. She should be given in wedlock and call the cold grave, 'son-in-law'.

A man who had no sons was called 'cut-off'. He had no progeny and no continuation; he was barren. Yet the word *kawthar* in the Koran means fullness, advantages, blessings as well as progeny and many children. God in answer to the disbelievers who called His beloved Prophet 'cut-off' gave the Prophet the good news that he would have many offspring.

In such an environment, the moment was ripe for fate to rend the veil. It was the time to direct the state of things. Life had become a stagnant, spoiled lagoon. It was time for a serious, creative revolution. It was the moment for a strong wind to blow. Suddenly an amazing plan was put into action, sweet but difficult. Two people were selected to carry out this plan, a father and a daughter. The Prophet (the father) must carry the heavy load and Fatima (the daughter) must reflect within herself the newly created revolutionary values.

CHAPTER EIGHT
THE BIRTH OF FATIMA

The largest Arab tribe was the Quraysh. The Kabah was in their hands which naturally gave them tribal nobility. They were divided into two families: the Bani Umayyid and the Bani Hashimi. The Bani Umayyid were the wealthiest but the Bani Hashimi were the most honorable for they were in charge of looking after the Kabah.

Abd al-Muttalib from the Hashimi clan had died. His son, Abu Talib, was the new leader of the Bani Hashimi, did not have the power that his father had. He had gone bankrupt in trading. He was living in poverty and had distributed his children (to be cared for) among his family.

A very strong rivalry had broken out between the two tribes. The Umayyids were trying to gain control of all of the property and honors of the Quraysh. They wanted to, at the same time, break the spiritual hold of the Hashimis. Among the Hashimi tribe, the family of Muhammad (ﷺ) had received new credit. The grandson of Abd al-Muttalib had just married Khadija, a wealthy, well-respected widow of Makkah. This gave him a stronger social position.

The honorable standing and personality which Muhammad (ﷺ) showed, the trust and credibility which he had among people and, in particular, among all the Hashimis and the leaders of the Quraysh, made everyone see that he reflected the honor of Abd Manaf and was the protector of the nobility of the Hashimis. People sensed he would be the reactivator of the honor and nobility which Abd al-Muttalib had possessed.

Hamza was a youth, an athlete. Abu Lahab was a man without credit. Abbas was wealthy but without character. Abu Talib honorable but without money. It was only Muhammad (ﷺ), who along with his wife, had character. He had youth as well. He and his wife had a respectable amount of wealth and were part of the family tree of the Bani Hashimi. Great developments were expected from this family. Their shadow fell over Makkah.

Everyone was waiting for the sons to be born to this family, sons to bring strength, credit and nobility to the family of Abdul Muttalib. The first child born was a girl, Zaynab. But the family was anticipating a son. The second child was a daughter, Ruqiya. The anticipation grew stronger and the need also increased. The third child was a girl, Umm Kulthum. Two boys, Qasim and Abd Allah were born. They held great promise. But they did not blossom. They died in infancy. Now there were three children in this house, and all three were girls.

The mother had aged. She was over fifty years old. The father, although he loved his three daughters, shared his tribe's feelings and their anticipation. Could Khadija, who was almost at the end of her life, bring forth another child? Hope had become very dim. Yes! Happiness and hope once again filled the house. The excitement reached a peak. This was the last chance for the family of Abd al-Muttalib, the last hope. But once again, a daughter. They name her Fatima.

The happiness and hope of the Hashimi tribe fell to the Umayyids. Enemies whispered, "Muhammad is cut-off. The man who was the last link in his family chain, had four daughters. Nothing more."

How sad. What a beautiful and strange game fate was playing. Life passed on. Muhammad (ﷺ) drowned in the storm of his mandate and his appointment as the Prophet of God. He conquered Makkah and freed all the Quraysh prisoners. All of the tribes were under his leadership and his shadow was thrown over the whole of the Arabian peninsula. His sword crushed the Emperors of the world. His song rang through the heavens and the earth. In one hand, strength, and in the other, prophecy: the full honors.

And now, Muhammad (ﷺ) was the Prophet. In the city, filled with waves of happiness, he had power and greatness the like of which a human being could never conceive. A tree, which did not grow from Abd Manaf nor Hashimi nor Abd al-Muttalib, grow, rather, from a light under the mountain of 'Hira'. It extended from one end of the desert to the other, from horizon to horizon. Till the end of time, it encompassed (and will continue to encompass) all of the future.

And this man had four daughters.

But no, three of them died before he did. And now, he had only one child, a daughter, the youngest, Fatima.

Chapter Nine
Islam Revolutionizes
the Position of Women

The Koranic Word, Kawthar

Muhammad (ﷺ) was heir to all of the family's honors, inheritor of a new kind of wealth based not upon blood, not land nor money but upon the phenomenon of revelation. Born of faith, struggle in God's Way (*jihad*), revolution, thought and sensitivity, he was beautifully woven. He received the highest spirit. Muhammad (ﷺ) was joined to the history of mankind, not to that of Abd al-Muttalib, Abd Manaf, the Quraysh nor the Arabs. He was the inheritor of Abraham, Noah, Moses and Jesus (ﷺ). Fatima was his only heir.

"*We gave you kawthar, oh Muhammad. For your Creator, establish the prayer and sacrifice a camel. It is he, that very hated enemy of yours who is cut-off*" [108]. His enemy with ten sons was cut-off. He was useless, cut-off without the highest form of inheritance. "*We gave you kawthar,*"—Fatima.' It was in this way that revolution appeared in the depths of the conscience of time.

Now, a daughter became the owner of the values of her father, the inheritor of all the honors of her family. She was the continuation of the chain of great ancestors, the continuation which began with Adam and passed through all of the leaders of freedom and consciousness in the history of mankind. It reached Abraham (ﷺ) and joined Moses (ﷺ) and Jesus (ﷺ) to itself. It reached Muhammad (ﷺ). The final link in this chain of divine justice, the rightful chain of truth was Fatima, the last daughter of a family who had anticipated a son. Muhammad had known what the hands of fate had in store for him. And, Fatima, also, had known who she was. Yes! This school of thought created such a revolution. A woman, in this religion, was freed like this. Isn't this the religion of Abraham and of them, his heirs?

THE HONOR BESTOWED
UPON A FEMALE SLAVE

Nobody had the right to be buried in a mosque. The greatest mosque in the world was the *Masjid al-haram* in Makkah. The Kabah. This house belonged to God. It was devoted to God. It was the direction to which all of the prescribed prayers were oriented. The house was ordered by Him and Abraham built it. It was a house which the Prophet of Islam honored with the mandate of freedom. He freed this 'House of Freedom', circumambulated it and went down in prostration towards it. All of the great prophets of history were servants of this house. But no prophet had the right to be buried there. Abraham built it, but he is not buried there. Muhammad freed it, but he was not buried there. In the whole history of humanity, there was one, and one person only, who had been given this privilege. The God of Islam allowed one person to be buried in this way. Who?

A woman. A slave. Hagar, the second wife of Abraham and mother of Ishmael. God ordered Abraham to build the greatest house of worship of humanity and, alongside it, the grave of this woman. Humanity must forever gather around the tomb of Hagar and circumambulate it

The God of Abraham chose a woman from among this great human society as his unknown soldier. God chose a mother and a slave. In other words, The God of Abraham chose a creature who, in all systems of humanity, lacked nobility and honor.

THE HONOR BESTOWED
UPON THE PROPHET'S DAUGHTER

Yes, in this school of thought such a revolution took place. A woman was freed in this manner in this religion. This is how Islam appreciated the position of womanhood. The God of Abraham has chosen Fatima. Fatima, a girl, replaced a son as the inheritor of the glory of her family, maintaining the honorable values of her ancestors and continuing the family tree and prestige.

In a society that felt the birth of a daughter to be a disgrace which only burying alive could purify, where the best son-in-law a father could hope was called 'the grave', Muhammad (ﷺ) knew what fate has done to him. Fatima knew who she was. This is why history looked in amazement at the way Muhammad (ﷺ) behaved towards his young daughter, Fatima, at the way he spoke with her and at the way he praised her.

We see that the house of Fatima was next to the house of Muhammad (ﷺ). Fatima and her husband, Ali, were the only people who lived next to the Prophet's mosque. Only a court-yard of two meters separated the two houses. Two windows faced each other, one from the house of Muhammad, the other from the house of Fatima. Every morning the Prophet opened his window and greeted his young daughter.

We see that whenever the Prophet went on a journey, he knocked at the door of Fatima's house and said good-bye to her. Fatima was the last person who bade farewell to him. Whenever he returned from a journey, Fatima was the first person he sought out. He knocked on the door of her house and he asked how she was.

It is recorded in some of the historic documents that the Prophet would kiss the face and hands of Fatima. This sort of behavior was more than just the relationship of a kind father and his daughter—a father kissed the hands of his daughter, his youngest daughter! Such behavior struck a revolutionary blow against the inhumane relationships of that time. "The Prophet of Islam kissed the hands of Fatima." Such a relation-ship opened the eyes of important people and politicians. The majority of the Muslims gathered around the Prophet in amaze-ment at the greatness of Fatima.

This sort of behavior on the part of the Prophet of Islam taught humanity to discard bad habits and fantasies of history and traditions. It taught man to come down from his Pharaoh-like throne, to put aside his pride and rough oppression and to bow his head when meeting a woman. It taught women to aspire to the glory and beauty of humanity and to put aside old feelings of inferiority and baseness.

This is why the words of the Prophet not only show the kind-ness of a father but also bring out his responsibilities and strict duties. He showed his appreciation for Fatima and spoke about her in the following terms: "The best women in the world were four: Mary, Asiyah [the wife of Pharaoh who brought up Moses], Khadija and Fatima." And, "God is satisfied with her contentment and becomes angry from her anger." Or, "The contentment of Fatima is my contentment. Her anger is my anger. Whosoever loves my daughter Fatima loves me. Whosoever makes Fatima content makes me content. Whosoever makes Fatima unhappy makes me unhappy." And, "Fatima is a part of my body. Whosoever hurts her, has hurt me, and whosoever hurts me has hurt God."

Why all this repetition? Why does the Prophet insist upon praising his young daughter? Why does he insist upon praising her in front of other people? Why does he want all of the people to be aware of his special feelings towards her? And finally, why does he so emphasize the contentment and anger of Fatima? Why does he so often use the word 'hurt' in relationship to Fatima.

The answer to this is very sensitive and important. It is clear. History has answered it all: the secret of these wondrous actions was unveiled, in the few short months after the death of her father.

THE MOTHER OF HER FATHER

History not only speaks of the 'great ones', it also attends to them. Children were always forgotten. Fatima was the youngest child in the family. Her childhood passed in a storm. Her birth date is debated. Tabari, Ibn Ishaq and Ibn Hashim give it as five years before the Prophet's mission. Murravij al-Zahib Masudi mentions it as five years after the Prophet's mission. Yaqubi says, "After the revelation." Thus, there is a difference of opinion among the recorders of the Traditions. The Hanafi, Malikis, Hanbalis and Shafiis, say, five years before the mandate of the Prophet, and the Jafari say five years after his mission.

We leave it to the scholars to enlighten us as to the exact date of her birth. We are concerned with Fatima herself and the reality of Fatima. Whether she was born before or after the mission of the Prophet does not concern us here

That which is clear is that Fatima remained in Makkah alone. Her two brothers died as infants and Zaynab, her oldest sister, who acted as the mother of this beloved child, went to the home of Abi al-Aas. Fatima bitterly accepted her absence. Then Ruqiya and Umm Kulthum's married the sons of Abu Lahab. Fatima remained even more alone—if we accept her birth as having been before the mission of the Prophet. If we accept the second date, then, essentially, from the time she opened her eyes, she was alone. At any rate, the beginning of her life coincided with the heavy mandate of the Prophet. It was filled with great struggles, difficulties and punishments whose shadows fell upon the house of the Prophet.

While her father bore the mandate of consciousness for mankind upon his shoulders and suffered hatred from the enemies of the people, her mother consoled her beloved husband. Early in childhood, Fatima tasted the suffering, sadness and anger of life. Because she was very young, she moved about freely. She made use of this freedom to accompany her father. She knew her father had no life of his own, had no opportunity to take hold of his child's hand and walk freely and easily down the streets and into the bazaar. He always went alone. In the sea of the town's enmity, he swam with dangers on all sides. The small girl, who knew her father's fate, never let him go alone.

Many times she saw her father standing amidst a crowd of people. He spoke to them softly and they, in turn, harshly sent him away. Their only answers were to mock him and show him enmity. He felt lonely and friendless again. But quietly and patiently he gathered another group. He began his speech all over again. At the end, tired and having achieved no result, like fathers of other children who returned home from their jobs, he also returned home seeking a bit of rest. He then returned once more to his work.

Once when he had gone into the *Masjid al-haram*, where he was vilified and beaten, Fatima, still a small child, stood alone a short distance from the scene. She watched and then returned home with her father.

One day while prostrating himself in the mosque, his enemies threw the intestines of a sheep at him. Suddenly, little Fatima, reached towards her father, picked up the intestines and threw them away. Then with her small, loving hands, she cleaned her father's head and face, comforted him and led him to their home .

People who saw this thin, weak girl, alone, beside her champion father, saw how she comforted him. She supported him through his troubles and sufferings. With her pure, child-like heart, she sympathized with him. It was because of this that she came to be called *umm al-abiha*, the mother of her father.

Chapter Ten
The Confinement

The black and difficult years of hunger began in the valley of Abu Talib. The Hashimi and Abd al-Muttalib families were imprisoned—with the exception of Abu Lahab who has joined the enemies. Men, women and children were placed in this hot, dry valley. A notice was written by Abu Jahl, in the name of all the wealthy people of the Quraysh, and it was placed on the Kabah wall: "No one should have any contact with the Hashimi tribe. All relationships with them are cut-off. Do not buy anything from them. Do not sell anything to them. Do not marry any of them."

They were forced to live in this stony prison until loneliness, poverty, hunger and the difficulties of life made them surrender to either the idols or to death! They all had to bear torture—both those who had accepted the new religion and those who have not yet turned to the new religion.

Those who had not yet embraced Islam, nevertheless admired Muhammad (ﷺ) and presented a united front to the enemy. They defended him and even though they did not know Islam, they knew the Prophet. They had faith in his purity. They knew he was not interested in personal gain. They sensed his faith. They heard what he had to say about the worship of the Truth. They knew he sincerely wished to free the people.

They were worth far more than the intellectuals filled with fear—such as conservatives like Ali ibn Umayyid, who, having discovered progressive ideology, supposedly opposed reactionaries, the foulness of aristocratic society and the Arab regime with its class distinctions. Yet, these same people, knowing all of this, in order to protect the wealth of their fathers, their social position and physical health remained on the side of Abu Jahl and Abu Lahab. They watched the torture of Balal, Ammar, Yasser and Somayyeh. They did not move their lips to object.

Throughout these difficult years, these men left their compatriots and their friends in this small compound, alone. They busied themselves with their lives in the bazaar, their homes and families. They past their time with the pagan leaders. They even joined hands. Years later, the followers of this way and its religion were more than the followers of the religion of the Prophet himself.

On the opposite side was Ali, Abu Dharr, Fatima, Husayn, Zaynab and all of the Emigrants and Companions. But those like Ali ibn Umayyid were the first Muslims to continue the practice of dissimulation [pious fraud]—even though the Prophet had forbidden it. They remained loyal to this principle and did not relinquish it until their death.

It is when the fire of a new faith lights up their spirits and a movement full of danger begins in society (based upon experiment, choice and obligatory tests in which one speaks to the self clearly and without deceit) that the wonders of humanity appear. The glories were accompanied by feelings of inferiority, by feelings of strength as well as weakness. All these were hidden within the spirit, and all of them revealed themselves.

Now in this frightening compound were people who, although not Muslims, yet bore the difficulties with patience, silence and three years of hunger and loneliness. They shared the shadow of danger. They also took part in God's great revolution for humanity. In this most sensitive moment of the beginning of the history of Islam, they shared the pain, and understood the position of the Prophet and his Companions.

But the black cloud of ignorance covered the comfortable and happy city filled with conservatism, contradiction, and shamelessness. Some Muslims could be seen whose skirts were contaminated and their hands frail. They were busy gaining security and comfort. Were they the viewers or the players in this tragedy? The question arises because in their imagination, they believed they had religion. They loved religious people. They felt themselves to be enlightened.

The families of the Hashimi tribes cut themselves off for three years from their city, their people, their freedom and even their means of livelihood and lived in this confinement. Was it possible to leave the valley in the middle of the night and, hidden from the eyes of the spies of the Quraysh, get food for the hungry waiting in jail? Could it be that a liberal family member or friend might, out of kindness, bring some bread. Hunger sometimes reached the point that they looked like 'black death'. But as they had prepared themselves for a 'red death', they were patient.

Saied ibn Ali Vaqas, confined with the others, wrote, 'Hunger had brought on such dizziness that, if at night I kicked a soft, wet material, without even realizing it, I would put it in my mouth and suck it. Two years later, I still do not know what it was.'

All of the Prophet's family bore the difficulties of hunger, loneliness and poverty for his sake. The Prophet personally assumed responsibility for them. When a child cried from the pain of hunger, when a sick person cried from lack of medicine and lack of food, when an aged person (man or woman) reached the limits of suffering after three years of hunger, physical torture and the rigors of the climate, they hid all their suffering within themselves. The light and blood drained from their faces, yet they denied any problems when speaking to the Prophet.

At the same time, despite all the difficulties, they remained loyal and generous in faith and love. All of this was an expressions of spirit and of faith and greatly affected the sensitive heart of the Prophet.

Know for sure that whenever food arrived in the darkness of the night and was given to the Prophet to be shared among the people, the portion of his wife and daughter was the least of all.

The family of the Prophet, in this compound, consisted of Khadija, their small daughter, Fatima, and her sisters, Umm Kulthum and Ruqiya, the daughters-in-law of Abu Lahab. After the mission of the Prophet, Abu Lahab ordered his sons to divorce Ruqiya and Umm Kulthum in order to hurt and show contempt for the Prophet. But Uthman, a young, wealthy, handsome man, married Ruqiya—thus answering the act of Abu Lahab. Ruqiya then immigrated to Ethiopia with Uthman. Umm Kulthum, whose life had fallen apart and who had lost her happiness because of her faith in her father, now found herself in the compound. She preferred hunger and remaining with her generous and heroic father in the way of faith and freedom to living in comfort and ease with her malicious and conservative husband, Utayba.

The days passed with difficulty in this compound separated from life. At night, the black tent of darkness fell upon the residents of this mountainous area. Weeks, months and years of hardship passed slowly over their tired bodies and spirits, but all continued in sympathy with each other and with the Prophet. The family of the Prophet had a special position in the midst of this group. The head of the family bore the heavy weight of their bitter fate upon his shoulders.

Umm Kulthum, her happiness destroyed, had moved from the home of her husband to that of her father. His other daughter, Fatima was still a young girl of either two or three or twelve or thirteen—depending on whose reckoning we follow. She has a weak constitution, but a sensitive spirit full of feelings.

Khadija, his elderly wife, had lived through the ten years of the Prophet's mission and three years in the compound. She had suffered hunger. She had witnessed the constant torture of her husband and daughters. She had borne the death of her two sons. She has not lost patience, but her body had been severely weakened. At every instant death appeared to her. In this state, hunger cried out so loud that the aged, sick Khadija (who had lived her life in wealth and had now given everything in the way of the Prophet) put a bit of leather in water and held it between her teeth.

Fatima, the young, sensitive girl was worried about her mother. Her mother was worried about her last, frail daughter whose great love for her mother and father was common knowledge among the people. In the last days of their imprisonment, Khadija, who sensed the approach of death, was bed-ridden. Fatima and Umm Kulthum sat beside her. Her father had gone outside to distribute the rations. Khadija, aged, weak, remembering the difficulties she had lived through, said with a sense of regret, "If only my approaching death could wait until these dark days pass and I could die with hope and happiness."

Umm Kulthum, crying, said, "It is nothing, mother, do not worry." Her mother replied, "Yes, for me, by God, it is nothing. I am not worried about myself, my daughter. No woman among the Quraysh has tasted the blessings that I have tasted. There is no woman in the world who has received the generosity which I have received. It is enough for me that my fate in this life, in this world, has been to be the beloved wife of God's choice. As to my fate in the other world, it is enough that I have been among the first who believed in the Prophet and that I am called 'the mother of his followers'." Then whispering to herself, she continued, "O God, I cannot count the blessings and kindnesses that you have given me. My heart has not grown narrow because I am moving towards you, but I do wish to be worthy of the benefits you gave me."

The shadow of death fell upon the house. Silence and deep sorrow filled Khadija, Umm Kulthum and Fatima. Suddenly, the Prophet appeared illuminated with hope, faith, strength and victory. It was as if three years of loneliness, hunger and heavy spiritual asceticism had produced no effect upon the body and spirit of the Prophet other than to increase his courage, will power and faith.

CHAPTER ELEVEN
FREEDOM, TRAGEDY,
SPIRITUAL STRENGTH

KHADIJA DIES

The dark years of confinement ended. Khadija lived to see the salvation of the Muslims and to care for her beloved husband and her noble and loyal daughters. The Prophet experienced his first great victory over the Quraysh. But the destiny which had been sent to change our history allowed no peace or pleasure, for two great tragedies fell upon him simultaneously.

Abu Talib and Khadija both died within a few days of each other and within a few days of their freedom. Abu Talib had raised the orphan Muhammad (ﷺ) and had made up for his missing father, mother and his grandfather, Abd al-Muttalib. He had looked after the young man, Muhammad (ﷺ), and cared for him. He had found work for him in the service of Khadija. Finally, it was he who acted as the father at the marriage of Khadija and Muhammad (ﷺ). He had supported the prophecy of Muhammad (ﷺ). With all of his influence, character, personality and social credit, he had protected him. He even bore the three years in confinement, bore the difficulties and hunger and yet remained with him. It was because of him that the Prophet was saved from death and the horrible torture which his companions suffered. Now, he had lost Abu Talib, his only protector against the anger, danger and hatred of the city.

And Khadija was the woman who had given up the privacy of their life to his destiny the woman who at forty or forty-five had married Muhammad, the twenty-five year old orphan and

171

poor shepherd. He came to know her through love with the faith of a fellow sufferer and thinker. He sought refuge in her from the difficulties of poverty and life. He received the kindness of a friend and the love of a mother which he had never had. He benefited from her advice and the great protection which she gave him.

Later, when he was appointed as God's Prophet, she was with him, step by step. She was beside him, beside his heart, beside his spirit. During the whole time of the thunderstorm of difficulties, fears, dangers, loneliness, during years of hatred and enmity, during battles, fights and treacheries, she was with him from the first moment of the revelation until the final moments of her death. She was with him during all of the moments of his life. She gave all of her life, love, faith, and wealth at the moment when he needed it most.

Now the Prophet had lost his protector and compassionate, fellow sufferer, the first person who believed him, the greatest giver of sympathy and, finally, the mother of his Fatima. Fatima had lost her mother.

Difficulties and tortures increased. Abu Talib had died. The Prophet was left defenseless before hatred. Hatred and enmity became violent when they witnessed the patience, perseverance and faith of the Prophet and his Companions. The roots of hatred become firmer and more merciless. The Prophet was very much alone. Abu Talib was no longer in the city, and Khadija was no longer at home.

Fatima now more than ever sensed the heavy burden of the hatred and grudges. She was called 'the mother of her father'. At the time that her sisters went to their husbands' homes, she was still tied to her mother's skirts. "Mother, I never want to replace this home with another one. Mother, I will never leave you," Fatima may have said. Khadija smiling, may have answered, "They all say that and we say, 'My daughter, the time will come.'" Fatima, imploringly, might have continued, "No. I will never leave my father. No one will separate me from him." Her mother would then remain silent.

Fatima sensed she had such a mandate. Her message was not a child's desires. Her faith in her mandate gained strength when she heard her father speak.

How surprising that the Prophet called upon her in the presence of the leaders of the Quraysh and the leaders of the

Hashimi tribe and the Abd Manafs. Her? A young girl? She alone and only she from among her family?

The child-like feelings and loving kindness of the young girl, who hundreds of times reiterated that she would never marry and that she would never leave her father, were growing into a serious covenant and took on the quality of a responsibility and a commandment.

The first years of her life coincided with the first years of the mission and the difficulties and tortures of the beginning of the mandate. Fatima, from among all of the children of the Prophet, was the worthiest to bear the suffering to bear the heavy weight of the responsibilities of the mandate which lay upon her father's shoulders. She was aware of her fate and so were her mother and father.

On one of the last days of her life, Khadija, worried, turned to her and said, "After me what things will you see, my daughter. My life will end today or tomorrow. Zaynab and Ruqiya, your two sisters, are at peace beside their kind husbands. My mind is not worried about Umm Kulthum because her age and experience are enough to keep her. But, you, Fatima, are drowned in difficulties. You have to suffer many sorrows and tribulations which increase daily."

Fatima, who shared in bearing the burdens which had been placed upon her father's shoulders, answered, 'Rest assured, mother. "Don't worry about me. The idol-worshipping Quraysh will torture and punish Muslims and they will show no mercy. The souls and hearts of Muslims must rejoice in accepting this despotic torture."

Fatima was the most worthy, having suffered great torture. She was special because the blessing of being the daughter of the Prophet was offered to her and because of the kindness and respect which continue to be shown her.

CHAPTER TWELVE
A NEW HISTORY BEGINS

After the death of Abu Talib, enmity and hatred reached its peak. One group of the Companions and followers of the Prophet went to Abyssinia, while another group suffered loneliness and poverty under the increasing torture of the Quraysh. The Prophet, then fifty years old, whose life had been spent in difficulties, was living alone with Fatima, his young daughter.

But...no. The hand of fate brought a son to this house and no one knew what role he would play.

Yes. Ali did not stay in his father's house. He did not grow up there. From childhood he lived beside Fatima. He was raised in the home of Fatima's father. The fate of this young boy was strangely connected to the fate of this father and this girl.

Destiny was taking its course. In the mysterious quiet, full of ambiguity, a stormy design was nourished to break the stone idols that had created barriers and discrimination. The first of the deceitful priests of the royal court died in the fire temples of the Persians. The great, frightening palaces of Madaen were pulled down. The lustful, blood-thirsty Emperor of Byzantine was pushed into the sea.

But the greatest of all to fall, to be erased in the hearts and minds, was the rusted tradition and the chains of habit, the pus of superstition and rotted myth, the prejudice and discriminatory beliefs that poison humanity .

They were dismantled. They were washed. The previous values and honors were turned upside down and changed. In an environment polluted with vile fairy tales of racism and pride, with aristocracy and power, with epics of plunder, the worship of blood and idols always causes the earth to revolt against false gods. All these things, large or small, prevent freedom, equality, justice, spiritual struggle and self-awareness for the unknown masses who lack glory and tribe. Instead of seeking history in rotten bones, fallen gravestones and rich rulers of the sword, seek history in the blood, life and poverty of the people!

Seek the line which begins with the heirs of the last chosen Prophet! Each one had a finer cloak of martyrdom than his predecessor. Each one either spent his life on the battlefield or teaching people or in the prison of the oppressors. This important mandate in history began with Fatima.

It is the kind hand of poverty which caused the child of Abu Talib (even though he had a father) to go to the house of his uncle's son so that his spirit might not become polluted by his own family's ignorance. He was present from the time of the first revelation. He was there from the moment that the mission began. He lived through the purifying fire of difficulties and problems so that he could play the difficult role he had to play in the migration, so that he could participate in the battles of Badr, Uhud, Khaybar, Fath and Hunayn, thereby guaranteeing the victory of the Islamic Revolution, so that he could grow up close to Fatima and, finally, so that with Fatima, he could establish the 'exemplary family' which (in the continuation of the work of Abraham) began a new history .

MIGRATION

Thirteen years of difficulty, resistance, confinement and, torture in Makkah ended. Fatima, from early childhood, patiently stood alongside her father in the city, in their home and in their imprisonment. Even with her weak constitution, she withstood the angry blows of envy and the difficulties of resistance in the savage environment of ignorance. With her little hands, she caressed her hero father like a mother.

The migration began. Muslims went to Madinah. The Prophet and Abu Bakr secretly left Makkah. Fatima and her sister, Umm Kulthum also left Makkah. Suddenly one of the evil men of the Quraysh, who had a history of causing the Prophet difficulties, caught up with them and violently threw them down. Fatima, who had a weak constitution and who had suffered from the effects of three years in prison, was greatly affected by this event. She suffered pain the entire way to Madinah. This uncalled for act of Huyrath ibn Naqiz had such an effect upon the Muslims and the Prophet that, even eight years later when conquering Makkah, they had not forgotten what he had done. His name was mentioned among those who should not be spared. They said that even if he were hanging on the cloth of the Kabah, he should be killed. It was no accident that Ali carried out this order.

IN MADINAH

Now they were in Madinah. The Prophet had built his mosque and, next to it, his house which he constructed from mud and the leaves of palm trees. Then he announced the ceremony of 'the covenant of brotherhood'. "Every two should become brothers in the way of God." Jafar ibn Abu Talib became the brother of Maaz ibn Jabal, Abu Bakr became the brother of Khariji ibn Zahir, Umar ibn Khattab became the brother of Utayba ibn Malik and Uthman became the brother of Aas ibn Sabet. But what of Ali? Then the Prophet said, "I am his brother." Muhammad (ﷺ) became the brother of Ali.

Once again, from among all the figures, Ali was placed beside the Prophet. Ali took another step closer to the Prophet. Fatima bint Asad, the mother of Ali, had nursed the Prophet. Abu Talib, the father of Ali, had protected the Prophet. The Prophet grew up in the house of Ali. Ali grew up in the house of the Prophet, beside his daughter Fatima. Ali was nourished in the lap of Khadija, the mother of Fatima. The son of the uncle of the Prophet, the child of the Prophet, had now become the brother of the Prophet.

THE SEALING OF THE LINK

There remained one more step before Ali could reach the final stage foreseen for him in the fate of the Prophet and in the honor of Islam.

Fatima has kept her promise. In the home of her father, she lived quietly alone. She rejected Umar and Abu Bakr's offers of marriage. All of the Companions knew that Fatima had a very special fate, and they knew that the Prophet would never give her hand in marriage without consulting her.

Fatima grew up with Ali. She saw him as a dear, older brother and as a beloved butterfly around her father. Fate threw these two together for very special reasons. Neither one of them was tied to the age of ignorance. They both grew up from the beginning with the mission. They developed under the light of the revelation.

What feelings did Fatima have towards Ali? What appeared from the great, brave, courageous heart of Ali towards Fatima? We may conceive of them but the words to express them are missing. How can we describe the complicated feelings which arise from faith, love, spiritual strength, and worship. How can we describe the kindness of a brother and a sister who share the same belief. How can we describe the familiarity of two spirits. They shared the difficulties and troubles of fate together. Fellow travelers, step by step, moment by moment for their whole lifetime, they encountered kindness and inspiration mixed with faith. Why was Ali silent? He was twenty-five years old. Fatima had reached puberty. She was either nine years old or nineteen.

In my opinion, the obstacles before Ali were clear. Fatima had promised herself to her father. She knew herself to be the mother of her father and to be a person who ran his house. How could Ali take her from this house where the daughter was so attached to her father that they could not be separated? How could Ali ask the Prophet for her hand in marriage? Ali shared the same feelings as Fatima.

Suddenly the picture changed. Ayisha came into the house of the Prophet. The Prophet, for the first and last time in his life, took a young, alive, virgin as his wife. Fatima, little by little sensed that her father's young bride would replace Khadija and herself—not in his heart —but undoubtedly in his house. Ali also sensed that the moment which destiny has prepared for them had arrived. But he had nothing.

He was a boy who had grown up in the Prophet's house, who had spent his youth struggling in the way of his beliefs. He did not have an opportunity to gather or save things. The only capital he had in the world was the faithful sacrifice he had made for the Prophet. Capital? Not even a house or a piece of furniture. Nothing.

At the same time we see that he approached the Prophet. He was seated next to him. He had put his head down and spoke with his beautiful shyness. "What do you want son of Abu Talib?" asked the Prophet. Ali answered full of modesty and inner peace, "I want to take the hand of Fatima, daughter of the Prophet." The Prophet answered, "Wonderful! Congratulations!" The next day in the mosque the Prophet asked him, "Do you have anything?" Ali replied, "Nothing, oh Prophet." The Prophet asked, "Where is the shield I gave you in the battle of Badr?" "It is with me," Ali replied. The Prophet said, "Give that." Ali quickly went, got the shield and returned and handed it to the Prophet. The Prophet ordered that it be sold in the bazaar and with its small price, he should begin his life. Uthman bought the shield for forty-seven dirhams. The Prophet called his Companions together, and he himself performed the wedding ceremony. He said, "Fatima, daughter of the Prophet, according to the ruling traditions, is given to Ali."

They prayed for their progeny and then brought out a dish of dates. And this was the wedding ceremony. The list of Fatima's property? A hand mill, a wooden bowl and a cotton rug.

At the beginning of the second year of the migration, Ali found a house beside the mosque of Quba, and he took Fatima there. Hamza (one of the first martyrs, the great hero of the religious crusades, and uncle of the Prophet and Ali) sacrificed two camels and invited the people of Madinah to his home for the wedding celebration.

The Prophet instructed Umm Salama to accompany the bride to Ali's house. Then Bilal called the people to the evening prayer. After the prayer, the Prophet went to Ali's house. He asked for a bowlful of water and after reciting some verses from the Koran, he asked the bride and groom to drink from that water. He then made his ablution with it and sprinkled it upon both of their heads. When he began to leave, Fatima began crying. It was the first time that she would be separated from her father.

The Prophet comforted her with these words, "I am leaving you with a person of the strongest faith, a man who is the most knowledgeable among those with knowledge, the most ethical among those with ethics and the highest of spirits among the spiritual."

STRUGGLES CONTINUE TO RENEW THE SPIRIT

This departure from the Prophet began the second part of Fatima's life. Destiny brought new difficulties and sorrows to this most beloved and precious being of humanity. Fatima, who had grown up in poverty and with hardships in the home of her father, now had come to the home of Ali, a home whose only decoration and furniture was love and poverty.

The difficulties of life in Ali's house began. But the greatest difficulty of all was that Fatima had the same responsibilities she previously had had, but they were now in connection with Ali. A youth whom she had, until yesterday, looked upon as a brother became a husband. Fatima knew that the life of Ali would remain such. She knew that he only thought about spiritual struggle in God's Way, about God and ab out the people. He would return home with only empty hands. Fatima found herself more responsible here than when she was in her father's home. She had the responsibility of being the wife of a man who was more serious than lucky and who was greater than life.

Fatima ground the wheat herself. She baked the bread. She worked in the house and brought the water from outside her home. Ali, who knew the generosity and majesty of Fatima (whom he loved for many reasons) knew the difficulties of her childhood which had made her physically weak. He, therefore, was sorrowed by all the work and labor which she had to perform.

One day in a tone of sympathy, he said, "Fatima Zahra, you have placed yourself in so many difficulties that my heart breaks for you. God has given many workers to Muslims. Ask the Prophet to give one of them to you." Fatima sought out her father. "What is it my daughter?" he asked. "I came to see how you are," she said. She returned home and told Ali she was too ashamed to ask anything of her father. Ali, struck with wonder, called Fatima, and they returned together to the Prophet. Ali himself asked the question. The Prophet answered without hesitation, "No! By God I will not give you even a prisoner of war. The stomachs of the Companions are hungry. If I find nothing to give them, I have to exchange the prisoners for food to give to the hungry Companions."

Ali and Fatima thanked him and, with empty hands, returned home. It is recorded. The husband and wife returned home to an empty house. Both remained silent thinking about what they had asked of the Prophet. The Prophet thought all day about the answer he had given his beloveds. Suddenly the door opened and the Prophet appeared. It was not only the darkness of the night but also its coldness which caused Ali and Fatima to shiver He saw that they had placed a thin cloth upon themselves. It was so short that when they pulled it up over their heads, their feet were exposed and when they covered their feet, their heads were exposed.

Softly he commanded them, "Do not move from your places." Then he added, "Do you want to know about something which is better than what you had asked of me?" "Of course, O Prophet of God," they replied. "It is something which Gabriel brought for me which I now share with you. After every ritual prayer, say *Allahu akbar* (God is Greater) ten times. Say *al-hamd al-Lah* (praise belongs to God) ten times and *subhan al-Lah* (Glory to God) ten times. When you have quietly crawled into bed, say *Allahu akbar* thirty-five times, *al-hamd al-Lah* thirty-three times and *subhan al-Lah* thirty-three times.'

Once again, Fatima took this as a lesson and a gentle reminder. She learned something which reached the depths of her being: She is Fatima.

This was a lesson which she knew. Although she had learned it from childhood, such lessons must follow continuously. They required successive teaching and learning. This was not a lesson in knowledge but rather a lesson in becoming. 'Becoming Fatima' was not easy. She was a holy trust. It required that she ascend many steps and fly many flights into higher worlds while remaining step by step and wing to wing with Ali. She must share with Ali in his sorrows and in his difficulties. She had the greatest responsibility in the history of freedom, *jihad* and humanity. She was the link in a chain which extended from Abraham to the Prophet, from Husayn to the Guided One (*mahdi*), from the beginning to the end of history.

Fatima had the responsibility of being the link between prophecy and the Guided One (*mahdi*). These were the values of Fatima herself. For her to 'be Fatima' obliged the Prophet to be strict with this special and exceptional companion. She must not have a single moment of peace in life for that might keep her from constant 'becoming'. Sorrow and loneliness were the water and earth of this girl who must grow under the light of revelation and bear the burdens of freedom and justice. She was the pure roots of the tree, each branch of which was appointed to take the 'fire of God' from heaven and give it to the people on earth. She must carry the heavy globe of the earth upon their shoulders. This is why Fatima must always learn. Her learning must be as light and air and food are to a tree—never ending.

A word instead of a servant! Only this wonderful bride and

groom could understand that one can live by a word. They were happy. They drank it and ate it and were filled by it.

These words, like the rain, must continue to fall and only these two thirsty creatures grown from among the highest form of humanity, were obliged to drink it and grow with it. The sudden sound of the Prophet in that dark night and his meaningful silence heralded the blessed coming of this rain..

It was not without reason that Ali, a man engaged in religious struggle, full of effort and work, a man who prayed not out of habit (just busy moving his tongue and chin) twenty-five years after this night, said, "May God be my witness that from the night that I received this lesson from the Prophet, I have not forgotten it for a single night."

In amazement, they asked, "Even the night of Siffin?" And Ali said again, emphasizing even more, "Even the night of Siffin."

Fatima also lived with this lesson until she died. These prayers were registered in her name. It was these heavenly words which came to help her in her home instead of a servant. They were the wedding present the Prophet gave his daughter.

The Prophet was very strict with his beloved daughter, Fatima. He has learned this method from God. There was no Prophet in the whole of the Koran who was so punished and so criticized as the Prophet. Why? Because none of the other Prophets were so beloved in the eyes of God and none of them were so responsible to the people.

One day, like any other day, the Prophet entered Fatima's home. His eye fell upon a patterned curtain. He frowned, said nothing and left. Fatima sensed it . She knew what her sin was. She also knows what her repentance was.

She immediately took the curtain from the wall and sent it to her father so that he could sell it and give the money to the needy of Madinah. Why so rough and strict? Zaynab, her sister, lived in luxury and splendor in Abu al-Aas's house. From the Prophet's way of expression and his type of discipline with her, it is clear that Fatima was something special, another kind of daughter. The Prophet addressed her, "Fatima, work now, because tomorrow I can do nothing for you."

You can see the distance between this Islam and the Islam which says, "One tear for Husayn will put out the fires of hell," or "Even if one's sins are greater than the foam of the oceans, the grains of sand and the stars in the sky, they will be forgiven," or "Friendship with Ali will turn all of one's sins into benefits on the Day of Judgment."

This means, essentially, that anyone who does not sin in this world or who sins little, is a fool because he can do nothing which can not be changed into benefits in the next world. More terrifying than this are the words which God is supposed to have said, "The friends of Ali are in heaven, even if they disobey me. The enemies of Ali are in hell, even if they obey me!"

INTERCESSION

There are not two religious systems—one of God and one of Ali. The system is very strict. The Prophet cannot even support Fatima when she stands in the presence of the Creator for God's judgment in the other world. He cannot protect her from deviation. Fatima must become Fatima herself. Being the daughter of the Prophet does not mean anything there, but it might be useful here in order for her to become Fatima. If she does not become Fatima, she is lost.

Intercession means this: not cheating at an exam or 'knowing the right people' or being at the mercy of one's family relationships in accounting for the truth and justice of God or changing the numbers in the record book of this world or bringing in relatives over the wall and through hidden doors to paradise. According to the Koran, the Prophet and Imams can only intercede with God's permission, a permission given only to those who are capable.

Fatima knew this. The Prophet had taught her. He has also taught others. This Islamic intercession takes the books and responsibilities which religion brings into account. It is quite different from the intercession referred to in the Age of Ignorance, where people appealed to their idols to intercede for them. They committed murder and thousands of dirty deeds, then offered a cow or a camel to Lat, Uzza or their other large and small idols and, through cries of regret or pleas of sympathy, sought intercession from them.

I not only accept the intercession of the Prophet but also that of Fatima and even the intercession of the Companions and great martyrs. What are we saying? I also believe that visiting the grave of Husayn removes sins. I believe that the spirit and thoughts of human beings who meditate on such great examples of humanity can be altered. The faith of such people can bring about a revolutionary change in them.

Faith in intercession transforms people. It kills weaknesses, fears, idol worshipping, and the worshipping of one's own self. From this spring comes the inspiration for human wisdom, beliefs and virtues. It inspires institutions to struggle in God's Way. It inspires permanence, sincerity and the blossoming of spiritual meanings. It brings about a new set of values. It strengthens human values. It does away with sicknesses of the will, habits, and sinful, attitudes deep in one's mind. It builds a great person. It is natural and logical that the past errors belong to the past and no longer exist and will never again be.

Hurr, the great hero or Karbala, through the intercession of Husayn, came out of the hell of slavery and was saved from being a sinner and murderer. With just a few steps, he reached the highest peak of liberty, truth and humanity.

And Fatima, through the intercession of the Prophet became Fatima. In Islam, intercession is the means of reaching 'the most worthy of salvations'—not a means of 'saving the unworthy'. It is the individual who must receive the intercession of an intercessor and—through this means—change his or her fate. In other words, the individual must change his character and behavior in order to become worthy of changing his destiny. Yes, an individual takes that from an intercessor. But an intercessor does not give that to an individual. No polluted and valueless person can pass the exam on the day of judgment unless he has learned in this world how to pass through to the next world using the techniques of life, struggle, work and service.

An intercessor is one such teacher—not a supporter of the illegal. Husayn acts as an intercessor for people who love him, have faith in him, and who, remembering him and his story, recall his having been a martyred warrior and nourish him through their recollection. He guides those who are wandering in the ways of ignorance.

"Fatima, work today because tomorrow I can do nothing for you." No exceptions are made for her in God's system of justice and the laws of Islam. She is responsible for her position. She must answer for every step that she takes. One day a Quraysh woman who had become a Muslim stole something. The Prophet heard of this. Her fingers must be cut-off," he said.

Many people's hearts bled for her. The large families of the Quraysh, who were the wealthiest of the Arab tribes, counted this as an insult, the stain of which would remain with their tribe. They went forward to seek intercession.

They asked Fatima to intercede with God for this woman. She did not accept. They went to Usama, the son of Zayd, who was the step-son of the Prophet. The Prophet loved Zayd and his son, Usama, very much. His special kindness towards the young Usama was famous in history. Usama, with all of his personal kindness and special closeness to the Prophet, with his reputation for loyalty and sacrifice and with the prestige of his father who had been Khadija's servant and the dear one of the Prophet, came from the Quraysh to ask that the sin of this woman be overlooked. He asked the Prophet to forgive her.

The Prophet answered in no uncertain terms, "Do not speak to me, Usama. Whenever the law is in my hands, there is no way of escape. Even if she were the daughter of the Prophet, Fatima, her fingers would be cut-off."

Why did he choose the closest among all of his beloved, the daughter of the Prophet? And why the name, Fatima? The answer to this question is clear. When he spoke of his calling, he chose his youngest daughter, Fatima from among all of his close family. It was only to her that he spoke of Islam.

With his clear announcement, Fatima was to become one of the four highest women in the history of humanity: the other three were Mary, Asiyah, and Khadija. Why was Fatima the last? Because she was the last complete link in the chain (among all of the creatures) for the whole duration of time, for all of the cycles of history, the last. Among the saints, she was the last. She was Fatima, an ideal image of the day of judgment.

The value of Mary lies with Jesus Christ whom she delivered and nourished. The value of Asiyah, the wife of Pharaoh, lies with Moses, whom she nourished and befriended. The value of Khadija lies with Muhammad (ﷺ) whom she befriended and with Fatima to whom she gave birth and who she nourished.

And the value of Fatima? What can I say? To whom does her value belong? To Khadija? To Muhammad? To Ali? To Husayn? To Zaynab? To herself!!

CHAPTER THIRTEEN
WHY FATIMA?

Ali and Fatima were now in their home outside of the city. They lived away from the daily bustle of the city, near the village of Quba (eight kilometers to the south of Madinah) next to the Quba Mosque. During the migration, the Prophet rested for one week at Quba where Ali, following three days behind, eventually joined him. After that, the Prophet went for the first time to Madinah and established Islam freely in that city. He laid the foundation for his new mosque, and history began.

Fatima and Ali later moved back to Madinah where they lived next door to the house of the Prophet which functioned as a mosque. The similarities between the beginnings of the Quba mosque and the Madinah mosque are most exciting to whomever is acquainted with the story of the Prophet's mosque and the house of the Prophet. If people do not understand it logically, they will emotionally sense it.

THE SPIRIT OF MUHAMMAD

While Fatima and Ali were far from the Prophet in Quba, it was most difficult for the Prophet. These two—the spirit of the Prophet's house—lived far from him, outside the city, in a home fraught with difficulties and poverty but also filled with love and faith.

Ali, from the beginning of his childhood, had lived with poverty, loneliness, difficulties, hatred, religious struggle and asceticism. He had borne his hard and bitter life in Makkah patiently. His youth and early childhood had been nothing other than immersion in belief and religious struggle. He was a very serious spirit, who had no thought about a house, life, pleasure,

187

wealth or comfort. He had a thirst which was only satisfied by bitterness. He was formed built from worship, asceticism, thought and work.

Fatima was also a product of sorrow, piety and poverty. She bore the tortures that her father, her mother, her sisters and Ali had borne for years in Makkah. They left a deep impression upon her body and upon her spirit. Her body was weak, but her feelings were deep. She had a most sensitive heart. Now in the house of Ali, she forced herself once again to live with difficulties, work, poverty and asceticism. Ali did not bring trivial entertainment to their house. Fatima also brought no routine desires and petty excitements to their new home. She did not pull Ali from heaven to earth nor drain his internal strength, depth and seriousness.

It was only the Prophet alone who would bring about the happiness of his beloveds through good feelings and words. Each kindness contained an ocean of meaning, sweetness and power for Ali and Fatima.

The Prophet was himself aware of this. He knew the needs of his beloveds who lived because they loved. He knew, "Whosoever loves Him has no life and for whosoever loves Him, this is life itself." He brought his Fatima and his Ali close to him. He made their house next door to his. It was made just like his of branches and palm leaves. Its door opened to the mosque—wall to wall. The windows of the house of Fatima directly faced the window of the Prophet's house.

These two windows which faced each other spoke of two hearts open to each other—the heart of a father and the heart of a daughter. Each morning their windows opened onto each other. Each morning there were greetings and laughter. Each evening, promises to meet the next day. It is this window about which it is said, "The Prophet, everyday, without exception, unless he was on a journey, sought out Fatima and greeted her."

Why from among all of the Companions, from among all of his close family, from among all of his daughters, should only Fatima live next to the mosque and share a wall with his home? The house of the Prophet was the house of Fatima. The family in which Ali was the father, Fatima the mother, Hasan and Husayn, the sons, and finally, Zaynab and Umm Kulthum the daughters, was the family of the Prophet. The family of the Prophet was this unique family, this unique home so emphasized in the Koran and the Traditions. The family of the Prophet, cleansed of all impurities, was chaste and protected for all generations to come.

Whosoever knows this family does not need reasoning and lengthy explanations. Even if there were no words expressed, intelligence itself would admit its uniqueness.

Now in Madinah, sharing a wall with the house of Ayisha, this house built within the mosque, Fatima's family grew. Hasan, Husayn, Zaynab, and Umm Kulthum were born. A new history had begun. With the dawn of these stars, new horizons had been found. The Prophet found the meaning of life Islam found the proof of belief. Humanity found the witness of all things!

THE CONTINUATION OF THE PROPHET

In the third year of the migration, one year and a few months after Fatima and Ali married, Hasan was born. Madinah celebrated the end of its waiting for its messenger. The Prophet, who for the first time during sixteen long and drawn out years (filled with torture, hatred, ugliness, treachery, with news of the torture of his friends and the death of his beloveds) now tasted the new and sweet message of the birth of Hasan. This news soothed his tired spirit .

Full of happiness, he entered Fatima's house. He held the first fruit of the union of Ali and Fatima in his arms. He recited the call to prescribed prayer in the baby's ear and finally distributed silver to the poor people of Makkah (silver in an amount equal to the weight of the hair on the baby's head).

A year passed. Husayn was born. The Prophet now had two 'sons'. Fate decreed that his two sons, Qasim and Abd Allah should not live. Thus the sons of the Prophet came through Fatima. As the Prophet said, "The generation of each Prophet was from his own body, but mine is from Fatima."

It is the Prophet's progeny who continued. These two spirits joined to produce the successive generations. In the mission of the Prophet, Ali was present and in the succession of Ali, the Prophet was present. In the pure faces of these two children (Hasan and Husayn), the Prophet saw three faces in these two: Ali, Fatima and his own.

Fate decreed that Hasan and Husayn should take the place of his sons. These two were the fruits of the union of Ali and

Fatima—Fatima, the mother of her father. All the Companions knew 'his smallest and most beloved daughter'. And Ali was his guardian, his brother and, through Fatima, the father of his beloved grandsons.

The roots which join Ali and the Prophet to each other cannot be counted. Both stemmed from Abd al-Muttalib. The mother of Ali looked after the Prophet from the time he was eight years old, and Ali's father, Abu Talib, was like the Prophet's father for seventeen years. The Prophet grew up in Ali's house from the age of eight to twenty-five, and Ali grew up in the Prophet's house from early childhood until the age of twenty-five. Khadija was like Ali's mother, and the Prophet was like his father!

What more similar and close union could there have been! Their relationships were comparable in every way. These two human beings were symmetrical, were twins and reflections of each other.

Ali was the second person who accepted Islam from the Prophet. His wife Khadija had been the first. Ali extended his hand to the Prophet when the Prophet was preaching in secret and alone. They joined together and, from then on, stood together through all dangers and difficulties until the Prophet's death.

Before the mission, Ali was a small boy of six or seven years old when the Prophet took him alone to Mt. Hira. Ali participated in the depth of asceticism and wonderful prayers. Ali accompanied the Prophet day and night.

The Prophet would stand in the moonlit silence in the cave on Mt. Hira or sit down or slowly pace back and forth. Sometimes underneath the rain of inspiration, his head fell forward. Sometimes he raised his head to the heavens and cried until he found his way. He was waiting. He saw something still unknown to him. During all of this, a small child, like his shadow, was with him— sometimes on his shoulder and sometimes beside him.

Once when Ali was a child of nine or ten years old he entered the room of Khadija and the Prophet! He saw them kneel on the ground, sit for awhile and then rise and say something under their lips. Both did this together. Neither one noticed him. He remained in wonder. Finally he asked, "What are you doing?"

The Prophet answered, "We are performing our prescribed

prayers. I have been sent as the messenger to spread the word of submission (*islam*) and to call people to the worship of the One God and my own mission. Ali, I call you as well to it."

Ali was still a child of no more than a few years, living in the house of the Prophet, drowned in his kindness and his greatness. Ali did not say yes without thinking. Faith had to filter through his wisdom and then find its way to his heart. At the same time, his tongue had the tone of his years. He said, "Allow me to talk to my father, Abu Talib, and then make my decision."

Immediately afterwards, he ran up the stairs to his room to sleep. But this invitation was not an ordinary invitation which Ali, even though only eight or ten years old, could take quietly. He stayed awake thinking until dawn.

No one knew what effect the words that night had on the thoughts of this boy, but in the morning, they heard his footsteps, light, but decisive and quiet. They stopped behind the door of the Prophet. Then the sweet beautiful voice of Ali was heard: "Last night, I thought to myself, 'God, in creating me, had not consulted Abu Talib, first. So why should I now ask his opinion about worshipping Him?' Tell me about Islam."

The Prophet spoke to him saying, "I accept." From then on Ali found himself upon this way and in the midst of this union. He directed every second of his life towards this end. He became a wonderful symbol of one who worshiped God, was loyal to the Prophet, a friend to humanity and devoted to the spirit. He joined the heart and mind of the Prophet in a thousand ways, both hidden and manifest. Everyone knew this. The Prophet knew it more than others. He sensed the thousands of rays of light falling from his spirit upon Ali. One day, much later when his spirit was filled with the light which shone upon him from the Prophet, he became excited. His heart deeply desired to hear the Prophet's feelings towards him. He asked, "Among these two, which is the most beloved of the Prophet, his daughter, Fatima Zahra, or her husband, Ali?"

The Prophet was at the other end of a difficult question. At the same time that he was required to answer 'an impossible question', while smiling kindly and softly, he had to find an answer right for all concerned. With a tone full of the pleasure of victory, he answered, "Fatima is more beloved to me than you, and you are dearer to me than she."

The Prophet never tried to show himself different from others. Rather, it was the opposite. He would say, "I am a human being like you. The only difference is the revelation which I receive." He always declared that he did not know the hidden world and other than that which was told him, he knew nothing. He always tried not to stand out or seem peculiar and, as far as possible, not to call attention to himself.

One day an old woman approached him to ask him something. All the things that she had heard about him and the greatness she knew he had, so affected her that when she found herself in his presence, she trembled and stuttered. The Prophet, who sensed that she had been struck by his presence, moved simply and quietly forward. He placed his hand kindly upon her shoulder and in a gentle and intimate tone, said, "Mother. What is it? I am the son of that Quraysh woman who milked sheep."

The depth of his sensitivity, sympathy and the softness of his heart was most amazing. Sometimes, inside the house, he would so humble himself that the hands of little Ayisha easily reached him. He kissed the hands of Fatima. His analogies which came from kindness were something special: "Ammar is as the space between my two eyes," "Ali is from me, and I am, from Ali," "Fatima is a part of my body."

And now Hasan and Husayn were born. What things did the Prophet not do with these two beloved children! He loved them, the mirror and fruit of his 'most beloved and dearest ones' and 'the dearest of his beloveds'. He had always showed special kindness to Fatima and given her spiritual strength the extent of which cannot even be found among men today. And now, from his only remaining daughter came two sons whom he must have loved very dearly. He was so fond of them that everyone expressed amazement.

One day, he entered Fatima's house as he did everyday from the time the children were born. He saw that both Ali and Fatima were asleep, and Hasan was hungry and crying. He found nothing to eat. The Prophet could not bring himself to wake his dearest and his most beloved. Quietly, with bare feet, he found their sheep, milked it and gave the milk to the child until he became quiet.

One day, when he was hurriedly passing Fatima's house, the cries of Husayn reached his ears. He returned and entered the house. With his whole body shaking, he shouted at Fatima,

"Don't you understand that his crying causes me pain!"

Usama ibn Zayd (whom we have mentioned before) said, "I had business with the Prophet. I knocked at his door. He came out. As I was talking to him, I realized he had something hidden under his clothes. He was holding onto it with difficulty, but I did not know what it was. When I had finished saying what I had come to say, I asked, 'What is that which you are holding, Prophet of God?'

"The Prophet, while his face filled with delight and pleasure, pulled apart his cloak and I saw Hasan and Husayn. At the same time that he wanted to explain his unusual behavior to me, he could not take his eyes off of them. In a tone full of joy and happiness, as if speaking to himself, he said, 'These are my two sons, the sons of my daughter.'"

Then as his voice, full of wonder, in a melody which cannot be expressed, continued, "Oh, God, I love these two. I love these two and love those who love them."

In the words of a contemporary Arab, "If they were to have asked the Prophet which of his daughters should continue his line and which son-in-law, he would have chosen the same two which God chose."

The children of Fatima and Ali felt that the Prophet was their grandfather, father, friend, relative of the family, guardian, companion and playmate. They were closer to him, more intimate and free than with their own mother and father. One day, during one of the congregational prayers, the Prophet went down in prostration. The prostration continued for such a long time that the people who were praying behind him began to wonder what had happened. [In the congregational prayer, the congregation performs the prayer behind an Imam or leader whose movements they follow in unison.] The Prophet had always been swift in his prescribed prayer. He always took the weakest people into consideration.

They thought something had happened or, else, that a revelation had reached him. After the ritual prayer, they asked him. He said, "Husayn had climbed on my back when I had gone down in prostration. As he had the habit of doing this in my home, I could not bring myself to hurry him, so I waited until he himself crawled down. This is why the prostration took so long."

The Prophet insisted that all people, especially the

Companions, know and see with their own eyes how he loved these two children, Hasan and Husayn and their mother and their father with more love than anyone's heart can hold.

If not, why did he treat Fatima with so much respect? Why did he kiss her hand and her face in the mosque so much and with such insistence? When he spoke from the pulpit, he constantly tried to show everyone his feelings for this family. After his prayers, he added the words, "God love them as well," referring to Hasan, Husayn, Fatima and Ali. "Their satisfaction is my satisfaction and my satisfaction is God's satisfaction. God, whoever bothers them, has bothered me, and whoever bothers me, bothers You."

Why these words? Why all these expressions of feelings of love? Why this show of affection especially for this family? The near future answered all of these 'whys'. The fate of this family, the fate of each and every member of this family, gave the answer to these 'whys'. They all began with the Prophet. The first sacrifice was Fatima. Then Ali. Then Hasan. Then Husayn, and, finally, Zaynab.

In the 5th year of Ali and Fatima's marriage, one year after Husayn, a girl was born to this family. She had to be born, and had to closely follow Husayn. She was Zaynab. In the following year, another girl, Umm Kulthum was born. Zaynab and Umm Kulthum—they had the same names as the daughters of the Prophet.

Yes. Fatima was becoming 'everyone' to the Prophet. She was his 'only one'. His Zaynab died. Ruqiya and Umm Kulthum also died. In the 8th year of the migration, God gave him a son, Ibrahim, but he also died. Now there was the Prophet and his only remaining child, Fatima—Fatima, and her children. This was the family of the Prophet. The love of the Prophet for Hasan and Husayn increased. These two children had become his whole life, and he spent all his free time with them.

THE COMPASSION OF MUHAMMAD (ﷺ)

The Prophet was a man who showed great strength of will and speech, whose sword was feared by all the caesars, kings and powerful rulers of that time. His enemies trembled before his anger. At the same time, he was a most sensitive person. His heart beat with kindness. His spirit was excited by the slightest touch of truth, sincerity and kindness.

At the terrible battle of Hunayn, where his enemies united to put him under their swords and destroy him and to drag him down to defeat and death, miraculously 6000 enemies were taken prisoner and 40,000 camels, sheep and other plunder were seized. A man came out from among the defeated enemies and said, "O, Muhammad, among these prisoners are your wet-nurse and your aunts and uncles." He then added, "If we were in the presence of your nurse, we would expect kindness from her, and you are greater than any of us."

They brought a woman forward who said, "I am the nurse of your Prophet." The Prophet asked, "What sign do you have?" She bared her shoulder and said, "These are the marks of your teeth which you made when I carried you on my back and you became very angry and bit me."

The memories flooded his mind as he recalled the kindness of his nurse and her daughters and the time of his childhood in the desert amidst this tribe. He was so affected and put into such a state of wonder that tears gathered in his eyes, and he said, "I give away my share and the shares of all of the children of Abd al-Muttalib. Be present in the mosque tomorrow. After the ritual prayer, announce your request to the gathering. I will give my family's answer to you, and perhaps other tribes will follow me." The next day he did as he said he would and freed all of them. The few victorious warriors who objected to giving back everything were satisfied when promised something later.

In his home and among his family, he was like this. To the outside world, he was a warrior, a politician, a commander full of strength and power. But inside the home, he was a kind father, a humble husband—simple and intimate. Even though his wives were sometimes rude to him, he never once struck them [wife-beating was customary before the mandate of the Prophet]. They caused him to suffer by complaining about the poverty in his home.

He would leave them and go out and sleep in the storage area. He would put up a ladder and sleep on the second floor, or he would sweep the floor and sleep on the earth. He lived like this for one month.

Finally, his wives, who both loved him and had faith in him, would surrender and became still, ashamed of their greedy behavior. He told them to choose divorce and this world or him and poverty. All, except one, preferred the second proposal and remained with him.

Whenever he left his home and wherever he went, whether walking in the streets or the bazaars of Madinah, he carried either Hasan or Husayn on his shoulders.

In the mosque, he went to the pulpit to speak to the people standing and listening to him. His grandchildren were in the house next to the mosque. They left the house, began walking and fell down. Suddenly the Prophet's eyes fell upon them. He could not take his eyes off of them. He saw that they walked with difficulty. They fell and got up again. He could no longer bear it. He stopped in the middle of his words, anxiously came down from the pulpit, picked them up and (as he had done when they were babies) held them in his arms and again returned to the pulpit. He saw the people were amazed. They were surprised by the extent of the spiritual sensitivity of this powerful man. They sensed that he wished to ask their pardon. For the sake of his children, he had interrupted his sermon.

Kindly holding the children, he returned to the pulpit and said, "God spoke rightly when He said, 'Your children and your wealth are your trials and tribulations.' My eyes fell upon these two children. I saw that each step the children took, they fell down. I could not bear it so I stopped speaking and went and got them."

They say his compassion towards Husayn was different. The power and depth of his sensitivities exceeded all limits He took hold of Husayn's shoulders, played with him and sang for him. He put his feet upon Husayn's chest and took his hand. Full of love and tenderness, he kissed him and from the bottom of his heart, he said, "God love him. Love him."

One day he had an invitation to go some place. He left the house with a few of his Companions. In the bazaar his eyes suddenly fell upon Husayn who was playing with his playmates. The Prophet stood before the children. He extended his hands to take his grandchild, but the child ran from one corner to the other. The Prophet, trying to catch him and laughing, caught hold of him. He put one hand on the back of the child and with his other, he took hold of his chin, kissed him and said, "Husayn is from me and I am from Husayn. God love whoever loves Husayn." His Companions wondrously looked on. One turned to another and said, "The Prophet treats his grandchild in such a manner. By God, I have a son, and I have never kissed him."

The Prophet turned to him and said, "Whosoever shows no kindness, receives no kindness."

Days and nights came and went. Fatima tasted the sweet moments of happiness and the bitter memories of the past. The poverty she had suffered faded.

The Battle of Khaybar came. The Jews gave the grazing area of Fadak to the Prophet. He gave it to Fatima. Fatima, who now had four children, found life less difficult.

THE CONQUEST OF MAKKAH

Makkah was conquered. Fatima accompanied her victorious father and hero husband who held the flag in his hand. They enter Makkah. She witnessed the greatest victory of Islam. She revisited the city where she had been born. She remembered the good and bad times she had had in Makkah. The Mosque of the Kabah and what had happened, the house of her father, her life with her sisters who were no longer alive, the 'birthplace of Fatima,' the valley of Abu Talib and the grave of her mother, Khadija.

She returned full of the happiness of victory and satisfaction, drowned in honors and goodnesses. Her father was little by little freed from the hatred of his enemies. His shadow fell upon the whole of the peninsula. Her husband was a force to reckon with at the battles of Badr, Uhud, Khandaq, Khaybar and the conquest of Makkah. One blow of his at these battles (or even at Hunayn and Yemen) was worth more than the prayers of men and jinn until the day of judgment.

She had her children—the only fruits of a life of sorrow and difficulties, the fruits of the union of love and faith and the only continuation of the seed of her father and of she herself. Her children were the heart of the family, center of the home and center of the pure family of the Prophet. Yes, it was as if Fatima had been compensated for all of her sorrow and bitterness, as if she had been rewarded for her virtues. That which fulfilled her the most was the fact that her children so filled the heart and soul of her father. She compensated for the sufferings of her beloved father, for whom no son remained and all of whose daughters, except herself, die in their youth.

Now, with her beloved children, Hasan and Husayn, Zaynab and Umm Kulthum, she felt blessed. As for the Prophet, the sweet taste of seeing them erased the rawness and bitterness of his life. He at last had a chance to become familiar with the happiness and pleasure which life can offer. Now aged over sixty, his feelings and needs for these children grew more than ever.

Life had been kind. A sweet smile appeared upon Fatima's face. A halo of goodness, honor and generosity fell around her house. Fatima, enjoyed the unexplainable kindness of her father, the greatness of her honorable husband and the pleasure which her children brought her. She ascended a throne of good fortune with her desires and aspirations fulfilled.

But all of this peace was just the quiet before the storm .The storm came. It was black, frightening and like a whirlwind. It took all of her peace and destroyed her home.

The Prophet was bed-ridden. He could no longer rise.

THE DEATH OF THE PROPHET

All images suddenly changed in her eyes. The pure and good Madinah now writhed with hatred and fear. Politics pushed faith and piety from the city of the Prophet. The promises of brothers were broken, and tribal oaths again renewed. The Prophet was no longer a leader. Ali was sent for Ayisha and Hafsa called their fathers.

The voice of Umar was heard saying the ritual prayer, then the voice of Abu Bakr. The army stood without words. Against the words and even insults to her father, they would not move. From all corners came objections about the choice of Usama as the leader of the army, although the Prophet had himself chosen Usama and had given him the banner of leadership.

It was Thursday, and what a Thursday. "A rain of tears fell from the eyes of my father. He ordered, 'Bring a tablet and a pen so that something can be written. Then that when I am gone, you will not be led astray.' Those opposed caused an uproar. They did not allow it. They said he was just mumbling. They said the book of God existed, and there was no need of anything more.

As Fatima recalled: "And now, father no longer spoke. The house of Ayisha, which shared a wall with my house, was silent. The Prophet's head was in Ali's lap. His eyes were beginning to close. He spoke to me only with his eyes.

"I could no longer bear all of these difficulties. He was my father, and I was his mother. I feared he might leave me in this city in this uproar!

"He did not take his eyes off me. He was very worried about me. He read in my face that I was suffering. His heart bled for me, Fatima, his daughter, his youngest daughter, his most beloved daughter.

"He indicated things to me with his eyes. I leaned my face forward and placed it on his. He whispered to me that his sickness was death. 'I will die.'

"I picked up my head. Misery and terror so overcame me that I lost all my strength. The misery of remaining alive after my father almost tore my heart apart.

"'Why did he give just me this message? I who am the weakest among all the rest?' I wondered.

"But his look was fixed upon me. His heart burned for his youngest daughter who, like a baby, needed him. He again indicated that I should draw near. It was as if he wanted to continue what he had been saying, 'But, you, my daughter, will be the first person from among my family who will come after me and who will join me.' Then he added, 'Are you not satisfied, Fatima, that you will be the leading woman of these people?'

"What a significant condolence. Only this news could lessen the pain of my misery over the death of my father! 'May God bless you, father. How well you know how to give condolences to Fatima.' I understood why among all these people, I alone must hear the news of his death. Now I had found the strength to cry and mourn. The man was dying. The protector of orphans and the refuge of widows was dying

"Suddenly the Prophet opened his eyes and said, 'Fatima, this poem is in praise of Abu Talib. Don't recite a poem in my praise. Recite the Koran. Recite!'

"Then the Prophet continued: 'Muhammad is no more than a Prophet. Other prophets have been sent before him. If he dies or is killed, you will go backwards and return to the reactionary, despotism of ancient time.'

"Then he said, 'God curse those who set up the graves of their Prophets as places of worship.' While whispering to himself, he said, 'Is there a place in hell for oppressive dictators?'

"He continued, 'We have given that home in the next world to those who do not oppress and create corruption. Whosoever opposes oppression and corruption should not seek them and should not do them.'

"The politicians did not allow him to write anything, but asked him to just say what he wanted to write. 'What do you want to write?' Annoyed, he looked at them and said, 'What I intend to do is better than what you call me for.' He also answered, 'I counsel you to three things: first, push the polytheists out of the Arabian peninsula; second, accept the agents of the tribes in the way that I accepted them; third, ...!

"Suddenly they all looked at Ali. He was silenced by his sorrow. The father was silent. His silence continued. Looking into a corner, tears welled up in his eyes, and he pondered long.

Fatima continued: "I screamed in pain. My grief was from your grief, father. In a tone of peace, in answer to me, he said, 'There will never be any sorrow for your father again.'

"My father's lips were sealed, the lips which recited the revelation, the lips which had kissed me and my children. He looked at us for awhile, and then his eyes closed. Blood flowed from his throat. His head rested upon Ali's chest. Ali kept a frightening and heavy silence. It was as if Ali died before my father. Ayisha lamented upon my father's head, as did his other wives.

"The moments passed in the silence of death. Suddenly his hands, which were in a position of prayer upon Usama's head, fell to his sides and his lips moved, 'To my highest Friend.' Then all things ended.

"Father, oh father! You accepted God's invitation. You have gone to Gabriel,' I cried.

"Outside there was an uproar. The city was crying without hesitation or fear. I heard the cries of Umar, who said, 'The Prophet has not died. He rose to heaven like Jesus Christ. He will return. Whosoever says the Prophet has died is a hypocrite. I will cut-off his head.'

"Several hours passed. It became quiet. I saw that Abu Bakr and Umar entered the room. Abu Bakr pulled back the covering over my father's face. He cried and left. Umar also left.

"Ali began the work of ablution and putting on the white cloth of the dead. My husband, Ali, Abu al-Hasan [father of Hasan, one of Ali's titles], washed the pure body of my father while he continued crying. He poured water upon him and fire upon my soul. People had lost their Prophet. People remained without refuge, the Companions without a leader but Ali and I lost everybody and everything. Suddenly, I sensed that in this city, in the world, we were exposed.

"All at once everything turned around. Faces changed. Terror fell from the door and wall. Politics replaced truth. The handshakes which had bound brothers together in their oaths moved apart, and relatives moved closer [that is, old tribal blood ties began to replace the new national, religious ties]. The elders and aristocracy took on a new life beside the cold body of my father, the Prophet of God and Messenger to the people.

"For Ali and myself the event was so terrible that we could think of nothing but the death of the Prophet. The city was full of plans, plots and conflicts. For us existence, all at one time, emptied itself. The shadow of fear upon his face, Abbas, our oldest uncle, came and in a tone full of meaning and fear, addressed Ali. 'Put your hands forward so that I can give my allegiance. Then they can say the uncle of the Prophet of God gave his allegiance to the son of the uncle of the prophet of God. The members of your family will also give their allegiance to you. When this is finished, no one will be able to oppose it.

"What? Is there someone who wants this position?' asked Ali.

"'Tomorrow you shall know,' replied Abbas.

"Ali sensed the danger. But this sense of danger passed through him like lightening and left. He was inwardly overflowing with sorrow. The Prophet was his relative, his father, his guardian, his teacher, his brother, his friend. The Prophet embodied all his faith and feelings. The Prophet was the existence of Ali. Ali could not bring himself to think about the events taking place outside of this home. He sensed the Prophet's spirit under his hands. He sensed a trembling. He did the ablution. He was busy with the Prophet and with his children, our children."

Hasan was seven, Husayn six, Zaynab five and Umm Kulthum only three. Destiny had planned a life of enmity for the young children after the Prophet's death. Outside the city at Saqifa, the Helpers of the Prophet gathered together to choose the Prophet's representative from among themselves. They felt that the Quraysh of Makkah had their own plans. Abu Bakr, Umar and Abu Ubaydah arrived and convinced them that the Prophet had said, 'Leaders are from among the Quraysh.' They reasoned that the replacement for the Prophet must be from among his family. As a result, Abu Bakr was chosen at Saqifa.

RECALLING FATIMA'S LIFE

Fatima 's childhood occurred after her mother had given all of her wealth for the cause of Islam. The peacefulness of the life of her father and the happiness of her youth with her sisters had passed. Her mother had become old and broken. Her mother's age was beyond sixty-five. Happiness, wealth and the good fortune of life were replaced by weakness, poverty, difficulties, an environment of hatred, and the treachery of strangers.

Her mother, Khadija, before being the mother of Fatima and wife of the Prophet, had been the first associate and the greatest companion of a man on whom the heavy mission of heaven had fallen, the mission of removing the blackness of ignorance, the mission of returning the fire of God to mankind, the mission of freeing people from the chains of bondage by changing the economic system of slavery and the mission of freeing people from the mental prison of idol worship, Khadija was now the mother of Fatima, but completely occupied with the Prophet who had received inner inspiration about that which is above life and happiness. Around Khadija a fire full of hatred, the troubles of the worship of materialism and enmity spread. The mother of Fatima was busy with the difficulties and the revolution of the Prophet. The Prophet lived amidst his troubles and his revolution giving the message of God to his people.

There is no heart which could sense what Fatima was feeling. The love of Fatima for the Prophet was much more than the love of a daughter for her father. She was the daughter who was also the mother of her father, the sympathizer with him in his exile and loneliness, the acceptor of his troubles and his sorrow, the companion in the religious struggle, the link in the chain of his line; his last daughter and, during the last years of his life, his only child. After his death, she was his only survivor, the light of his home, the only pillar of his family and, finally, the only mother of his children, his inheritors.

Just when Fatima needed the love of her mother and the kindness of her father, she sensed that her mother and father, (both of whom had lived only with pain, loneliness and misery) needed her child-like kindness and caresses.

There is a saying that a heart which finds a friend through

trouble and sorrow develops a friendship which, when compared to a love based on happiness and pleasure, is much deeper and more certain. The feeling with which one views how one has lived one's life and how one's friend has answered one's needs is not the same as the feeling of familiarity one senses from the friend in one's own being. For when one sees that one has sacrificed one's life and that the needs of the friend have been met, the spirit—in the heights of its subtleness and the depths of its feelings—forms another spirit within the self—the spirit of friendship.

And Fatima gave such friendship to the Prophet that there is no comparison to one who gives love to one's father. The intimacy and purity of feelings which she had for him created a continuous link and a situation incapable of being described. With the spirit of her father within herself, she was able to bear the years of difficulties, hatred, fear and torture. She bore the fact that her hero father was sacrificed and remained a stranger in his own country, unknown in his own city, alone among his family, alone among those who spoke his language. He remained without anyone to whom he could talk. He had to stand face to face with ignorance and idol worship. He had to stand face to face in savage conflicts with untamed elders, petty aristocrats and hated slave dealers.

His shoulders were bent under the heavy weight of the divine mission of the One God. He was alone in this long walk from slavery to freedom, from the dark valleys of Makkah to the peaks of the mountain of light, alone and without a companion while his soul was suffering from the hatred, plots and blindness of the people. His body was wounded from the troubles and blows of the enemy. He tried harder than anyone else to bring happiness and salvation to his tribe, and yet he and his family suffered because of the trouble his tribe caused him. They treated him as a stranger.

On the one hand, he was alone, a suffering spirit, bearer of the revelation and on the other, he was a storm of love and fiery faith. Tribal enmity, the blindness of the people, the loneliness of not having anyone and the heavy weight of the load of the 'trust' he had brought caused him anguish. God had offered the burden of bearing this weight to the heavens and the earth, but they had rejected it. Only mankind was willing to accept the responsibility. In following this, the Prophet, everyday from morning until night, cried out a warning (to whomever passed by the Safa hill) of danger to people who were asleep and passive. He did this under the rain of problems that sought him out each day.

He announced the message in the sacred precinct of the Masjid al-Haram beside the *dar al-madweh*, the meeting place of the wealthy Quraysh aristocrats and before the eyes of 330 dumb, senseless, spiritless idols who were the gods of the people. He called the people to awaken. He cried for freedom. At the end of the day, tired and exhausted, wounded internally, his heart overflowing with pain, he returned to a silent home empty-handed, followed by mockery. Within his home there was a woman broken by the sufferings of life, her body and her whole existence full of love, her two eyes waiting in anticipation, watching the door.

Fatima, a young girl, weak, moved step by step with her father through the streets of hatred to the *Masjid al-haram* under the taunts of curses, mockery, and contempt. Whenever he fell he became like a bird that had fallen out of the nest. When a bird falls from its nest, the possibility arises that it will fall into the claws and beaks of wild animals or birds. Fatima threw herself upon her father. With all of her strength, she protected him. With her small, fine hands, she took her hero into her arms. With the edge of her small, fine fingers, alive with kindness, she cleaned the blood from her father's head and hands. She healed his wounds with her soft words She encouraged the man who carried the Word of God. She returned him to their home.

She was a link of kindness, attraction and love between a suffering mother and a suffering father. When her bloodied father returned from Taif, she alone came forward to greet him and with her child-like, endearing efforts, attracted him to herself, despite of all of his worries and troubles. She attracted his heart towards her warm reception.

In the valley of the confine she lived three years beside her sad, bed-ridden, elderly mother and her suffering father covered with difficulties. She bore hunger, sorrow and loneliness. After the death of her mother and the death of the uncle of the great Prophet, she filled the sudden emptiness his life with her kindness and endless understanding. The Prophet was now alone both inside the home and outside of it.

She acted as a mother to her father who was now very much alone. She devoted love, faith and all the moments of her life to her father. Through her kindness, the feelings of her father were satisfied. Through her devotion and faith in the mission of her father, she gave him energy and honor.

By going to Ali's house and by accepting his noble poverty, she gave him hope. Through Hasan, Husayn and Zaynab she offered her father the sweetest and dearest fruits of her life. Her children compensated the Prophet for his terrible losses: the deaths of his three infant sons and the deaths of his three grown daughters. The roots of Fatima's lifelong love were deeper than the feelings of a child of eighteen or twenty-eight years. She was stronger than life, purer than will and faith. All the golden webs of the beyond were created in the soul, depth and conscience of Fatima. They joined her with the spirit of her father.

And now this delicate web was torn by the thorn of the death of her father. Fatima must 'remain' without him and 'live'. How terrifying and heavy was this blow to the frail heart and weak body of Fatima, this girl who lived only through love of her father, faith in her father. She lived because of her father.

It is no accident that the Prophet, upon his deathbed, consoled her and gave her the strength, the strength to bear her father's death. This strength was the only gift from the death of her dear one. The special news was that she would join him sooner than any of the others.

CHAPTER FOURTEEN
HER FINAL STRUGGLE

SHE SEEKS OUT
THE SOIL OF HER FATHER'S GRAVE

Now the only meaning she found in life was the kind soil of her father's grave and the hopeful news he gave her when he said, 'Fatima, you will be the first person to join me from among my family.'

But when? What an exciting prospect!

Her suffering spirit, like a wounded bird whose wings have been broken,was further wounded by three inescapable sights: the silent and sorrowful face of her husband, the saddened faces of her children and the sight of the silent, cold earth upon her father's grave in the corner of Ayisha's house.

Whenever the pain in her heart increased and she lost her breath from crying, she sensed that she was in need of the kindness and condolences of her father. She sought him out. She fell upon the silent earth of his grave. She stared at his grave and suddenly it was as if she had just heard of the death of her father for the first time. She cried out.

She pushed her fingers into the earth. She filled her empty hands with it. She tried to see him behind the curtain of her tears. She put the earth upon her face and smelt it. For a moment she was at peace. She had found condolence, but, suddenly, in a voice which broke with tears she said, "Anyone who smells the earth of Ahmad (Muhammad) has lost nothing if he never again smells any other musk. O father, what miseries have fallen upon me after you. If they had fallen upon a bright day, they would turn it into night." Gradually she would grow silent. The earth of her father's grave poured through her senseless fingers. She looked at it with painful amazement. Then she became motionless and silent.

She put all of her sorrows in the death of her father. Each day was like the first day of his death. Her impatience grew everyday, and her cries became more painful. The wives of the Helpers gathered round her and cried with her. The waves of sorrows pressed upon her heart and caused her eyes to bleed.

Her sorrow was more disturbing than anyone could conceive. No one could console her or ask her to be patient. Nights and days passed like this. The Companions were warmed by their power, riches and conquests. Ali was lost in sorrow and Fatima in thoughts of death. She became impatient to receive the gift her father had promised her.

THE DEATH OF FATIMA

Each day that passed she became more impatient for death. The only way she could bear to remain alive was to seek refuge in her father, to draw near him when her faith and spirit overflowed with complaints and pain.

How great was her need for such a refuge, for such a peace? But time passed slowly. Ninety-five days had passed since her father promised her death, and death would not come.

It came. On Monday, the 3rd of Jamadi al-thani, in the 11th year of the migration, in the year of the death of her father, it came. She kissed each one of her children.

Now was the moment to bid farewell to Ali. How difficult it was! And Ali had to remain alone in the world for thirty more years. She sent for Umm Rafia to come. Umm Rafia had arranged the Prophet's funeral.

She said, "O servant of God. Pour water on me so that I may wash myself." With patience and peace, she performed the ablution. Then she put on the clothes which she had not worn since the death of her father, the clothes she had put away. It was as if she had put aside the memory of her mourning and now was going to see a dear friend.

She said to Umm Rafia, "Put my bed in the middle of the room." Softly and quietly she stepped into the bed. She faced the Kabah and she waited. A moment passed, moments. Suddenly cries were heard within the house. She closed her eyes to the world and opened her eyes upon her beloved awaiting her. A candle of fire and sorrow was extinguished in Ali's house. And Ali remained alone, with his children.

She had asked Ali to bury her at night so that no one would recognize her grave or follow her corpse. Ali did as she had asked. But no one knew how. And they still do not know where. In her home? Or in Baqia'? It is not clear. And where in Baqia? It is not clear. That which is clear is the pain of Ali, that night, next to the grave of Fatima.

Madinah was silent in the night. All Muslims were asleep. The night was only broken by the quiet whisperings of Ali. Ali was very much alone both in the city and in his home—without the Prophet and without Fatima. Like a mountain of pain, he sat upon the earth of the grave of Fatima. Hours passed. Night, quiet and silent, listened to the pain of his whispering. Baqia was peaceful, fortunate. Madinah was without loyalty. All remained in silence. The awakened graves and sleeping city listened!

The wind of the night took the words flowing with difficulty from the spirit of Ali (as he sat beside Fatima's grave) towards the house of the Prophet: "To you from me and from your daughter, who followed you in such haste, greetings O Prophet of God.'

"My patience and my ability have weakened from the fate of your dearest, O Prophet of God. But how can I seek patience with such terrible misfortune and los?

"I placed you in the grave, but you still exist in my heart. We are all from God and unto God we shall return. But my sorrow is eternal, and my nights sleepless until God takes me to the home in which you are now.

"Right now your daughter will tell you how your tribe joined each other against her and took away her rights. Insist that she tell you everything that happened. All these things happened even though not much time has passed since your death, and people have not forgotten you .

"Greetings to both of you, greetings from a man who has neither anger nor sorrow."

He remained silent for a moment. He suddenly sensed the exhaustion of a whole lifetime. It was as if with every word pulled from the depths of his being, he gave up a part of his existence.

He was alone. He did not know what to do. Stay? Return home? How could he leave Fatima here alone? How could he return alone to his home? The city looked like a devil in the darkness of the night. Schemes, treacheries and shamelessness awaited him.

How could he stay? His children, the people, truth, responsibilities and a heavy mission awaited him. His pain was so heavy that it destroyed his strong spirit. He could not decide. Hesitation gripped his soul. Go? Stay? He sensed that he was unable to do either. He did not know what he would do. He explained to Fatima: "If I leave you it is not because I do not want to stay near you. If I stay here [die] have I not renounced the fate that God promises those who bear patiently?"

Then he arose, stood and faced the Prophet's house, with a passion which overflowed into words. He wanted to say that he, Ali, was returning that which had been entrusted to him. 'Listen to what she says. Ask her to tell you everything precisely. Have her recount all the things that she saw after you, one by one!'

EPILOGUE

Fatima lived like this and died like this. After her death, she began a new life in history. Fatima appeared as a halo around the faces of all of the oppressed who later became the multitudes of Islam. All of the sufferers, all of those whose rights had been destroyed, all who had been deceived, all took the name of Fatima as their emblem.

The memory of Fatima grew with the love and wonderful faith of the men and women, who throughout the history of Islam, fought for freedom and justice. Throughout the centuries they were punished under the merciless and bloody lash of the caliphates. Their cries and anger grew and overflowed from their wounded hearts.

This is why in the history of all Muslim nations and among the deprived masses of the Islamic community, Fatima has been the source of inspiration for those who desire their rights, for those who seek justice, for those who resist oppression, cruelty, crime and discrimination.

It is most difficult to speak about the personality of Fatima. Fatima was the ideal that Islam wanted a woman to be. The form of her face was fashioned by the Prophet himself. He melted her and made her pure in the fires of difficulties, poverty, revolution, deep understanding and the wonder of humanity.

She was a symbol for all the various dimensions of womanhood. She was the perfect model of a daughter when dealing with her father. She was the perfect model of a wife when dealing with her husband. She was the perfect model of a mother when raising her children. She was the perfect model of a responsible, fighting woman when confronting her time and the fate of her society.

She herself was a guide—that is, an outstanding example of someone to follow, an ideal type of woman, one whose life bore witness for any woman who wishes to 'become herself'—through her own choice.

She answered the question of how to be a woman with her wonderful childhood and adulthood, her constant struggle and resistance on two fronts (inside and out) in the home of her father, in the home of her husband, in her society, in her thoughts and behavior and in her life as a whole.

I do not know what to say. I have said a great deal. Still much remains unsaid.

In the symphony of all the amazing aspects of the great spirit of Fatima, that which causes the most wonder in me, is this : that Fatima was the traveling companion, was the one who stepped in the same steps of her father was the one who flew together with the great spirit of Ali through the heights of humanity towards perfection and completion was the one who passed through all the stages of the ascent of the spirit and the psyche.

She was not just a wife to Ali. Ali looked upon her as a friend, a friend who was familiar with his pains and his great aspirations. She was his endless refuge, the one who listened to his secrets. She was the only companion of his loneliness. This is why Ali looked at her with a special look and also at her children.

After Fatima, Ali took other wives and he had children from them. But from the beginning, he separated the children who were from Fatima from his other children. The latter are called 'Bani Ali',[that is, sons of Ali] and the former, 'Bani Fatima' [the children of Fatima].

Isn't it strange! The children of Ali derived their names from Fatima. And we saw that the Prophet also saw her with different eyes. Among all of his daughters, he would only discipline Fatima. He relied only upon her. From an early age, she accepted the great invitation.

I do not know what to say about her or how to say it? I wanted to imitate the French writer who was speaking one day in a conference about the Virgin Mary. He said, "For 1700 years all of the speakers have spoken of Mary. For 1700 years, all philosophers and thinkers of various nations of the East and West have spoken of the value of Mary. For 1700 years, the poets of the world have spent all of their creative efforts and power in their praise of Mary. For 1700 years, all of the painters and artists have created wonderful works of art showing the face and form of Mary. But the totality of all that has been said and the efforts of all the artists and thinkers throughout these many centuries have not been able to better describe the greatness of Mary than the simple words, 'Mary was the mother of Jesus Christ.'"

And I wanted to begin in this manner with Fatima. I got stuck. I wished to say, 'Fatima was the daughter of the great Khadija,' but I sensed this would not fully describe Fatima. I wished to say, 'Fatima was the daughter of Muhammad,' but I sensed this would not fully describe Fatima. I wished to say, 'Fatima was the wife of Ali,' but I sensed this would not fully describe Fatima. I wished to say, 'Fatima was the mother of Hasan and Husayn,' but I sensed this would not fully describe Fatima. I wished to say, 'Fatima is the mother of Zaynab,' but I still sensed this would not fully describe Fatima.

No, these are all true, and none of them is Fatima

FATIMA IS FATIMA

APPENDICES:
GUIDE TO SHARIATI'S
COLLECTED WORKS

In the publishers notes, explanation is given about the arm or logo of the Husayniyah which comes from a calligraphy

in Jalal al-Din Rumi's place of burial which says, "Oh
Master Mu*la*na." The *la* comes from Mu*la*na.

VOLUME 2: REVOLUTIONARY SELF-DEVELOPMENT   328pp

2.1 Preface   3-9
   1970/1349   April-May   Ordibehesht
   Text written for *Iqbal and Us* but repeated here. First time
   printed in Persian. Title by editors.

2.2 How to Remain   11-57
   1977/1355   January 2   Muharram 11th 1397AHL
   Tape. Also called "Conversations with the 11th Night."
   Recorded in a private gathering. Among those present on
   the 11th of Muharram were Hejazi, Khamene'i and
   Mutahhari. Issues were presented by Shariati. The group
   expressed its views and Shariati spoke seeking an answer.
   Title from the text by editors. First time printed in
   Persian.

2.3 Mysticism, Equality, Freedom   59-90
   Tape. Date unknown. Also in letters (vol. 1, p. 143). First
   time printed in Persian. Translated into English and published in *Marxism and Other Western Fallacies* (Berkeley:
   Mizan Press, 1980).

2.4 Love-Monotheism   91-113
   Text. Date unknown. Also called Love. First time printed in
   Persian.

2.5 Freedom, Auspicious Freedom   115-128
   Text. Date unknown. Title by editors. First time printed in
   Persian.

2.6 Revolutionary Self-development   129-184
   1976/1355   Summer
   Text.

2.7 Knocking on the Door of Truth   185-196
   1976/1355   December-January   Dey
   Tape. Private. Title from a verse in Jalal al-Din Rumi's
   Mathnawi based on a Tradition from the Prophet. First
   time printed in Persian.

2.8 Peace (*salam*) in the Ritual Prayer   197-210
   Private meeting. Date unknown. Written after 18 months
   in prison. First time printed in Persian.

2.9 Hurr: Man Caught Between Tragedy and Salvation   211-247
   1976/1355   Fall
   Text. Read in a private session in Muhammad Humayun's
   home. Ashura night 1397/ December 31, 1976/ Dey 10,
   1355. Most complete text here. Includes notes in the
   margin of the manuscript.

2.10 Night of Power (*qadr*)   249-254
   Text. Date unknown. No title.

2.11 The Night Journey (*mi'raj and isra*)   255-263
   In response to Questions and Answers. Date unknown.
   First time printed in Persian.

VOLUME 3: ABU DHARR   286pp
Book One
3.1 Abu Dharr Ghifari   1-200
    1954/1334
    First time printed in Persian. Translation of a text in
    Arabic by Jawdat al-Sahar. Shariati's Introduction to the
    translation has been translated into English and published
    in *And Once Again Abu Dharr* (Tehran: Abu Dharr
    Foundation, 1985).

Book Two
3.2 And Once Again Abu Dharr   201-263
    1972/1351   July-August
    Text. Husayniyah Irshad. Text consists of a speech given
    before the play. He had been told that a bomb had been
    planted to kill the players. He then continued his
    Introduction so that if anyone be killed, it would be him.
    English translation published (Tehran: Abu Dharr
    Foundation, 1985).

VOLUME 4: RETURN   477pp
Book One
4.1 Return to Self   3-33
    Speech at Jundi Shapur University. Date unknown.
    Printed along with other speeches:
4.2 When the Ranks are Clear
4.3 The Miracle of Faith and Consciousness
Book Two
4.4 Return to which self?   35-401
    Text. Date unknown. First time printed in Persian. Written
    during his last years. Shariati edited the typed version.
Contains:
4.5   The Fate of Thoughts
4.6   Contemporary Reformers
4.7   Revolutionary Political Leftists
4.8   Society and History
4.9   Where are we in history?
4.10 Philosophy and Science of History
4.11 Marxism and the Course of History
4.12 The Responsibility of Intellectuals
4.13 Determinism of History
4.14 The Mission of the Intellectual
4.15 Assimilated
4.16 Discontinuity of History
4.17 Historical Conscience
4.18 Feeling for the Past and Coming to Know Historic Self
      in the East
4.19 Pretending to be Modern
4.20 Colonialism and Assimilation
4.21 Serving and Reforming
4.22 Intellectual vs Pseudo-Intellectual

            All sections of Volume 5: *Iqbal and Us* dealing specifically
            with Iqbal Lahouri have been translated into English in
            addition to Author's Preface printed in Volume 2 of the
            Collected Works, under the title: *Iqbal: Manifestation of the
            Islamic Spirit*. Publication date, spring, 1990 (Joint
            Publication of ABJAD Book Designers and Builders,
            Albuquerque and Crescent International, Canada).

Distributed through KAZI Publications, Chicago.

VOLUME 6: HAJJ: REFLECTIONS ON ITS RITUALS 266pp
6.1 A Word to the Reader
    Volume 1: 23 Years in 23 Days
    Volume 2: The Place of the Covenant (*miyad*) with Abraham
    Volume 3: Hajj: Reflections on its Rituals

Part One
6.2 Introduction to the Shorter Pilgrimage (*umrah*)
6.3 The Season (*musum*)
6.4 *Ihram* at the Place of the Appointed Time (*miqat*)
6.5 Making Your Intention Known (*niyyah*)
6.6 The Ritual Prayer in the Place of the Appointed Time
6.7 Prohibitions (*muharramah*)
6.8 The Kabah
6.9 Circumambulation (*tawaf*)
6.10 The Black Stone (*hajar al-aswad*) and the Oath of Allegiance (*bayat*)
6.11 The Station of Abraham (*maqam*)
6.12 The Search (*sa'y*)
6.13 The Cutting of Nails or Hair (taqsir) and the End of the Longer
    Pilgrimage (*umrah*)
Part Two
6.14 Introduction to the Longer Pilgrimage (**tamatu**)
6.15 Arafah
6.16 Mashar
6.17 Mina
6.18 Stoning the Satans (*rami*)
6.19 The Sacrifice (*adha*)
6.20 The Trinity of Idols
6.21 The Festival (*id*) of the Sacrifice
6.22 The Pause (*wuquf*) After the Festival
Conclusion
6.23 A General Look
6.24 After the Festival of Sacrifice: Stoning
6.25 The Last Message of Revelation
6.26 A Final Word
6.27 The Return
    1971
        This volume was completed and published sometime in
        1971. Translated into English in an abridged form and
        published by FILINC: Houston, 1978. Complete translation
        published 1994 (Joint Publication of ABJAD Book
        Designers and Builders, Chicago. Distributed by KAZI
        Publications, Chicago under the title *Hajj: Reflections on
        its Rituals.*

VOLUME 7: SHI'ISM 363pp
Book One
7.1 Shi'ism: A Complete Political Party 3-168

Lecture 1:
    1972/1351   October 24
Lecture 2:
    1972/1351   November 12
        Speech. Husayniyah. Two lectures. Lecture 1 previously
        printed in Persian. Lecture 2, first time printed in Persian.
        Shariati edited the texts of both lectures. It was as a result
        of the second lecture that the Husayniyah Irshad was
        closed and ten months later Shariati put into solitary con-
        finement for 18 months.

Book Two

    1972/1351   September 12
        Speech. Husayniyah. Printed before in Persian. Text edited
        by Shariati.

Book Three

    1971/1350   November 6
        Speech. Husayniyah.

Appendix:

VOLUME 8: PRAYER 195pp
Book One
    1959/1338   Summer
        Translation of the book by Alexis Carrel (1873-1944).
        Translation printed in Paris.

Book Two
    1970/1349   April 2
        Speech. Husayniyah.

Book Three
        Two writings. Dates unknown. One given at the end of the
        above lecture and the other is an older text. Part of the lat-
        ter was translated into English in *Martyrdom* (Tehran: Abu
        Dharr Foundation, 1985).

Book Four
    1972/1351   September 13
        Speech. Husayniyah.

VOLUME 9: ALID SHI'ISM/SAFAVID SHI'ISM 315pp
        Date unknown. Introduction to a play on the Sarbedaran
        which was not allowed to be performed by the regime.
    1971/1350   October 31
        Speech. Husayniyah.

Contains: Introduction; Setting the Stage; Movement and Institution; The Ottomans and the West; Suddenly an Attack from Behind; An Example of the Logic of Safavid Shi'ism; The Logic of a Shi'ite Alim; The Assembling of Religion and Nation Nationhood: The Shu'ubi Shi'ite Movement; Religion: The Shi'ite Shu'ubi Movement; Negating Shi'ism Through Shi'ism; Western Christianity and Safavid Shi'ism: Foreigners in Karbala; The Ideological Bases of the Two Sects

Husayniyah.
Contains: Introduction; Eastern and Western Spirit and Attitudes;
Characteristics of Western Spirit and Culture

Contains: Basis for Eastern and Western Thought; China; Islamic Thought
and Science are Two Different Things; Religious Philosophy of History is
Based on Contradiction; Where is the way of salvation?

Contains: Education Has Two Stages; Hinduism

Contains: Hinduism; Metamorphosis of Thought and Words; On the Verge of
Hope

VOLUME 15: HISTORY AND KNOWLEDGE OF RELIGIONS (II)337pp

Contains: Introduction; Shi'ism; Why Iran Chose Islam; Justice and
Leadership; Why the General of the Khorasan Army Was Sent to Fight the
Arabs; Alid/Safavid Shi'ism; Equity and Justice; Imamate (Leadership);
Difference Between Dictatorship and Revolutionary Leadership; Selection

Contains: Introduction; Intellect and Welfare; The Vedas; Way of Salvation;
Me; Brahmanism

Contains: Introduction; Abraham; Tribal Evolution; Relation Between
Welfare and Absurdity; Life of Buddha

Contains: Introduction; Buddha

Contains: Hinduism

Contains: Ancient Iranian Religions

Contains: Zoroastrianism
Appendix:

Speech. Mashhad. After release from prison. Also called "Method of Approach to the Quran." Tape called "Quranic Terminology" and "Key to the Understanding of Quranic Terminology."

29.3 Civilization: The Logical Outcome of Migration
    1971/1349   January 24
    Madinah.
29.4 Study of Types of Migration
    1971/1349   January 25
    Madinah.
29.5 The Salvation of the Young Generation
    1971/1349   January 26
    Madinah.
29.6 Migration, *Ummah* (Community) and *Imamate* (Leadership)
    1971/1349   January 27
    Makkah.
29.7 Reflections on the Hajj Rituals
    1971/1349   February 5
    Arafah.
29.8 The Islam of Muhammad: Reviver of Abraham's Religion
    1971   February 6
    Mina.
29.9 Sacrifice Your Ishmael
    1971/1349   February 7
    Mina.
29.10 Selection and/or Election
    1971/1349   February 8
    Mina. Translated into English and published (Tehran: Ham-dami Foundation, 1980).
29.11 What must be done?
    1971/1349   February 16
    Makkah.
29.12 A Glance at the Life of Muhammad (ﷺ): From Birth to Actualization of Prophethood
    1971/1349   February 17
    Mt. Hira.
29.13 Twenty-three Years in Twenty-three Days
    1972/1350   January 14
    Madinah.
29.14 The Importance of Migration in Islam and a Study of Five Kinds of Migration in the Holy Quran
    1972/1350   January 15
    Madinah.
29.15 A Sketch of the Prophet's Mosque and its Environs: The Vital Necessity for Coming to Know Fatima (ﷺ)
    1972/1350   January 16
    Madinah.
29.16 Monotheism: The Infrastructure of All Actions, Rules and Feelings
    1972/1350   January 20
    Makkah.
29.17 Now that you have reached the Ka'bah, do not remain there.
    1972/1350   January 26
    Arafah.

the Muslim world against the West. Hopkins had invited
Kashf al-Ghita to attend an anti-communist conference to
be held in Lebanon. The latter refused and instead sent a
letter in which he took an anti-imperialist stance. An
English translation of the letter has been published
(Tehran: IPO, 1987) under the title *Islamic Anti-
Imperialism*.

VOLUME 35: MISCELLANEOUS WORKS (2 vols)   558pp

A. Index to the Translated Titles of the Volumes of the Collected Works

B. Index to the Transliterated Titles of the Volumes of the Collected Works

Abu Dharr 3
'Ali (ﷺ) 26
Athar-eh gounah goun 35
Ba mokhatib-ha yeh ashna 1
Baz gasht 4
Bazshenasi-yeh hoveyat-eh irani-yeh eslami 27
Che bayad kard 20
Ensan 24
Ensan-eh bi khod 25
Eslamshenasi 30
Eslamshenasi I 16
Eslamshenasi II 17
Eslamshenasi III 18
Gofteguha-yeh tanhayi 33 (2 vols.)
Honar 32
Hossein (ﷺ): varith-eh Adam 19
Hubut dar kavir 13
Jahanbini va id'iologi 23
Jehat-giri-yeh tabeqati-yeh eslam 10
Khod sazi-yeh engelabi 2
Ma va eqbal 5
Madhhab alayheh madhhab 22
Miyad ba Ebrahim 29
Nameh-ha 34
Niyayesh 8
Ravesh-eh shenakht-eh eslam 28
Shi'ah 7
Tah lili az manasek-eh haj 6
Tarikh-eh tamadon (I) 11
Tarikh-eh tamadon (II) 12
Tarikh va shenakht-eh adiyan I 14
Tarikh va shenakht-eh adiyan II 15
Tashayo'-eh 'Alavi/ tashayo'-eh Safavi 9
Vijehgi-ha-yeh qarn-eh jadid 31
Zan 21

C. INDEX TO THE TRANSLATED TITLES
CONTAINED IN THE COLLECTED WORKS

T

U

V

W

We Have Several Historic-Cultural 'Self's' 4.39*
What does 'civilization' mean? 11.2*
What I Infer from Religion 4.27
What is poetry? 32.7*
What must to be done? 20.8*
What must be done? 29.11
What need is there for 'Ali (ﷺ)? 26.5
When the Ranks are Clear 4.2*
Where are we in history? 4.9*
Which Religion? 4.46*
Who is a responsible intellectual? 20.9*
Who is Muhammad (ﷺ)? 30.2
Why is mythology the spirit of all world civilizations? 11.6*
Wishes 25.10*
Word to the Reader, A 6.1
World View 23.1*
World View and Environment 12.3*
World View Based on Logic, Consciousness and Orientation 4.44*

Y

Yea Brother! That's the way it was! 22.3
Years of Decision-making. What should be done? 4.33*

*Undated or exact date unknown.

D. INDEX TO THE TRANSLITERATED TITLES CONTAINED IN THE COLLECTED WORKS

E. Dated Works According to Dates— Fall 1968-Fall 1972

1968 October 25,26   1347 Aban 3,4
 Approach to the Understanding of Islam, 28.2
1968 December 11,12   1347 Azar 20,21
 Complete Human Being, 25.6
1968 December 28   1347 Dey 7
 Human Being and History, 24.5
1969 March 6,7   1347 Esfand 15,16
 Ali (ﷺ): A Myth-like Reality, 26.6
1969 March 19-22   1347-48 Esfand 28,29, Farvardin 1,2
 Appointment with Abraham I-IV, 29.1
1969 March 31-April 3   1348 Farvardin 11-14
 Ummah (Community) and Imamate (Leadership), 26.10
1969 May 10   1348 Ordibehesht 19
 Civilization and Modernism, 31.9
1969 October 12   1348 Mehr 20
 A Glance at Tomorrow's History, 31.6
1969 December 2   1348 Azar 11
 Ali (ﷺ) is Alone, 26.4
1969 December 3-5   1348 Azar 12-14
 Ali (ﷺ): His Fruitful Life After Death, 26.9
1969 December 10   1348 Azar 19
 The Scientific Method, 31.2
1969 December 14   1348 Azar 23
 About the Book, 25.9
1969 December 26,27   1348 Dey 5,6
 Migration and Civilization, 23.11
1970 February 1   1348 Bahman 12
 Advice and a Story, 32.8
1970 April 2   1349 Farvardin 13
 School of Sajjad (ﷺ): Consciousness, Love, Need and *Jihad* in
 Prayer (The Philosophy of Prayer), 8.2
1970 August 7   1349 Mordad 16
 History and its Value in Islam, 29.20
1970 August 13, 14   1349 Mordad 22,23
 Religion vs Religion, 22.1
1970 August 21, 22   1349 Mordad 30, 31
 Intellectuals and Their Responsibility to Society, 20.2
1970 August 23   1349 Shahrivar 1
 Philosophy of History in the View of Islam, 19.8
1971 January 23   1349 Bahman 3
 Madinah: The City of Migration, 29.2
1971 January 24   1349 Bahman 4
 Civilization: The Logical Outcome of Migration, 29.3
1971 January 25   1349 Bahman 5
 Study of Types of Migration, 29.4
1971 Januray 26   1349 Bahman 6
 Salvation of the Young Generation, 29.5

1971 January 27 — 1349 Bahman 7
Migration, *Ummah*(Community) and *Imamate* (Leadership), 29.6
1971 January 31 — 1349 Bahman 11
Monotheism and Multitheism, 23.2
1971 February 5 — 1349 Bahman 16
Reflections on the Hajj Rituals, 29.7
1971 February 6 — 1349 Bahman 17
The Islam of Muhammad (ﷺ): Reviver of Abraham's Religion, 29.8
1971 February 7 — 1349 Bahman 18
Sacrifice Your Ishmael, 29.9
1971 February 8 — 1349 Bahman 19
Selection and/or Election, 29.10
1971 February 16 — 1349 Bahman 27
What must be done?, 29.11
1971 February 17 — 1349 Bahman 28
A Glance at the Life of Muhammad (ﷺ): From Birth to Actualization of Prophethood, 29.12
1971 March 5 — 1349 Esfand 14
An Insight into Shi'ite History, 19.6
1971 March 7 — 1349 Esfand 16
Husayn (ؑ): Adam's Heir, 19.1
1971 April 9 — 1350 Farvardin 20
Lesson 1: History and Knowledge of Religions, 14.1
1971 April 22 — 1350 Ordibehesht
Lesson 2: History and Knowledge of Religions, 14.2
1971 April 27 — 1350 Ordibehesht 7
Permanent Standands of Education, 29.23
1971 May 7 — 1350 Ordibehesht 17
Lesson 3: History and Knowledge of Religions, 14.3
1971 May 21 — 1350 Ordibehesht 31
Lesson 4: History and Knowledge of Religions, 14.4
1971 June 4 — 1350 Khordad 14
Lesson 5: History and Knowledge of Religions, 14.5
1971 June 17 — 1350 Khordad 27
Lesson 6: History and Knowledge of Religions, 14.6
1971 July 2 — 1350 Tir 14
Fatima is Fatima (ؑ), 21.1
1971 July 13 — 1350 Tir 22
Death: A Message for Life, 29.26
1971 July 16 — 1350 Tir 25
Lesson 8: History and Knowledge of Religions, 14.8
1971 August 28 — 1350 Shahrivar 6
Machine at the Service of Machinism, 31.8
1971 October 29 — 1350 Aban 7
Lesson 9: History and Knowledge of Religions, 14.9
1971 October 30 — 1350 Aban 8
Mothers! Fathers! We are to blame!, 22.2
1971 October 30 — 1350 Aban 8
Awaiting the Religion of Protest, 19.7
1971 October 31 — 1350 Aban 9
Alid Shi'ism/Safavid Shi'ism, 9.2

1971 November 6   1350 Aban 15
Responsibility of Being a Shi'ite, 7.3
1971 November 7   1350 Aban 16
What need is there for Ali(ﷻ)?, 26.5
1971 November 10   1350 Aban 19
Ali (ﷻ): Founder of Unity, 26.6
1971 November 11   1350 Aban 20
Yea Brother! That's the way it was!, 22.3
1971 November 12   1350 Azar 1
From where should we begin?, 20.6
1971 November 26   1350 Azar 5
Lesson 11: History and Knowledge of Religions, 15.4
1971 December 10   1350 Azar 19
Lesson 12: History and Knowledge of Religions, 15.5
1971 December 14   1350 Azar 23
Round Table, 22.7
1971 December 24   1350 Dey 3
Lesson 13: History and Knowledge of Religions, 15.6
1972 January 7   1350 Dey 17
Lesson 14: History and Knowledge of Religions, 15.7
1972 January 14   1350 Dey 24
23 Years in 23 Days, 29.13
1972 January 15   1350 Dey 25
The Importance of Migration in Islam, 29.14
1972 January 16   1350 Dey 26
Sketch of the Prophet's Mosque and its Environs, 29.15
1972 January 20   1350 Dey 30
Monotheism: The Infrastructure of Our Actions, Rules and Feelings,
29.16
1972 January 26   1350 Bahman 6
Now that you have reached the Ka'bah, do not remain there, 29.17
1972 January 27   1350 Bahman 7
Review and General Conclusion, 29.18
1972 January 29   1350 Bahman 9
Promise for the Future, 29.19
1972 February 4   1350 Bahman 15
Lesson 1: School of Thought and Action, 16.1
1972 February 11   1350 Bahman 22
Lesson 2: School of Thought and Action of Islam, 16.2
1972 February 18   1350 Bahman 29
Lesson 3: Introduction to the Study of Monotheism, 16.3
1972 February 24   1350 Esfand 5
Martyrdom, 19.3
1972 February 25   1350 Esfand 6
Lesson 4: Three Phases of Monotheism, 16.4
1972 February 26   1350 Esfand 7
After Martyrdom, 19.4
1972 March 3   1350 Esfand 13
Lesson 5: Four Visages of Monotheism, 16.5
1972 March 10   1350 Esfand 20
Lesson 6: Let Us Arise and Take a Step Forward, 16.6

1972 April 7   1351 Farvardin 18
    Lesson 7: Monotheism: A Philosophy of History, 16.7
1972 April 14   1351 Farvardin 25
    Lesson 8: Philosophy of Ethics, 16.8
1972 April 21   1351 Ordibehesht 1
    Lesson 9: Hajj: Objective Embodiment of Monotheism, 16.9
1972 April 28   1351 Ordibehesht 8
    Lesson 10: History in the View of the Quran and Schools of Thought,
    17.1
1972 May 5   1351 Ordibehesht 15
    Lesson 11: Toynbee's Thesis and the Dynamic Activator of History, 17.2
1972 May 12   1351 Ordibehesht 22
    Lesson 12: Marxism in the Three Cycles of History, 17.3
1972 May 19   1351 Ordibehesht 29
    Lesson 13: The Popularization of Schools of Thought, 17.4
1972 May 26   1351 Khordad 5
    Lesson 14: The Relationship Between Thought and Action, 17.5
1972 June 2   1351 Khordad 12
    Lesson 15: Marxism in the 19th Century, 17.6
1972 June 9   1351 Khordad 19
    Lesson 16: Scientific Marxism and State Marxism, 17.7
1972 June 16   1351 Khordad 26
    Lesson 17: Alienation and the Dialectic of Work/Need in Marxism, 17.8
1972 June 23   1351 Tir 2
    Lesson 18: Introduction to Husayn (ﷺ): Heir of Adam, 17.9
1972 June 25   1351 Tir 4
    Expectations from the Muslim Woman, 21.2
1972 July 13-15   1351 Tir 22-24
    Seminar, 21.3
1972 July 14   1351 Tir 23
    Lesson 19: Capitalism and Surplus Value, 18.1
1972 July 21   1351 Tir 20
    Lesson 20: Products of the School of Islam, 18.2
1972 August 25   1351 Shahrivar 3
    Our Century in Search of Ali (ﷺ), 26.3
1972 September 12   1351 Shahrivar 21
    Revolutionary Role of the Reminders and Reminding in History, 7.2
1972 September 13   1351 Shahrivar 22
    The Most Beautiful Worshipped Spirit, 8.4
1972 September 22   1351 Shahrivar 31
    Lesson 21: Those Addressed by We Intellectuals, 18.3
1972 September 29   1351 Mehr 7
    Lesson 22: Historic Determinism, 18.4
1972 October 6   1351 Mehr 14
    Lesson 23: Social Dialectics, Socialism, Negation of Ownership, 18.5
1972 October 13   1351 Mehr 21
    Lesson 24: Capitalism and Compromise, 18.6
1972 October 18   1351 Mehr 26
    Third Way, 20.4
1972 October 19   1351 Mehr 27
    Consciousness and Deception, 20.5

1972 October 24   1351 Aban 2
  Shi'ism: A Complete Political Party, part I, 7.1
1972 October 26   1351 Aban 4
  Followers of 'Ali (ﷺ) and Their Anguishes, 26.8
1972 October 27   1351 Aban 5
  Lesson 25: Capitalism Wakes Up, 18.7
1972 October 27   1351 Aban 5
  Message of Hope to the Responsible Intellectual, 20.1
1972 October 29   1351 Aban 7
  Qasitin, Mariqin, Nakithin, 26.7
1972 November 1   1351 Aban 10
  Introduction to the Lecture of Hasan al-Amin, 31.9
1972 November 3   1351 Aban 12
  Lesson 26: Commentary on Surah Anbiya, 18.8
1972 November 10   1351 Aban 19
  Lesson 27: School of Existentialism, 18.9
1972 November 12-Friday   1351 Aban 21
  Shi'ism: A Complete Political Party, part II, 7.1

The Husayniyah is closed by the security forces. Ten months later, Shariati is arrested and is sent to solitary confinement for 550 days.

ENDNOTES TO THE INTRODUCTION

I: FINAL MIGRATION

1. He died in 1987, ten years after his son.

2. It is common practice among Muslims to consult the Quran when faced with a difficult decision. Three important issues appear in the verses that Shariati opened: The verses refer to the Battle of Tabuk and the *jihad* which was issued by the Holy Prophet in 631AD (9AH) to meet the aggression of the Roman Emperor. Verse 40 refers to the migration of the Holy Prophet from Makkah to Madinah. This important moment in Islamic history is referred to three times in the Quran: here, 2:194 and 8:30. The verse here refers to the Holy Prophet telling his Companion, Abu Bakr, who was in the cave with him as they hid from the Makkans, "Fear Not. Surely God is with us," whereupon "God sent down His Tranquility and strengthened him with hosts of angels."

3. *Collected Works* (CW), vol. 1, p. 46.

4. Interview printed in *Shariati as didgah du ustad* by Ali Muhammadi Garmsari.

II: FROM MAZINAN TO FRANCE

1. Interview with Muhammad Taqi Shariati printed in *Shariati as didgah du ustad* by Ali Muhammadi Garmsari.

2. Translated into English by Gh. A. T. in the Introduction to *On the Sociology of Islam* (Berkeley: Mizan Press, 1979).

3. *Op. cit.*, Interview.

4. His ideas were so developed at this stage that this essay formed the basis for all of his future work. This is a relative extensive translation because of its importance to the history of his ideas.

5. *CW*, vol. 31, pp. 5-7.

6. *Op. cit.*, Interview.

7. In *CW*, vol. 5, *Iqbal and Us*, in "Iqbal: the 20th Century Reformer," he says he was in France in 1958 at the peak of the Algerian Liberation Movement.

III: TO FRANCE AND BACK

1. Interview with Muhammad Taqi Shariati printed in *Shariati as didgah du ustad* by Ali Muhammadi Garmsari.

2. *CW.*, vol. 30, pp. 6-7.

3. The title comes from a poem in Jalal al-Din Rumi's *Mathnavi* which, in turn, draws upon a prophetic tradition in which the Holy Prophet said that the movements of *ruku* (beinding forward) and *sujud* (prostration) when performed in the ritual prayer are like double door knockers whereby one knocks on the doors of Truth.

4. *CW*, vol. 30, p. 44.

5. *CW*, vol. 30, p. 115.

V. FROM THE HUSAYNIYAH TO THE ZAYNIBIYAH

1. Interview with Muhammad Taqi Shariati printed in *Shariati as didgah du ustad* by Ali Muhammadi Garmsari

2. The following is an extensive quote from his letter because of its importance in understanding his program of revitalizing Islam. See *CW*, vol. 1, pp. 134-148.

3. Shariati is referring to an idea he developed based on his study of religion that the rightful religion of monotheism has throughout history been opposed by the religion of *kufr* (disbelief, infidelity, covering over the truth of religion, atheism) which takes on the form of multitheism (too many gods!) and idolatry. These latter positions on religion have been implemented through three specific agents, referred to by Shariati as the trinity in Islam, namely, rulers who rebel against God's Commands (*taghut-ha*), the wealthy class who live in ease and luxury (*mala* and *mutrif*) and pseudo-religious priests or scholars.

The first usurp the power, use it for their own self-interests and then because they are usurpers they are inevitably obliged to maintain their power and the status quo through force and coercsion in total disregard of God's promises to the deprived and oppressed.

The second group maintain control over the status quo through the use of their wealth, 'buying off the opposition', so to speak or employing the opposition to serve them instead of or in place of serving the One God.

The third group protect their position by deceiving the people in the Name of God through religious legitimations. The weak, abased and oppressed are told that they will be rewarded for their poverty in the next world or that God is the final judge between the just and the unjust so leave it to Him to decide. "Don't get involved," or 'What's it to you who is in the right and who is in the wrong? Leave it to Him to decide." All of which leads to humanity's backing off from responsibility and commitment to God's Way and the Straight Path.

4. Red Shi'ism or Truthful Shi'ism is another idea developed by Shariati and it is the Shi'ism which says, "No," to oppression and injustice in spite of all of their self-interests which will inevitably be sacrificed because of their beliefs and principles.

It is seen opposed by Deceitful Shi'ism which compromises at every point and which raises the Imams beyond the divinity so the question not even arise that their lives be as models for Muslims because they are so sacred that an average human being is not even expected to follow their lives as exemplary Muslims. It is a view which is historically demonstrated through Safavid rule in Iran which is very different than Alid or Red Shi'ism and the stand that Ali (ﷺ) took against oppression and injustice.

5. The program outlined by Shariati has been translated into English and published in *What should be done?* (Houston: IRIS, 1987).

6. The Algeriers Accord, a valid international agreement, was signed between the Shah and Saddam Hossein of Iraq. After the victory of the Islamic Revolution in 1979 and the Shah's fleeing Iran, Saddam Hossein tore up the agreement on national television just before he initiated an all out air, sea and land attack of aggression against Iran in September 1980 which led to the Iraq-Iran war when Iran retaliated in defense of its country.

VI. EPILOGUE

1. Interview with Muhammad Taqi Shariati printed in *Shariati as didgah du ustad* by Ali Muhammadi Garmsari.

2. *Ibid.*

3. *Ibid.*

4. *Ibid.*

GLOSSARY

Abd al-Rahmans: Abd al-Rahman ibn Awf, a Companion of the Prophet, was made head of a council to elect a new caliph upon the death of Umar. He made Uthman caliph. When Abd al-Rahman died he had over 3,000,000 gold dinars according to Ibn Khaldun. It would appear that this was in disregard of the Quranic injunction against hoarding. "Those who treasure up (kinz) gold and silver and do not expend them in the Way of God— give them the good tidings of a painful chastisement, the day when they shall be heated in the fire of hell and therewith, their foreheads and their sides and their backs shall be branded: *'This is the thing you have treasured up for yourselves; therefore, taste you now what you were treasuring.'"* (9:34-35). Shariati then used his name as a generic term to refer to those who hoard their wealth.

Abu Dharr: One of the earliest Companions of the Prophet, he was born Jundab ibn Junadah from the Ghifar tribe outside of Makkah.

Carrel, Alexis: (1873-1944) French surgeon, sociologist and biologist who received the Nobel Prize for Medicine in 1912. His writings include *Man, the Unknown* (1935) and *Reflections on Life* (1952).

Commanding to Good and Preventing Evil: "That which is described in the language of intellectuals in the world today as 'human and social responsibility', has been accurately described and determined in Islam as *amr b'il ma'ruf wa nahy an al-munkar.*" See *CW*, vol. 5, p. 52.

Comte, Auguste: (1798-1857) Exponent of Positivism who named and systematized the science of sociology. Positivism is a system of thought and knowledge proposed as capable of providing a basis for political organizations in modern industrial society.

Fanon, Franz: (1925-1961) A psychoanalyst from Martinique, he joined the Algerian Liberation Movement in 1954 and in 1956 became an editor of its newspaper *El-Moudjahid* published in Tunis. He wrote *Black Skin, White Masks* in 1952 which reflected his personal frustrations with racism. In 1961, just before his death of cancer, he wrote *The Wretched of the Earth* which established him as a prophetic-like figure, the author of a social gospel that urged colonized peoples to purge themselves of their degradation in a "collective catharsis" to be achieved by violence against their European oppression. He is also author of *For the African Revolution.*

Greater occultation: In the Shi'ite view, the Mahdi (ﷺ) is in greater occultation and will appear at the end of Time to bring justice, equity and truth to all of mankind.

Gurvitch: (1905-1965) Shariati says he spent five years in his classes where be became familiar with his thoughts. He describes Gurvitch's life, "He was a former communist who fled Russia. His life resembled a myth. He had fought alongside Lenin and Trotsky but disagreed with Stalin. He spent twenty years in Europe and America trying to escape from the Nazis who had put a price on his head as well as from the Stalinists." See *CW*, vol. 13, pp. 320-321.

Hurr: The word means 'inward liberation' and is the name of a man who was serving in Yazid's army in 61AH (682 AD) and on the 10th of Muharram, knowing that Imam Husayn's (ﷺ) Companions could not defeat Yazid's army, yet he chose Husayn (﷽). Shariati writes, "The visage of Hurr is a visage which is clear and reflects independence. His was in the position of committing a crime yet he passed the distance from 'criminal' to 'person who serves God', from an instrument in the hands of Yazid to follower of Husayn (﷽), from worldly fame to martyrdom, from the dirtiest of assignments as an executioner to a great and free human being in just half a day with the choice he made. On the morning of Ashura he was an officer in the army of Yazid and after a few hours, he was among the victims in the ranks of Imam Husayn (﷽) and one of his dearest helpers. How could just one or two hours be sufficient for all of this? Did he change his mind as a result of studying? Did his view of faith and belief change? Did his principles of jurisprudence change? "No. The only change that took place between the Hurr of Ta'sua and the Hurr of Ashura was his change in choice of leadership. In this great transformation it is only the leader that changes. It is this change of leadership which transforms an individual criminal into the highest of stations one can attain in life. The change in leadership developed a person from one who should have suffered the eternal fires of hell into an inspiring person who is full of nobility and self-sacrifice. The story of Hurr retells this truth—to what extent the choice of change in leadership and knowledge of a rightful leader can effect a human being." (*CW*, vol. 2, pp. 215)

Husayniyah: An institution in Iran traditionally used for the performance of passion plays during the first ten days of the month of Muharram, the first month of the lunar calendar, in memory of the martyrdom of Imam Husayn (﷽).

Imam Husayn (﷽): (4/626-61/680) The grandson of the Prophet and third pure Imam who was martyred on the plains of Karbala by the forces of Yazid.

Jihad: Spiritual and religious struggle in the Way of God.

Ka'b al-Ahbars: Kab al-Ahbar was a Jewish rabbi who became a Muslim during the rule of Uthman and was considered by the latter to be a religious scholar whose opinion on religious issues was more highly valued than that of the Companions of the Holy Prophet. In return for this attention, Kab al-Ahbar would say whatever Uthman wanted to hear. Shariati then used his name as a generic term to refer to religious scholars who support a regime without regard to right or wrong, truth or falsehood thereby using religion to legitimate an unjust regime.

Karbala: A place on the Iraqi plains near Kufa where Imam Husayn (﷽) stood with 72 Companions against the attack of 30,000 men because he refused to give his allegiance to a usurper caliph who ridiculed Islam and this, just thirty years after the death of the Prophet of Islam.

Kufr: To deny or cover over the truth of religion and it is itself a kind of religion. It is translated as disbelief, infidelity or atheism.

Mashhad: A city in north-west Iran, it is an important area of pilgrimage because it holds the shrine of the eighth pure Imam, Imam Rida.

Mahdi (﷽): The Savior who will come at the end of time.

Massignon, Louis: (d. 1967) Shariati studied and worked with him from 1960-1962. Massignon's greatest contribution to Islamic scholarship is his study of the mystic Hallaj.

Minbar: A wooden structure in a mosque with stairs leading to a platform upon which the speaker sits.

Muawiyah: See Umayyid.

Mujahids: Social activists. The word comes from *jihad* and means those who engage in the spiritual and religious struggle upon God's Way.

Proudhon, Pierre-Joseph: (1809-1865) French libertarian socialist and journalist whose doctrines became the basis for later radical and anarchist theory.

Russell, Bertrand: (1872-1970) English logician and philosopher, best known for his work in mathematical logic and for his social and political campaigns.

Saint-Simon, Claude-Henri: (1760-1825) French social scientist, one of the chief founders of Christian socialism.

Sartre, Jean Paul: (1905-1980) French novelist, playwright and exponent of Existentialism—a philosophy acclaiming the freedom of the individual human being. He was awarded the Nobel Prize for Literature in 1964 but he declined it. He took over the phenomenological method from the German philosopher Edmund Husserl, which proposes careful, unprejudiced description rather than deduction.

SAVAK: The Shah's secret police who were responsible for the torture and death of many Muslims before the victory of the Revolution.

Ulama: Religious scholars. *Alim* is the singular.

Umayyids: A 'caliphate' monarchy begun in 41/661 when Muawiyah, the son of Abu Sufyan, usurped the power. The Umayyids remained in control of the Prophet's caliphate for 100 years when they were overthrown by the Abbasids who proved to be no better in their 'Islamic' rule.

Uthmans: This is a term used by Shariati to refer to rulers who disregard God's Commands.

Yazids: Yazid was the son of Mu'awiyah who began the Umayyid 'caliphate' monarchy. It was Yazid who order the massacre at Karbala in 61AH. As his is a good example of a despot tyrant-oppressive ruler, Shariati refers to this type of rulers throughout history as 'Yazids'.

Zaynab: The granddaughter of the Prophet and sister of Imam Husayn (ﷺ) who was taken captive after the battle of Karbala. It was she who took the message of the martyrdom of Imam Husayn (ﷺ) and his Companions to Damascus, Makkah and Madina.

GENERAL INDEX